Green
Fourth

V̵ ̵ ̵ ̵a̵ ̵ ̵my̵ ̵ ̵ ̵ ̵ ̵ts now – or are we?

Th̵ highly ac̵ ̵ ̵ ̵ ̵ .̵r̵o̵duction to green political thought is ṇ ̵w̵ av̵ ̵.able ̵i̵ a n̵e̵w̵ ̵.̵tion, having been fully revised and updated to take into account the areas which have grown in importance since the third edition was published.

The author describes and assesses the political ideology of 'ecologism', and compares this radical view of remedies for the environmental crisis with the 'environmentalism' of mainstream politics. Dobson examines the philosophical basis of ecological thinking, the potential shape of a sustainable society and the means at hand for achieving it. The relationship between ecologism and other political ideologies is also discussed.

New to this edition:

- Analysis of the 'green state'
- An account of 'hybridity' and the 'ecological footprint'
- The effect of globalization on ecologism
- Ecological citizenship
- Analysis of recent Green Party experience

Green Political Thought remains the starting point for all students, academics and activists who want an introduction to green political theory.

Andrew Dobson is Professor of Politics at Keele University, UK. Webpage: www.andrewdobson.com

D1628177

Green Political Thought
Fourth Edition

Andrew Dobson

Routledge
Taylor & Francis Group

LONDON AND NEW YORK

First Edition published 1990
by HarperCollins Academic
Reprinted 1991
Reprinted 1992, 1994
by Routledge

Second Edition first published 1995
Third Edition first published 2000
by Routledge
2 Park Square, Milton Park, Abingdon, Oxon OX14 4RN

Simultaneously published in the USA and Canada
by Routledge
270 Madison Ave, New York, NY 10016

*Routledge is an imprint of the Taylor & Francis Group, an informa
business*

Typeset in Times by RefineCatch Limited, Bungay, Suffolk
Printed and bound in Great Britain by
TJ International Ltd, Padstow, Cornwall

British Library Cataloguing in Publication Data
A catalogue record for this book is available from the British Library

Library of Congress Cataloging in Publication Data
Dobson, Andrew.
   Green political thought / by Andrew Dobson. – 4th ed.
      p. cm.
   Includes bibliographical references and index.

   1. Green movement. I. Title.
   JA75.8.D63 2007
   320.5'8 – dc22

ISBN10: 0–415–40351–0 (hbk)
ISBN10: 0–415–40352–9 (pbk)
ISBN10: 0–203–96462–4 (ebk)

ISBN13: 978–0–415–40351–1 (hbk)
ISBN13: 978–0–415–40352–8 (pbk)
ISBN13: 978–0–203–96462–0 (ebk)

Contents

Preface to the fourth edition

'The environment' is now a regular presence on the front pages of newspapers and in the headlines of TV news bulletins. This would have been unimaginable when the first edition of this book was published in 1990. The paradox, though, is that this increased exposure has not necessarily resulted in a better understanding of the causes and consequences of, and solutions to, environmental problems. In fact the range of analyses of unsustainability, and what to do about it, is quite often much narrower than it should be. The original aim of this book, then, which was to offer readers a contrast between 'radical' and 'reformist' environmentalism, is perhaps even more important now than it was in 1990. Many of the warnings of environmentalists that appeared outlandish in what we might call the 'pre-environmental' era have become common currency today, as we are confronted with evidence of environmental stress on a daily basis. We should at least be aware, therefore, of the variety of routes to sustainability – and the ideas about what the sustainable society itself might look like – that are available to us. That is what this book is about.

I would like to thank Craig Fowlie and Natalja Mortensen at Routledge for their work on this fourth edition, and to Ann King for her excellent and sympathetic copy-editing.

Andrew Dobson
Keele University, December 2006

Preface to the third edition

In the preface to the second edition of this book I noted the explosion of material on its central theme – ecologism – that surrounded publication of the first. This rush has shown no signs of abating – indeed, it has become even faster and more furious. The standard of this material is very high, and to the chapter-length analyses of ecologism referred to in the preface to the second edition, we must now add some outstanding longer reflections: for example, Goodin, 1992; Hayward, 1995, 1998; Dryzek, 1997; Smith, 1998; and J. Barry, 1999. These books form part of what we might call the 'second wave' of theorizing about environmental politics. The first wave was devoted to explaining and analysing the politicalideological aspects of environmental politics, and the first edition of this book was very much a part of that wave. Second-wave work, on the other hand, has focused more on political theory than on political ideology, and has taken the form of a critical exploration of the relationship between environmental politics and enduring themes and concepts in political theory such as democracy, justice and citizenship. Something of the influence of this second wave can be found in the third edition of Green Political Thought where I have added a section to Chapter 4 entitled 'Democracy and authoritarianism' and made references in Chapter 5 to the prickly relationship between social justice and environmental objectives. Chapter 5, indeed, has been changed rather radically. I have responded to the interest students have shown in the relationship between ecologism and other ideologies, and to some outstanding comparative studies by scholars working in that area, by expanding the coverage to include not only socialism and feminism, but liberalism and conservatism too. I have taken the opportunity this presented to cement the central theme of the book: that ecologism is a political ideology in its own right, distinct and different from the others with which it competes at the dawn of the twenty-first century. The sympathetic and not-so-sympathetic reactions to the development of ecologism which I identified and discussed in the Conclusion to the second edition have continued unabated. There is now a strong belief that the objectives of ecologism can be achieved without it, as it were. I think this is wrong, and I have updated the Conclusion once again to try to explain why. I am happy to report that the community of scholars working on environmental politics is strong, vibrant and still growing, and it continues to be an intellectual and social pleasure to work with them. It is particularly gratifying to see scholars from outside the 'green field' beginning to grapple with the intellectual challenges that environmental political theory has uncovered. I am, as ever, grateful to all those who have participated in this coruscating conversation for their influence on what I have written here. I am also grateful to my editor at Routledge, Mark Kavanagh, for inviting me to throw my hat in the ring once again. Finally, thanks to the building contractors at Keele University who unwittingly provided the material for Miho Suganami's cover photograph.

Andrew Dobson
Keele University August 1999

Preface to the second edition

It was only some time after the publication of the first edition of this book that I realized what I had been trying to do in it. The arrival of the owl of Minerva was prompted by many generous readings of Green Political Thought made by colleagues throughout the world, the collective weight of which made me see that securing a place for ecologism in the list of modern political ideologies was my prime intention first time round. Introductory textbooks on political ideologies have abounded for some time, but only recently has ecologism found its way into them. In 1989 I knew of no textbook of this sort that included a chapter on ecological political thought, but now there are several (for example: Ball and Dagger, 1991; Leach, 1991; Heywood, 1992; Macridis, 1992; Vincent, 1992; Dobson, 1993a; Kenny, 1994). The dawning realization of what I was up to has – I hope – sharpened the focus of the second edition, and I try (particularly in the Introduction) to embed my view of ecologism more firmly both in the theory of political ideology and in the context of popular overviews such as those mentioned above. This focus has also enabled me to hone further the distinction between environmentalism and ecologism: a distinction which is now part and parcel of environmental–political debate.

An overwhelming amount of literature on environmental politics has appeared in the past five years, and keeping track of it is a timeconsuming task. I have been pleasantly surprised to find that this often very sophisticated work has resulted in modulation of my earlier views rather than outright reconstruction (although how could I bear to say anything else?). I have, though, brought my remarks and examples up to date, and responded to challenges where they have been made.

The basic shape of the book has therefore remained the same. Attentive readers will spot that the material in Chapter 1 has been thrashed around somewhat due to the critical attention given it by a number of commentators. I hope to have made some of the arguments in Chapter

2 clearer than they were in the first edition, and I have a more catholic (yet simultaneously more principled) view of the shape of the sustainable society (Chapter 3) than I had in 1989. I have updated Chapter 4 and added a short section on direct action; and the sections on socialism in Chapter 5 have (I hope) benefited from contact with what is one of the largest growth areas in the literature – that which deals with ecosocialism. Ecofeminism seems to me to have bifurcated more obviously in recent years than it had by 1989, and I try to reflect this in my reworking of ecofeminist themes in Chapter 5. Finally, there has been a recent and significant swing towards the view that while environmentalism and ecologism might be conceptually distinct, they converge at all the points that really matter if the objective is protecting the environment. This debate provides the focus for the book's conclusion.

It is trite (but true) to say that this second edition of Green Political Thought would not have been possible without all the people who read (or otherwise absorbed bits of) the first edition, and told me what was wrong with it. It is invidious to mention just a few of them, but I shall do so anyway: Wouter Achterberg, Adrian Atkinson, John Barry, Ted Benton, Janet Biehl, Murray Bookchin, Anna Bramwell, Alan Carter, Brian Doherty, John Dryzek, Robyn Eckersley, Judy Evans, Bob Goodin, Peter Hay, Tim Hayward, Mike Kenny, Keekok Lee, Paul Lucardie, Mary Mellor, David Pepper, Dick Richardson, Mike Saward, Jan van der Straaten, Andrew Vincent, Albert Weale, Caroline Wintersgill, Marcel Wissenburg and Stephen Young.

Casting my eye over this list I realize that only one of these people was known to me personally in 1989. Perhaps the best thing to have come out of Green Political Thought is my good fortune at having come into contact with some outstanding scholars, a number of whom have turned into friends. One on the list, Caroline Wintersgill, is not an academic, but my editor at Routledge. I owe Caroline a debt for having cajoled me into the formative experience of preparing this second edition, and for having been the most longsuffering sounding board regarding what I should do with it. I hope that the result is worthy both of her persistence and of the attempts of my colleagues to illuminate my own intellectual darkness.

Andrew Dobson
Keele University, 1995

Introduction

Climate change. Deforestation. Acid rain. Species loss. Ozone depletion. Pesticide poisoning. Genetically modified food. These are the issues that invigorated political life in the late twentieth century and will continue to do so in the twenty-first. This is an extraordinary circumstance and it has happened extraordinarily quickly. Even thirty years ago, the development of a political movement around these issues would have been unimaginable. Knowledge of some of them – pesticide poisoning, for example – was restricted to a few scientists and even fewer social commentators, and there was no knowledge at all of others, such as global warming. Now it would be hard to find anyone in the 'developed' world who has never heard of these environmental problems, and probably even harder to find anyone in the 'developing' world who would not accept that environmental decay was either a cause or a symptom of their social, political and economic difficulties. Upon this realization, in both the North and the South, a vibrant environmental movement has been built – a movement which now has an influential presence both in civil society and in the more formal political world of parliamentary politics.

This movement has given rise to a veritable academic industry designed to analyse it, and this analysis takes many forms. There are introductory books covering the whole sweep of environmental politics (Doyle and McEachern, 1998; Dryzek and Schlosberg, 1998; Garner, 2000; Carter, 2001; Connelly and Smith, 2003). There are books and articles devoted to green political parties (Müller-Rommel and Poguntke, 2002), to environmental policy-making (Fischer and Black, 1995; Jordan *et al.*, 2003), to the sociology of the environmental movement (Doherty, 2002), and to the international relations of the environment (Thomas, 1992; Laferrière and Stoett, 1999; Paterson, 2000). There are journals that specialize in environmental politics – *Environmental Politics* and *Global Environmental Politics*. There are also books devoted to discussing and analysing the political and social ideas that lie behind the environmental movement (Atkinson, 1991; Hayward, 1995; Dryzek, 1997; Smith, 1998; Barry, 1999; Baxter, 1999; Blühdorn, 2000; Humphrey, 2001; Meyer, 2001; Whiteside, 2002; Dickens, 2004), and this is one of those books.

The first edition of *Green Political Thought* was published in 1990, when green political parties were a novelty and hardly anyone had heard of climate change. I wondered, then, whether the tender green plant of environmentalism was simply a version of already existing ideologies or whether it was a new ideology in its own right. The more I read about it the more I became convinced that we did indeed have a new ideology on our hands. It seemed to me that it made as much sense to say that environmentalism was 'like' other political ideologies as it does to say that socialism is 'like' liberalism, for example. Sixteen years later I am more convinced of this than ever. One of the most striking political transformations of the past two decades has been the way in which environmental concern has moved from the margins to the mainstream of political life. Everyone wants a piece of it. No serious candidate for political office can afford to buck this trend; it is as hard to find a politician opposed to sustainable development as it is to find one who is reluctant to kiss babies during election campaigns. This transformation has required of politicians that they assimilate 'the environment' into their respective political positions – and the result has been a series of severe cases of ideological indigestion. These attempts at the appropriation of environmental concern have made it more important than ever to stake out clearly the territory of the political ideology that has formed around environmental issues. Thus my principal objective here is the same as it was in 1990: to describe and assess that set of ideas regarding the environment which can properly be regarded as an ideology – the ideology of ecologism. This is a book about 'ecologism', then, in the same sense as you might read a book about liberalism, socialism, conservatism or fascism.

I shall be distinguishing between *ecologism* and its more visible cousin *environmentalism*. This book is about the former, not the latter, and the following may be taken as a rough-and-ready distinction between the two:

- *environmentalism* argues for a managerial approach to environmental problems, secure in the belief that they can be solved without fundamental changes in present values or patterns of production and consumption;

- *ecologism* holds that a sustainable and fulfilling existence presupposes radical changes in our relationship with the non-human natural world, and in our mode of social and political life.

So government ministers do not suddenly become political ecologists by trading in their limousines for hybrid (electric/petrol) cars.

I shall argue that environmentalism and ecologism need to be kept apart because they differ not only in degree but also in kind. In other words, they need to be kept apart for the same reasons that liberalism and socialism, or conservatism and nationalism, need to be kept apart. This may seem controversial because the standard view is that environmentalism and ecologism belong to the same family, with the former simply being a less radical manifestation of concern for the environment than the latter. It is less radical, of course, and this is not without importance, but I want to establish that the nature of the difference takes us beyond the question of radicalism into territory of a more fundamental kind – the kind of territory, indeed, that obliges us to distinguish liberalism and socialism as families and not simply, or only, as offspring of the same parents.

This is because, crucially, environmentalism is not an ideology at all. Most commentators ascribe the same three basic features to ideologies in the sense in which I am talking about them: they must provide an analytical description of society – a 'map' composed of reference points enabling its users to find their way around the political world. Second, they must prescribe a particular form of society employing beliefs about the human condition that sustain and reproduce views about the nature of the prescribed society. Finally, they must provide a programme for political action, or show how to get from the society we currently inhabit to the one prescribed by the ideology in question.

As far as the first characteristic is concerned, and in the context of keeping ecologism and environmentalism apart, it is important to stress that whatever problem is being confronted by any given ideology, it will be analysed in terms of some fundamental and (as it were) necessary feature of the human condition, and not in terms of contingent features of particular social practices. In our context, ecologism will suggest that climate change is not simply a result of inappropriate technologies for energy production, but rather that it is symptomatic of a misreading of the possibilities (or more properly here, constraints) inherent in membership of an interrelated biotic and abiotic community. My point is that while ideologies will disagree over analysis and prescriptions, they will always couch them in terms of fundamental 'truths' about the human condition. On this score, ecologism counts as political ideology while environmentalism does not.

A similar remark may be made in respect of the second point raised above: that of political prescription. The prescriptions made by political ideologies will not only be issue-based, but will be founded on some notion of the human condition and its associated limitations and possibilities. The prescriptions will probably be based on some principled vision of the way we should live our lives (the 'Good Life') and will contrast strongly with prescriptions that amount to no more than a set of technical adjustments or 'technological fixes'. Again, in these terms ecologism qualifies as a political ideology, but environmentalism does not.

So how do we go about defining this ideology of ecologism? We begin, in Roger Eatwell's words, by describing and assessing the 'intrinsic structure' of ideologies – their 'key tenets, myths, contradictions, tensions, even [their] morality and truth' (Eatwell and Wright, 1993, p. 1). This implies that each ideology has key tenets, myths and so on that distinguish it from other ideologies, and part of my task will be to outline what these are for ecologism – tenets that distinguish it from other ideologies and (I argue) from environmentalism, too. I am unashamedly involved, then, in producing an 'ideal type', and I say this early on so as to head off criticism that the ideology I describe is not that outlined in the latest manifesto of the Swedish Green Party (for example). Ecologism as presented here should 'not be confused with specific movements, parties or regimes which may bear [its] name' (Eatwell and Wright, 1993, p. 10; see also Talshir (2002) for a discussion of the relationship between green parties and ideology). The corollary of this is that one would not necessarily expect any single real-life political ecologist to subscribe in equal measure to all of the tenets and beliefs discussed in this book. This is to avoid the otherwise mistaken impression that 'the great majority of those who would consider themselves political ecologists in real life will not see their beliefs reflected in this description [of ecologism]' (Riechmann, 1997, p. 10; my translation). Real-life political ecologists may not subscribe to the totality of the ideas that are described and analysed here, but they will draw from the well of inspiration they provide.

Keeping ecologism and environmentalism apart, and focusing on the former, helps us to understand better the historical significance of green politics as a challenge to the political, social and scientific consensus that has dominated the past two or three hundred years of public life. Green politics self-consciously confronts dominant paradigms, and in this sense it is in a similar position to notions such as 'post-industrialism'. Michael Marien is right to suggest that, contrary to general opinion, there is not one but 'two visions of post-industrial society' and, importantly, that one of these is dominant and the other is subordinate. If we allow the subordinate one to disappear we risk intellectual sloppiness and are likely to mistake consensus for disagreement. The same goes for light-green and dark-green politics – or what I have called environmentalism and ecologism.

Marien writes that there are 'two completely different modes of usage: "Post-industrial society" as a technological, affluent, service society, and "post-industrial society" as a decentralized agrarian economy following in the wake of a failed industrialism' (Marien, 1977, p. 416), and suggests that the former is dominant with respect to the latter. Analogously, I have suggested that dominant and subordinate understandings of green politics have emerged from discussion of the topic as well as its political practice. The point is to remain open to the existence of these understandings rather than to let the bright light of the dominant one obscure the subordinate one behind.

In fact this is not simply an analogy. It just happens that Marien's dominant version of post-industrialism – a technological, affluent, service society – is a fair description of the twenty-first-century political aspiration to which most people would probably subscribe, if asked. We are certainly encouraged at every turn to aspire to it, at any rate. Now the content of post-industrialism in this dominant sense can work powerful magic on all with which it comes into contact – it moulds challenges to it in its own image and so draws their sting. This is, I think, precisely what has happened to environmental politics as it has emerged from the wings on to the main stage. There is now a perfectly respectable claim to be made that green politics can be a part of a technological, affluent, service society – a part, in other words, of Marien's dominant version of what post-industrial society both is and might be like. This is the green politics of carbon dioxide scrubbers on industrial chimneys, CFC-free aerosols, hybrid cars – and even nuclear power.

In this guise, green politics presents no sort of a challenge at all to the twenty-first-century consensus over the desirability of affluent, technological, service societies. But my understanding of the historical significance of radical green politics is that it constitutes precisely such a challenge, and that we shall lose sight of that significance if we conceive of it only in its reformist mode: a mode that reinforces conspicuous consumption and certain sorts of technology rather than calling them into question. Radical green politics is far more a friend of the subordinate interpretation of post-industrialism – a decentralized economy following in the wake of a failed industrialism – than of its dominant counterpart. Jonathon Porritt and Nicholas Winner assert that:

> the most radical [green aim] seeks nothing less than a nonviolent revolution to overthrow our whole polluting, plundering and materialistic industrial society and, in its place, to create a new economic and social order which will allow human beings to live in harmony with the planet. In those terms, the Green Movement lays claim to being the most radical and important political and cultural force since the birth of socialism.
>
> (Porritt and Winner, 1988, p. 9)

It is in these terms that I see green politics in this book; first, so as to keep a fuller picture of the movement in mind than is currently the case; second, to understand better the challenge it presents to the dominant consensus; and third, to establish ecologism as a political ideology in its own right. The latter is important because I believe Barbara Goodwin (among others) to be wrong in calling ecologism a 'crosscutting ideology' which 'falls into other existing ideological categories' (Goodwin, 1987, p. vii).

For the sake of convenience, but at the risk of blind blundering on territory where specialists themselves quite properly fear to tread, the world-view that modern political ecologists challenge is the one which grew out of the (early) Enlightenment. Norman Hampson has suggested a number of characteristics salient to the Enlightenment worldview: 'a period when the culture of the educated man was thought to take in the whole of educated knowledge' (Hampson, 1979, p. 11); 'that man was to a great extent the master of his own destiny' (ibid., p. 35); that 'God was a mathematician whose calculations, although infinite in their subtle complexity, were accessible to man's intelligence' (ibid., pp. 37–8); and that 'universal reason' was held to be preferable to 'local habit', principally because it helps to drive out superstition (ibid., p. 152).

All these characteristics are examined in detail by Adrian Atkinson (1991), and their general tenor is the exaltation of human beings and their particular faculties (e.g. reason) – the placing of the human being in a pre-eminent position with respect to the rest of not only terrestrial phenomena, but the universe at large. If Isaac Newton humbly saw himself as a boy playing on the sea-shore, finding only the odd shiny pebble while the 'great ocean of truth' lay before him, this was surely more because he hadn't the time to set sail than because he thought he lacked the equipment to do so. This belief in the centrality of 'man' and of his capacity for control of his circumstances was encapsulated in the principle of *bienfaisance,* or benevolence, according to which the world was the best of all possible worlds for human beings. Hampson quotes Pluche as writing that 'It is for him [Man] that the sun rises; it is for him that the stars shine', and goes on to observe that 'Almost everything could be pressed into service, from the density of water, which Fenelon considered exactly calculated to facilitate navigation, to the shape of the water-melon, which makes it easy to slice' (Hampson, 1979, p. 81). In these respects the Enlightenment attitude was that the world had been made for human beings and that, in principle, nothing in it could be kept secret from them.

In a tortuous way this attitude has remained dominant ever since in Western cultures and societies and those that have sought to emulate the Western model. They inform, too, Marien's dominant interpretation of what post-industrial society both is and ought to be: Baconian science has helped produce its technology and its material affluence, and the Promethean project to which the Enlightenment gave birth in its modern form is substantially intact. The historical significance of radical green politics is that it constitutes a challenge to this project and to the norms and practices that sustain it. This politics seeks explicitly to decentre the human being, to question mechanistic science and its technological consequences, to refuse to believe that the world was made for human beings – and it does this because it has been led to wonder whether dominant post-industrialism's project of material affluence is either desirable or sustainable. All this will be missed if we choose to restrict our understanding of green politics to its dominant guise: an environmentalism that seeks a cleaner service economy sustained by cleaner technology and producing cleaner conspicuous consumption.

These thoughts on the Enlightenment help to identify ecologism's current historical significance, but there is danger here, too. The analytic temptation is to see the ideology as a renewal of the Romantic reaction that the Enlightenment, and then early forms of industrialization, themselves brought about. So we cast ecologism in terms of passion opposing reason, of the joys of a bucolic life and of mystery as against transparency. And of course it is true that many manifestations of the green movement argue for a repopulation of the countryside and for the reawakening of a sense of awe in the face of natural phenomena.

At the same time, however, modern green politics turns out to be based on a self-consciously hard-headed assessment of the unsustainability of current political and economic practices – it is remarkable, indeed, to see the extent to which the success of modern political ecology has been mediated and sustained by scientific research. This could hardly be said of the Romantic reaction to the Enlightenment. Similarly, ecologism's political Utopia is (by and large) informed by interpretations of the principle of equality – a principle that was minted and put into circulation during the Enlightenment, and certainly not popular with the Romantics. And if we hold the green movement to believe that one can only recognize the value of the natural world through intuition (as we are likely to do if we see it merely as a resurgence of Romanticism), then we are blind to the enormous range and influence of rationalist attempts to account for such value, and which are of great importance to the movement's intellectual archaeology (Chapter 2).

So while (in terms of its present historical significance) radical green politics ought to be characterized as a challenge to the contemporary consensus over norms and practices that has its most immediate sources in the early Enlightenment, it would be a mistake to believe that it pays no heed whatever to those norms and practices. And this would be an especially big mistake if we were to jump to the conclusion that modern green politics is only a form of reincarnated Romanticism. To guard against this, we should say that its challenge most generally takes the form of an attempt to shift the terms of the burden of persuasion from those who would question the dominant post-industrial embodiment of politics and society (an affluent, big technology, high consumption, service society), on to those who would defend it. In doing so greens may sometimes speak, even if often *sotto voce*, in the Enlightenment idiom. Indeed, in the context of an extended enquiry into the relationship between ecology and enlightenment, Tim Hayward writes that 'the ecological challenge, precisely to the extent that it is a critical challenge, can be seen as a renewal of the enlightenment project itself' (Hayward, 1995, p. 39).

Finally, a remark needs to be made about the use of the word 'ideology' here. The study of ideology is immensely more complex than the standard 'functional' definition of the word would have us believe. At a more profound level than this, ideology 'asks about the bases and validity of our most fundamental ideas' (McLellan, 1986, p. 1) and as such involves us in critical thought about the most hidden presuppositions of current social and political life – even more hidden than those which political ecologists claim to have uncovered. Drawing on Marx, this conception of ideology urges us to take nothing for granted and suggests that words used in any given description of the world are opaque rather than translucent, and demand deciphering.

However, there is still something useful to be said about socialism, liberalism and conservatism from within the functional idiom, if only in the sense that we may indeed sensibly view political ideologies as providing 'the concepts, categories, images and ideas by means of which people make sense of their social and political world, form projects, come to a certain consciousness of their place in that world and act in it' (Donald and Hall, 1986, p. x). It is this functional understanding of ideology that informs the content of this book. I aim to set out the ideas with which radical greens describe the political and social world, prescribe action within it, and seek to motivate us to such action. This is an uncontroversial perspective in the context of describing political ideologies, but the understanding of 'ideology' that it presupposes is far from uncontroversial in the wider context of the study of ideology itself. In this wider context, both ecologism and the current book about it would have to be subjected to interrogation.

1 Thinking about ecologism

The British environmentalist Jonathon Porritt once said that 'Having written the last two general election manifestos for the Ecology Party, I would be hard put even now to say what our ideology is' (Porritt, 1984a, p. 9). In this chapter I want to establish some of the ground rules for this ideology, and in doing so I will build on two points established in the Introduction: first, that ecologism is not the same as environmentalism, and second, that environmentalism is not a political ideology.

I should say at the outset that these points set my views at odds with most of those who have written recently on political ecology as ideology. The more common position is that both environmentalism and ecologism need to be considered when green ideology is at issue, with writers typically offering a 'spectrum' of green ideology with all the necessary attendant features such as 'wings' and 'centres'. Elsewhere I have referred to these two approaches to green ideology as 'maximalist' and 'minimalist' (Dobson, 1993a). Maximalist commentators define ecologism tightly: 'people and ideas will have to pass stringent tests before they can be properly called political-ecological', while minimalists 'cast their net wider so that the definition of ecologism is subject to fewer and/or less stringent conditions' (Dobson, 1993a, p. 220). It will be clear that I take a maximalist position, partly due to the ground rules that I consider any description of any ideology must follow, which are betrayed by including environmentalism as a wing within a description of green ideology: partly because the submerging of ecologism in environmentalism is in danger of skewing the intellectual and political landscape, and partly because of how little the minimalist position actually ends up saying.

Andrew Vincent has written the most articulate and robust accounts from the minimalist position (Vincent, 1992, 1993) but even he concludes with some rather unspecific 'broad themes' in (what he calls) green ideology:

most [political ecologists] assert the systematic interdependence of species and the environment . . . [and] there is a tendency to be minimally sceptical about the supreme position of human beings on the planet. Furthermore there is a general anxiety about what industrial civilisation is actually doing to the planet.

(Vincent, 1993, p. 270)

The themes he identifies are rather watered down by the words 'tendency', 'minimally' and 'general', and they are so general as to be acceptable to a large number of people in modern industrial societies today – certainly a larger number than would style themselves political ecologists.

But it is only right to outline two advantages of the minimalist position, both of which are passed up in the approach adopted in this book. The first is that it reflects clearly the rather eclectic nature of the green movement itself. Many of the people and organizations whom we would want to include in the green movement are environmentalist rather than political-ecologist, and defining ecologism as strictly as I want to can obscure this very important truth about green politics.

The second advantage is that the minimalist approach allows us to see that the movement has a history – a fact which is less obvious from the maximalist point of view because it tends to date the existence of ecologism from the 1960s or even the 1970s. Minimalists will typically look to the nineteenth century for the beginnings of ecologism, but while some of the ideas we now associate with ecologism were indeed flagged over a hundred years ago, this is a far cry from saying that ecologism itself existed over a hundred years ago. Jesus Christ's cleaving to a measure of social equality did not make him a socialist, and nor does it mean that socialism existed in the first century AD. These, then, are the general issues at stake in thinking about ecologism, and they will resurface as detail in what remains of this chapter.

The need for a rethink of the values proposed in the radical green agenda is derived from the belief that there are natural limits to economic and population growth. It is important to stress the word 'natural' because green ideologues argue that economic growth is prevented not for social reasons – such as restrictive relations of production – but because the Earth itself has a limited carrying capacity (for population), productive capacity (for resources of all types) and absorbent capacity (pollution). This view was first put forward in its fullest form in *The Limits to Growth* report (Meadows *et al.*, 1974), a book which is of seminal importance to ecologism. It has been revised and updated twice (Meadows *et al.*, 1992 and 2005), but the message has remained substantially unchanged. 'The earth is finite,' write the authors of *Beyond the Limits*, sequel to the original *Limits* report, and '[G]rowth of anything physical, including the human population and its cars and buildings and smokestacks, cannot continue forever' (Meadows *et al.*, 1992, p. 7). From a green perspective, then, continuous growth cannot be achieved by overcoming what might appear to be temporary limits – such as those imposed by a lack of technological sophistication; continuous and unlimited growth is *prima facie* impossible. This theme will be pursued in Chapter 3.

At this point ecologism throws into relief a factor – the Earth itself – that has been present in all modern political ideologies but has remained invisible, either due to its very ubiquity or because these ideologies' schema for description and prescription have kept it hidden. Ecologism makes the Earth as physical object the very foundation-stone of its intellectual edifice, arguing that its finitude is the basic reason why infinite population and economic growth are impossible and why, consequently, profound changes in our social and political behaviour need to take place. The enduring image of this finitude is a familiar picture taken by the cameras of Apollo 8 in 1968 showing a blue-white Earth suspended in space above the moon's horizon. Twenty years earlier the astronomer Fred Hoyle had written that 'Once a photograph of the Earth, taken from the outside, is available . . . a new idea as powerful as any other in history will be let loose' (in Myers, 1985, p. 21). He may have been right. The green movement has adopted this image and the sense of beauty and fragility that it represents to generate concern for the Earth, arguing that everyday life in industrial society has separated us from it: 'Those who live amid concrete, plastic, and computers can easily forget how fundamentally our well-being is linked to the land' (Myers, 1985, p. 22). We are urged to recognize what is and has always been the case: that all wealth (of all types) ultimately derives from the planet.

Sustainable societies

The centrality of the limits to growth thesis and the conclusions drawn from it lead political ecologists to suggest that radical changes in our social habits and practices are required. The kind of society that would incorporate these changes is often referred to by greens as the 'sustainable society', and the fact that we are able to identify aspects of a green society distinguishable from the preferred pictures of other ideologies is one of the reasons why ecologism may be seen as a political ideology in its own right.

I shall outline what I understand the sustainable society to look like in Chapter 3, but two points about it should be borne in mind from the outset. First, political ecologists will stress that consumption of material goods by over-consuming individuals in 'advanced industrial countries' should be reduced; and second (linked to the first), that human needs are not best satisfied by continual economic growth as we understand it today. Jonathon Porritt writes: 'If you want one simple contrast between green and conventional politics, it is our belief that quantitative demand must be reduced, not expanded' (Porritt, 1984a, p. 136). Greens argue that if there are limits to growth then there are limits to consumption as well. The green movement is therefore faced with the difficulty of simultaneously calling into question a major aspiration of most people – maximizing consumption of material objects – and making its position attractive.

There are two aspects to its strategy. On the one hand it argues that continued consumption at increasing levels is impossible because of the finite productive limits imposed by the Earth. On this view our aspiration to consume will be curtailed whether we like it or not. Greens argue that recycling or the use of renewable energy sources will not, alone, solve the problems posed by a finite Earth – we shall still not be able to produce or consume at an ever-increasing rate. Such techniques might be a part of the strategy for a sustainable society, but they do not materially affect the absolute limits to production and consumption in a finite system:

> The fiction of combining present levels of consumption with 'limit-less recycling' is more characteristic of the technocratic vision than of an ecological one. Recycling itself uses resources, expands energy, creates thermal pollution; on the bottom line, it's just an industrial activity like all the others. Recycling is both useful and necessary – but it is an illusion to imagine that it provides any basic answers.
>
> (Porritt, 1984a, p. 183)

This observation is the analogue of the distinction made earlier between environmentalism and ecologism. To paraphrase Porritt, the recycling of waste is an essential part of being green but it is not the same thing as being radically green. Being radically green involves living a different kind of collective life. Greens are generally suspicious of purely technological solutions to environmental problems – the 'techno-logical fix' – and the relatively cautious endorsement of recycling is just one instance of this. As long ago as the *The Limits to Growth* thesis it was suggested that 'We cannot expect technological solutions alone to get us out of this vicious circle' (Meadows *et al.*, 1974, p. 192) and this has since become a central dogma of green politics.

The second strategy employed by green ideologues to make palatable their recommendation for reduced consumption is to argue for the benefits of a less materialistic society. In the first place they make a distinction between needs and wants, suggesting that many of the items we consume and that we consider to be needs are in fact wants that have been 'converted' into needs at the behest of powerful persuasive forces. In this sense they will suggest that little would be lost by some possessing fewer objects. The distinction between needs and wants is highly controversial and will be considered in more detail in Chapter 3.

Second, some deep-greens argue that the sustainable society that would replace the present consumer society would provide for wider and more profound forms of fulfilment than that provided by the consumption of material objects. This may profitably be seen as part of the contention made by some greens that the sustainable society would be a spiritually fulfilling place in which to live. There has recently been something of a boom in 'happiness studies', and it has been pointed out that there is no correlation between the raw wealth of a society and the happiness of its citizens (Layard, 2003, 2005). Western societies have become richer over the past fifty years, but they have not necessarily become happier. There are a number of reasons for this which it would be inappropriate to detail here; suffice to say that happiness research has lent some support to the long-standing green contention that fulfilment is not a necessary function of wealth, and that Gross Domestic Product is a poor proxy indicator for well-being.

A controversial theme in green politics which is associated with the issue of reducing consumption is that of the need to bring down population levels. As Fritjof Capra explains: To slow down the rapid depletion of our natural resources, we need not only to abandon the idea of continuing economic growth, but to control the worldwide increase in population' (Capra, 1983, p. 227). Despite heavy criticism, particularly from the left – Mike Simons has described Paul Ehrlich's proposals as 'an invitation to genocide' (Simons, 1988, p. 13) – greens have stuck to their belief that long-term global sustainability will involve reductions in population, principally on the grounds that fewer people will consume fewer objects: 'the only long-term way to reduce consumption is to stabilize and then reduce the number of consumers. The best resources policies are doomed to failure if not linked to population policy' (Irvine and Ponton, 1988, p. 29). The issue of population will be critically assessed in Chapter 3.

Reasons to care for the environment

In an obvious way, care for the environment is one of ecologism's informing (although not exhaustive) principles. Many different reasons may be given for why we should be more careful with the environment, and I want to suggest that ecologism advances a specific mix of them. In this sense, the nature of the arguments advanced for care for the environment comes to be a part of ecologism's definition.

In our context such arguments may be summarized under two headings: those which suggest that human beings ought to care for the environment because it is in our interest to do so, and those which suggest that the environment has an intrinsic value in the sense that its value is not exhausted by its being a means to human ends – and even if it cannot be made a means to human ends it still has value.

Most of the time we encounter arguments of the first sort: for example, that tropical rainforests should be preserved because they provide oxygen, or raw materials for medicines, or because they prevent landslides. This is not a complete list of reasons, though. The additional *ecological* perspective is neatly captured in *The Green Alternative* in response to the question, 'Isn't concern for nature and the environment actually concern for ourselves?':

> Many people see themselves as enlightened when they argue that the nonhuman world ought to be preserved: (i) as a stockpile of genetic diversity for agricultural, medical and other purposes; (ii) as material for scientific study, for instance of our evolutionary origins; (iii) for recreation and (iv) for the opportunities it provides for aesthetic pleasure and spiritual inspiration. However, although enlightened, these reasons are all related to the instrumental value of the nonhuman world to humans. What is missing is any sense of a more impartial, biocentric – or biosphere-centred – view in which the nonhuman world is considered to be of intrinsic value.
>
> (Bunyard and Morgan-Grenville, 1987, p. 284)

Lurking behind this statement are complex issues that will be discussed in detail in Chapter 2, but in this context of thinking about ecologism we need to make a distinction between the 'public' and the 'private' ecologist. The private ecologist, in conversation with like-minded people, will most likely place the intrinsic value position ahead of the human-instrumental argument in terms of priority, suggesting that the latter is less worthy, less profoundly ecological, than the former. The public ecologist, however, keen to recruit, will almost certainly appeal first to the enlightened self-interest thesis and only move on to talk about intrinsic value once the first argument is firmly in place.

Crisis and its political-strategic consequences

No presentation of ecologism would be complete without the appropriate (usually heavy) dosage of warnings of doom and gloom. Political ecologists invariably claim that dire consequences will result if their warnings are not heeded and their prescriptions not followed. The thirty-year update of *Limits to Growth* provides a typical example:

> we are much more pessimistic about the global future than we were in 1972. It is a sad fact that humanity has largely squandered the past 30 years in futile debates and well-intentioned, but halfhearted, responses to the global ecological challenge.
>
> (Meadows *et al.*, 2005, p. xvi)

The radical green's consistent use of an apocalyptic tone is unique in the context of modern political ideologies, and it might be argued that the movement has relied too heavily on these sorts of projections as a means of galvanizing people into action. The consequences of this have been twofold. First, there is the unfounded accusation by the movement's critics that it is informed by an overwhelming sense of pessimism as to the prospects of the planet and the human race along with it. In fact the movement's pessimism relates only to the likely life expectancy of current social and political practice. Greens are generally unerringly optimistic with respect to our chances of dealing with the crisis they believe they have uncovered – they merely argue that a major change of direction is required. As *Beyond the Limits* concludes:

> [T]his decline is not inevitable. To avoid it two changes are necessary. The first is a comprehensive revision of policies and practices that perpetuate growth in material consumption and in population. The second is a rapid, drastic increase in the efficiency with which materials and energy are used.
>
> (Meadows *et al.*, 1992, p. xvi)

The second and perhaps more serious consequence of the movement's reliance on gloomy prognostications is that its theorists appear to have felt themselves absolved from serious thinking about realizing the change they propose. This, indeed, is another feature of the ideology that ought to be noted: the tension between the radical nature of the social and political change it seeks, and the reliance on traditional liberal-democratic means of bringing it about. It is as though the movement's advocates have felt that the message was so obvious that it only needed to be given for it to be acted upon. The obstacles to radical green change have not been properly identified, and the result is an ideology that lacks an adequate programme for social and political transformation. Further comment on this will be made in Chapter 4.

Universality and social change

A related feature that ought to be mentioned, however, is the potentially universal appeal of the ideology. Up until now it has not been aimed at any particular section of society but is addressed to every single individual on the planet regardless of colour, gender, class, nationality, religious belief and so on. This is a function of the green movement's argument that environmental degradation and the social dislocation that goes with it are everybody's problem and therefore ought to be everybody's concern: 'we are *all* harmed by the ecological crisis and therefore we *all* have a common interest in uniting together with people of *all* classes and *all* political allegiances to counter this mutually shared threat' (Tatchell in Dodds, 1988, p. 45; emphasis in the original). Ecologism thus has the potential to argue more easily than most modern political ideologies that it is, literally, in everyone's interest to follow its prescriptions.

This is not so obviously true of other modern political ideologies. None of them is able to argue that the penalty for not following its advice is the threat of major environmental and social dislocation for everyone. The potentially universal appeal generated by this observation has undoubtedly been seen by the green movement as a positive characteristic, to be exploited for all it is worth. I shall examine this position in Chapter 4 and ask whether or not this belief is misplaced, and whether it has in fact been counterproductive in the sense of providing another reason for not attending sufficiently rigorously to the issue of social change. This thought has been prompted by the environmental justice movement in the USA which has pointed out that environmental degradation is suffered most acutely by the poor and the vulnerable, not by the rich. So poor communities get more than their fair share of landfill sites, and environmental disasters disproportionately affect the weak (Gerrard, 1995). For example, Hurricane Katrina, which struck the Florida coast in 2005 and devastated New Orleans, affected poor people more than wealthier ones, not so much because the disaster was any worse in the poorer suburbs but because people living in them were not able to cope with its effects. So people with money were more easily able to flee the city while those without private transport or the fare for buses and taxis had to stay behind. These observations have given rise to what Joan Martinez-Alier has called 'the environmentalism of the poor' (2002). Martinez-Alier contrasts a northern, post-materialist environmentalism with a southern material-ist environmentalism, with the latter aimed at securing a fair share of environmental resources for weak and vulnerable people. This kind of environmentalism calls into question the universalism discussed above, and suggests that poorer people have a stronger and more immediate interest in 'just sustainability' than those who are better-off.

Left and right: communism and capitalism

In standard political terms and in order to help distinguish ecologism from other political ideologies, it is useful to examine the widespread green claim to 'go beyond' the left–right political spectrum: 'In calling for an ecological, nonviolent, nonexploitative society, the Greens (*die Grünen*) transcend the linear span of left-to-right' (Spretnak and Capra, 1985, p. 3). Jonathon Porritt translates this into a transcendence of capitalism and communism, and remarks that 'the debate between the protagonists of capitalism and communism is about as uplifting as the dialogue between Tweedledum and Tweedledee' (Porritt, 1984a, p. 44). The basis for this claim is that from a certain green perspective the similarities between communism and capitalism can be made to seem greater than their differences:

> Both are dedicated to industrial growth, to the expansion of the means of production, to a materialist ethic as the best means of meeting people's needs, and to unimpeded technological develop-ment. Both rely on increasing centralisation and large-scale bureau-cratic control and co-ordination. From a viewpoint of narrow scientific rationalism, both insist that the planet is there to be conquered, that big is self-evidently beautiful, and that what cannot be measured is of no importance.
>
> (Porritt, 1984a, p. 44)

The name generally given to this way of life is 'industrialism', which Porritt goes so far as to call a 'super-ideology' within which commun-ism and capitalism are inscribed, and which he describes elsewhere as 'adherence to the belief that human needs can only be met through the *permanent* expansion of the process of production and consumption' (in Goldsmith and Hildyard, 1986, pp. 343–4). This observation is central to green ideology, pointing up both the focus of attack on contemporary politics and society – industrialism – and the claim that ecologism calls into question assumptions with which we have lived for at least two centuries. Ecologists argue that discussion about the respective merits of communism and capitalism is rather like rearranging the deckchairs on the *Titanic:* they point out that industrialism suffers from the contradiction of undermining the very context in which it is possible, by unsustainably consuming a finite stock of resources in a world that does not have a limitless capacity to absorb the waste produced by the industrial process.

Although the green movement appears to view 'left and right' and 'capitalism and communism' as synonymous pairs, I want to look at them separately, if only because the terms used to examine them will be different. It ought nevertheless to be said that the green claim in both cases has come in for criticism, especially regarding the second pair, and especially from the left.

In some respects we can talk of the green movement quite happily in terms of left and right because the terms we use to discuss the difference between the two can easily be applied to it. If, for example, we take equality and hierarchy as characteristics held to be praiseworthy within left-wing and right-wing thought respectively, then ecologism is clearly left-wing, arguing as it does for forms of equality among human beings and between human beings and other species. However, to argue that ecologism is unequivocally left-wing is not so easy. For instance, green politics is in principle averse to anything but the most timid engineering of the social and natural world by human beings. Since the French Revolution it has been a theme of left-wing thought that the existence of a concrete natural order of things with which human beings should conform and not tamper is a form of medieval mumbo-jumbo used by the right to secure and ossify privilege. The left has consistently argued that the world is there to be remade in the image of 'man' (usually) in accordance with plans drawn up by 'men' (usually), and in which the only reference to a natural order is to an abstract one outside of time and place.

The radical green aspiration to insert the human being in its 'proper place' in the natural order and to generate a sense of humility in the face of it appears to be 'right-wing' in this context:

> The belief that we are 'apart from' the rest of creation is an intrinsic feature of the dominant world-order, a man-centred or anthropo-centric philosophy. Ecologists argue that this ultimately destructive

belief must be rooted out and replaced with a life-centred or biocentric philosophy.

(Porritt, 1984a, p. 206)

Ecologists can only perversely be accused of using this idea to preserve wealth and privilege, but the understanding of the place of the human being in a pre-ordained and immensely complex world with which we meddle at our peril is nevertheless a right-wing thought. Joe Weston, writing from a socialist perspective, puts it like this:

> Clearly the green analysis of environmental and social issues is within the broad framework of right-wing ideology and philosophy. The belief in 'natural' limits to human achievement, the denial of class divisions and the Romantic view of 'nature' all have their roots in the conservative and liberal political divisions.

(Weston, 1986, p. 24)

John Gray (1993b) and Roger Scruton (2006) have picked up some of this and turned it into a virtue from a conservative point of view. Gray suggests that there are three 'deep affinities' between green and conservative thinking. The first is that 'both conservativism and Green theory see the life of humans in a multigenerational perspective'; second, '[B]oth conservative and Green thinkers repudiate the shibboleth of liberal individualism, the sovereign subject, the autonomous agent whose choices are the origin of all that has value'; and third, 'both Greens and conservatives consider risk-aversion the path of prudence when new technologies, or new social practices, have consequences that are large and unpredictable' (Gray, 1993b, pp. 136–7). Although Gray does not count a common opposition to 'hubristic humanism' in his list, he might have done (ibid., p. 139). The similarities which Gray outlines are well chosen, but there is plenty in the detail that may yet provide for lengthy arguments between political ecologists and conservatives (just what is to replace the shibboleth of the liberal individual? What are the rules for distribution across generations to be?) – and of course there is no mention of ecocentrism (as a fundamental distinguishing characteristic) at all. I shall examine the relationship between ecologism and conservatism in greater detail in Chapter 5. Generally, for now, the difficulty of describing ecologism as either obviously left- or right-wing is a legacy of its ambiguous relationship with the Enlightenment tradition referred to in the Introduction, and is consistent with its self-image of calling into question stock responses to that tradition.

Second, the green claim to transcend capitalism and communism, in the sense that ecologism calls into question an overriding feature common to them both (industrialism), has drawn heavy criticism from the left. There are two reasons for this. In the first place it brings back grim memories of the 'end of ideology' thesis of the 1960s. This thesis has been interpreted by the left as itself ideological in the sense of observing a putative veneer of agreement about the basic goals of society, and so obscuring and delegitimatizing alternative strategies. The 'end of ideology' position was buttressed by the convergence thesis, which argued that communist and capitalist nations were beginning to converge on a similar course of social and political action. The left pointed out that such analyses served to cement existing power relationships – particularly in the capitalist nations – and therefore performed a conservative social function. For socialists there is no more important political battle to be fought than that between capital and labour; and any politics that claims to transcend this battle is regarded with suspicion. The idea that the interests of capital and labour have somehow converged amounts to a betrayal, from the socialist point of view, of the project to liberate labour from capital. The interests of capital and labour are not the same, yet the green belief that both are inscribed in the super-ideology of industrialism makes it seem as though they are.

At root, proposes Joe Weston, the green movement's mistake is to refuse a class analysis of society It 'argues that traditional class divisions are at an end' (Weston, 1986, p. 22), and uses the concept 'industrial society ... to distinguish contemporary society from orthodox capitalism; it is not a neutral term' (ibid.). It is not neutral in the sense that it removes capitalism from the glare of criticism and thus contributes to its survival and reproduction. Similarly the original 'end of ideology' thesis was accompanied by an analysis of how policies are formulated and social conflicts resolved, collected under the term 'pluralism'. Socialists have always considered this to be a dubious description, principally because the apparently democratic diversity and openness it implies serve to obscure capitalism's hierarchy of wealth and power, based on the domination of labour by capital.

From Weston's point of view it is no accident, therefore, that the green movement's 'industrialism' thesis, kept company by the abandonment of a class analysis of society, also results in a political practice based around the pressure groups of pluralism. In this sense there is no difference between Daniel Bell and Jonathon Porritt. In the first place, Porritt's attack on industrialism prevents him from seeing that the real problem is capitalism; second, his failure to subscribe to a class analysis of society leads him to the dead-end of pressure-group politics; and third – and probably most serious from a socialist point of view – not only is he not attacking capitalism as he should, but he is contributing to its survival by deflecting criticism from it.

Porritt has recently shifted his position away from a thoroughgoing critique of capitalism to a cautious endorsement of it (Porritt, 2005). It is, he says, 'the only economic game in town' (Porritt, 2005, p. xiv), so if there is no hope for a sustainable capitalism, then there is no hope for sustainability, period. Greens of a more leftist persuasion, such as Derek Wall (2005) and Saral Sarkar (1999), will continue to argue that capitalism is part of the problem rather than part of the solution, principally because the drive for capital accumulation occurs without reference to or respect for the limits imposed by a finite planet (the 'limits to growth' argument).

So the left's belief that it is not possible to transcend capitalism while capitalism still exists makes it suspicious of claims to the contrary. David Pepper, for instance, has suggested that we should not see 'environmentalist concerns or arguments' as 'above or unrelated to traditional political concerns, but stemming from, and used very much as agents to advance, the interests of one traditional political side or the other' (Pepper, 1984, p. 187). The general conclusion the left draws is that ecologism serves the interests of the status quo by diverting attention from the real battleground for social change: the relationship between capital and labour. We will be in a better position to assess the green claim to transcend this battleground in Chapter 3 when ecologism's analysis and solutions to the crisis it identifies are set out, and I shall make more of ecologism's relationship with socialism in Chapter 5. The main point for now, though, is that it is undoubtedly a central feature of ecologism that it identifies the 'super-ideology' of industrialism as the thesis to be undermined, and it has been relatively easy for green ideologues to point to high levels of environmental degradation in Eastern Europe to make their point that there is little to choose – from this perspective – between capitalism and communism. It makes no appreciable difference who owns the means of production, they say, if the production process itself is based on doing away with the preconditions of its very existence.

Historical specificity

The issue of the history of ecologism has been the focus of considerable disagreement in recent commentaries. What is generally accepted is that there are three views in contention (Vincent, 1992; Dobson, 1993a). The first attempts to trace ecological sentiments back to the dawn of the human species, at least to the palaeolithic or neolithic period; the second 'dates the ecology movement from the 1960s and 1970s'; and the third 'identifies the roots of ecological ideas in the nineteenth century' (Vincent, 1993, pp. 210–11).

The first position is often associated with the view that many thousands of years ago there existed a golden age of peaceful coexistence with nature which ended – on Max Oelschlaeger's reading – with the onset of the neolithic era (Oelschlaeger, 1991, p. 28), and which we have (in the modern industrial world) failed to recapture to this day. Apart from the insecure nature of the evidence for such claims (disputed with some success in Lewis (1992, pp. 43–81), for example), the links between what human beings thought tens of thousands of years ago and modern ecology seem too tenuous to tell us much about the nature of a contemporary ideology.

The third view – that ecologism has its roots in the nineteenth century – is probably the most widely accepted (see e.g. Heywood, 1992; Macridis, 1992; Vincent, 1992), and is often based on a reading of Anna Bramwell's seminal *Ecology in the 20th Century* (1989). Among the similarities between nineteenth-century thinking (some of it, anyway) and contemporary ecologism, Vincent notes: 'a critical reaction to the European Enlightenment tradition . . . [E]cologism looks sceptically at the supreme value of reason', a denial of 'the central place of human beings and [the belief] that nature is without value and can simply be manipulated by humans', and finally the impact which Malthus and Darwin made for the integration of a 'strongly materialist and scientific perspective with an immanent and naturalistic understanding of religion and morality' (Vincent, 1992, pp. 211–12).

We might want to quibble over the detail of these claims, but it would be foolish to deny the broad parallels between the combination of scientific rationalism and Romantic arcadianism in both the nineteenth century and today's ecology movement. These (and other) parallels have been reaffirmed by Bramwell in the belief that the import of her earlier work has been largely accepted (Bramwell, 1994, pp. 25–33). Vincent believes that these parallels have been deliberately overlooked due to the reactionary political views associated with such positions in the late nineteenth and early twentieth centuries. Basing his argument largely on Bramwell's work, he suggests that the carriers of ecology in this period were primarily conservatives and nationalists (particularly of a 'folkish' persuasion) and, later, fascists and Nazis – it is by now *de rigueur* to point out that Himmler established an organic farm at Dachau concentration camp, and that both Himmler and Hitler were vegetarians (Bramwell, 1989, pp. 204 and 270, fn. 1). These, argues

Vincent, are embarrassing skeletons for today's predominantly left-leaning political ecologists, and so they are confined to the cupboard by the simple expedient of dating ecologism from, say, 1966 or 1973 rather than from 1866 or 1873 (the main contenders for when German biologist Ernst Haeckel first used the word 'ecology'; Bramwell, 1989, p. 253, fn. 2).

Quite how much there is in this political reason for making ecologism very contemporary rather than merely modern is hard to determine, but we do need to distinguish the search for the roots of ecologism from a description of the ideology itself. It is undeniable that ideas similar to those entertained by modern greens may be found in late nineteenth- and early twentieth-century industrial and industrializing societies – and although Vincent does not mention the 'energy economists' of France, Britain, the USA, Russia and Germany in the first quarter of the twentieth century, he might have done so (Bramwell, 1989, pp. 64–91). This is not, though, the same as saying that ecologism – as ideology – existed at that time, and two modern-day factors have served to bring ecologism fully into focus since then.

First, the scope of concerns in the modern age is new. Most of the resource, waste and pollution problems that were raised in earlier times had a fundamentally local character. Modern ecologism rests a large part of its case on the belief that environmental degradation has taken on a global dimension – most obviously in cases such as global warming and ozone depletion, but also in view of the potentially global climatic implications of deforestation (Dobson, 2004). Human beings have always interacted with their environment, of course, and not always wisely (Ponting, 1991). But greens believe that in the modern age the scale of human activity relative to the biosphere's capacity to absorb and sustain it has increased to the point where long-term human survival and the biosphere's integrity are put in doubt. This view – right or wrong – helps to distinguish ecologism from its more *ad hoc* environmentalist past and present.

Second, political ecologists believe that single-issue approaches to dealing with environmental problems do not address their seriousness at a sufficiently fundamental level. Greens campaign against acid rain, deforestation and ozone depletion, of course, but they do so by arguing that these problems stem from basic political, social and economic relations that encourage unsustainable practices. This systemic analysis leads to systemic prescriptions for change, and the interrelated and wide-ranging nature of the critique is a characteristic of modern ecologism missing from its nineteenth- and early twentieth-century progenitors. It is somewhat ironic that Green parties are criticized for being single-issue parties when the ideology – ecologism – from which they draw their inspiration is devoted to showing how it is the *connections* between various aspects of social, political and economic life that produce environmental problems.

It may be ill advised to try to be precise about dates in this context, but *The Limits to Growth* report of 1972 is hard to beat as a symbol for the birth of ecologism in its fully contemporary guise. As Eckersley has put it: 'the notion that there might be ecological limits to economic growth that could not be overcome by human technological ingenuity and better planning was not seriously entertained until after the much publicized "limits to growth" debate of the early 1970s' (Eckersley, 1992, p. 8). This is how the report expressed its principal conclusion:

> We are convinced that realization of the quantitative restraints of the world environment and of the tragic consequences of an overshoot is essential to the initiation of new forms of thinking that will lead to a fundamental revision of human behaviour and, by implication, of the entire fabric of present day society.
>
> (Meadows *et al.*, 1974, p. 190)

The sense of the radical change proposed by deep-greens is captured in the final phrases of this quotation, and clearly goes beyond the managerial environmentalism that I am keen to separate from ecologism proper.

Recognizing the historical situatedness of the ideology helps us to understand the nature of the ideology itself. We are provided with a boundary beyond which (in the past) ecologism could not have existed, and therefore any movement or idea behind that boundary can bear only an informing relation to ecologism as I think we ought to understand it. Rachel Carson's book *Silent Spring* (1965; first published in 1962), then, can only inform ecologism rather than 'be' it due to the absence of an overriding political strategy for dealing with the problems it identifies. My suggestion is that, in 1962, ecologism (and therefore the possibility of being radically green) did not exist, and that Rachel Carson's book and the period in which it was written are best viewed as part of the preconditions for ecologism. Looking at it in this way we shall avoid the mistake made in many commentaries on and anthologies of socialism, say, which talk of the cleric John Ball (who spoke on behalf of English peasants during the rebellion of 1381) as if he were a socialist. The most that can be said of him, living as he did well before the French and Industrial Revolutions that gave birth to socialism proper, was that his sentiments were socialistic. Similarly, the pre-1970 ideas and movements that have an affinity with ecologism are 'green' rather than green.

The final important consequence of historicizing the ideology is that it enables us to emphasize the novelty of its analysis. It has been remarked that, despite its claims to the contrary, the green movement's perspective is merely a reworking of old themes. Thus, for example, its warnings about population growth are substantially contained in the work of Thomas Malthus; its reluctance fully to embrace the mechanistic reason characteristic of the Enlightenment was a recurrent theme in the Romantic movement of the nineteenth century; and even its apocalyptic tone has been prefigured on countless occasions in countless Messianic movements. Such critics generally take these observations to indicate that, as has happened before, the subordinate themes associated with the green movement will eventually be submerged by their dominant and opposed counterparts. This interpretation fails to take full account of the historically specific nature of ecologism. For it is precisely the ideology's point that, while the terms of its analysis are not new in themselves, the fact of their being posited here and now gives those terms a novel resonance. So the critique of mechanistic forms of reason, for instance, cannot be directly mapped back on to similar critiques made in the nineteenth century. The additional factor to be taken into account, argues the green movement, is the potentially terminal state to which slavish usage of this reason has led us. In this way history defines the context within which ecologism operates (and therefore helps define ecologism itself), and provides the ground on which old themes acquire new resonances, coalescing to form a full-blown modern political ideology.

Conclusion

It needs to be stressed time and again that this is a book about ecologism and not about environmentalism. Most people will understand environmentalism – a managerial approach to the environment within the context of present political and economic practices – to be what green politics is about. I hope I have begun to establish that there is more to it than this. . Ecologists and environmentalists are inspired to act by the environmental degradation they observe, but their strategies for remedying it differ wildly. Environmentalists do not necessarily subscribe to the limits to growth thesis, nor do they typically seek to dismantle 'industrialism'. They are unlikely to argue for the intrinsic value of the non-human environment and would balk at any suggestion that we (as a species) 'nurture our spiritual capacity' (Porritt, 2005,

p. 145). Environmentalists will typically believe that technology can solve the problems it creates, and will probably regard any suggestions that only a reduction in material throughput in the production process will provide for sustainability as wilful nonsense. In short, what passes for green politics in the pages of today's newspapers is not the ideology of political ecology, properly understood. This is why the student of green politics needs to do more than scratch the surface of its public image in order to appreciate the full range of the debate that it has opened up.

2 Philosophical foundations

In 1855, Chief Seattle is supposed to have said:

> We know that the white man does not understand our ways. He is a stranger who comes in the night, and takes from the land whatever he needs. The earth is not his friend, but his enemy, and when he's conquered it he moves on. He kidnaps the earth from his children. His appetite will devour the earth and leave behind a desert. If all the beasts were gone, we would die from a great loneliness of the spirit, for whatever happens to the beasts also happens to us. All things are connected. Whatever befalls the Earth, befalls the children of the Earth.
>
> (quoted in Bunyard and Morgan-Grenville, 1987, p. 3)

Although it turns out that this speech was a fake, it has not stopped greens making liberal use of it and the sentiments it contains. Central to the theoretical canon of green politics is the belief that our social, political and economic problems are caused, in part, by our intellectual relationship with the world and the practices that stem from it (Benson, 2000).

In this regard, what sets ecologism apart from other political ideologies is its focus on the relationship between human beings and the non-human natural world. No other modern political ideology has this concern. Green, or environmental, *philosophy* is largely concerned with expressing what it is about the non-human natural world that political ecologists believe to be ethically important, and how best to defend it intellectually (Curry, 2006). These defences differ from the pragmatic 'limits to growth' arguments referred to in Chapter 1 and discussed in detail in Chapter 3. It is not just that the non-human world constitutes a set of resources for human use and that if we run them down we threaten the very basis of human life itself: it is that even if resources were infinite, there might still be good reason not to treat the non-human world in a purely instrumental fashion.

Political ecologists are moved by what Robert Goodin has called a 'green theory of value', which 'links the value of things to some naturally occurring properties of the objects themselves' (Goodin, 1992, p. 24). This theory of value is importantly different from other, more familiar ones associated with other political ideologies:

> It differs from a producer based theory of value in so far as it insists that . . . value-imparting properties are natural, rather than being somehow artefacts of human activities. And it differs from a consumer-based theory of value in so far as it insists that those value-imparting properties somehow inhere in the objects themselves, rather than in any mental states (actual or hypothetical, now or later) of those who partake of those objects.
>
> (Goodin, 1992, p. 25)

It is, then, the 'natural value' of things, imparted by their 'having been created by natural processes rather than by artificial human ones' (Goodin, 1992, p. 27) that political ecologists are particularly keen to preserve and promote. This is not to say that they are not interested in other types of things with different kinds of value, but what sets ecologism apart from other political ideologies is, precisely, its primordial interest in natural value and its promotion and preservation. This is, as Goodin says, the 'logical primitive' of green moral theory (Goodin, 1992, p. 120).

As a consequence of this, radical greens will have a particular view of what the much-vaunted objective of 'environmental sustainability' is about. Environmental sustainability, and its close cousin, sustainable development, have become all things to all people in the rush for environmental political correctness. It is possible, though, to bring some analytical clarity to the apparent chaos of meanings (see Dobson, 1998, ch. 2; Jacobs, 1999a), and political ecologists will give an unequivocal answer when asked what environmental sustainability means for them. Any definition of environmental sustainability must answer the fundamental question, 'What is to be sustained?' and while there are a number of possible responses, political ecologists will answer, 'natural value'. What they want to see sustained into the future is, to repeat Goodin, the value of things created by natural processes rather than by artificial human ones.

Just what these 'things' might be is open to some debate, of course. Individual animals? Species? Only living things? Or non-living things like mountains and rivers too? Environmental philosophy is not only concerned with preserving and promoting natural value, therefore, but also with deciding which possessors of natural value should be preserved and promoted. I shall try to give a flavour of all these debates in what follows, but my principal intention is to focus on the kind of environmental philosophy that I believe underpins the radical ideology of ecologism being examined in this book. Environmental philosophy seeks to judge between various reasons for restraint, and I shall suggest that not all reasons that can be given are radically ecological reasons, and that this leads to a distinction between what has come to be known as 'deep ecology' on the one hand, and the public face of ecologism as a political ideology on the other. I shall explore this below.

In green thinking, the general targets of attack are those forms of thought that 'split things up' and study them in isolation, rather than those that 'leave them as they are' and study their interdependence. The best knowledge is held to be acquired not by the isolated examination of the parts of a system but by examining the way in which the parts interact. This act of synthesis, and the language of linkage and reciprocity in which it is expressed, is often handily collected in the term 'holism'. Greater recognition of mutual dependence and influence, it is argued, will encourage a sensitivity in our dealings with the 'natural' world that discrete atomism has conspicuously failed to do.

Political ecologists often derive evidence for a holistic description of the universe from developments in physics during the twentieth century. It is no accident that one of the intellectual champions of the green movement, Fritjof Capra, is a teacher and researcher of theoretical physics, and his books *The Tao of Physics* (1975) and *The Turning Point* (1983) had a tremendous impact on its early intellectual development. In this context, if twentieth-century physicists Niels Bohr and Werner Heisenberg are popular figures in the green pantheon, then Francis Bacon, René Descartes and Isaac Newton are their complementary opposites. These three, according to the analysis of most green theorists, produced a world-view at variance in virtually all respects with that demanded by ecological survival in the twentieth century. Briefly, Bacon developed methods and goals for science that involved (and involve) the domination and control of nature; Descartes insisted that even the organic world (plants, animals and so on) was merely an extension of the general mechanical nature of the universe; and Newton held that the workings of this machine universe could be understood by reducing it to a collection of 'solid, massy, hard, impenetrable, movable particles' (Newton, quoted in Capra, 1983, p. 52).

In contrast, twentieth-century physics' exploration of the subatomic world has led to a very different picture of the nature of the 'physical' universe. The Newtonian atomic description has given way to a universe in which (at the subatomic level at least) there are no solid objects, but rather fields of probability in which 'particles' have a tendency to exist. Nor are these 'particles' held to be definable in themselves: rather, their nature is in their relationship with other parts of the system. As Niels Bohr commented: 'Isolated material particles are abstractions, their properties being definable and observable only through their interaction with other systems' (quoted in Capra, 1983, p. 69). Further, Werner Heisenberg's Uncertainty Principle (fundamental to the practice of quantum physics) shows that the observer – far from being independent of her or his experiment – is inextricably a part of it. Capra draws from this the requisite ecological-theoretical conclusion: 'We can never speak about nature without, at the same time, speaking about ourselves' (Capra, 1983, p. 77). Greens say that given these underlying connections in the physical world, it is a mistake to try to deal with problems in isolation from one another. In the UK, the current New Labour administration is fond of the idea of 'joined-up government', and if this aspiration were converted to reality Greens would be wholly in favour. For instance, the problem of climate change cannot be solved without coordinated action across departments with responsibility for transport and for trade and industry, as well as for the environment. I shall say more about interconnectedness when we discuss the limits to growth thesis, where it is of special importance, and in a later section of this chapter, on so-called 'deep ecology'.

Deep ecology: ethics as a code of conduct

Some years ago, 'deep ecology' was regarded as a keystone of radical political-ecological thinking (Curry, 2006, pp. 71–81). It was believed that a fundamental ethical shift was required that would dethrone human interests as the centrepiece of political life and extend ethical concern deep into the natural world. In recent years, this ethical move has itself been decentred in favour of a more political response which calls for an extension of political voice that would include nature. What these two moves have in common is a questioning of the overriding centrality – the 'trumping' effect – of human interests over those of other parts of the natural world. I shall say more about the democratizing move later in this chapter but the ethical arguments that paved the way for it are critical and I shall deal with them now.

The first influential use of the term 'deep ecology' is generally credited to the Norwegian Arne Naess. In September 1972 Naess gave a lecture in Bucharest in which he drew a distinction between what he called the 'shallow' and the 'deep' ecology movements. The distinction had to do with the difference between a shallow concern at 'pollution and resource depletion', for the damaging effects this might have on human life, and the deep concern – for its own sake – for ecological principles such as complexity, diversity and symbiosis (Naess, 1973, p. 95). I suggest that deep ecology informs a certain type of radical green politics in a way that will not be obvious to those who make such politics synonymous with environmentalism. Indeed, ecologism's being informed by deep ecology is precisely what (partly) helps distinguish it from environmentalism: environmentalists will be happy with so-called 'shallow' ecological reasons for care for the environment, while deep ecologists will want to advance 'deeper' reasons which take the natural world as an entity worthy of moral concern in its own right.

The first question to which any ethical theory must have an answer is: To whom or to what should it apply? This is tied to a second question: In respect of the possession of what attributes do we admit a subject to membership of the ethical community? One ethical theory might hold, for example, that it should cover human beings (and only human beings), and that this is in virtue of their possession of the capacity to reason. In this way, the attribute (possession of a rational faculty) defines the boundaries of the ethical community. Environmental philosophy in general, and deep ecology in particular, may be regarded as a series of answers to these two questions. In this context the influence of the animal rights movement and its intellectual backers has been profound. It is largely true to say that the extension by the animal rights movement and its theorists of the ethical domain from human to (some) animals has until recently been seen by ecophilosophers and deep ecology theorists as the right course to pursue in their aim to produce an ethic for non-sentient nature.

An ethic for animals is by no means the same as an ethic for the environment, but, to the extent that it constitutes a foray across the species divide, it is a start. As long ago as the third century BC, Epicurus argued that just as humans can experience pleasure and pain so can animals, and more recently Peter Singer has famously turned this argument into reasons for moral constraint in our behaviour towards animals (Singer, 1975). Tom Regan builds a different bridge across the divide by arguing that human beings and some animals may similarly be regarded as 'subjects-of-a-life', and that if this is the reason why we regard humans as morally considerable, it would be inconsistent to deny (some) animals similar moral considerability too (Regan, 1988).

Neither Singer nor Regan get anywhere near an environmental ethic, however. Singer restricts moral considerability to sentient beings, while Regan's extension of the moral community is even more circumscribed: besides humans it includes no more than 'normal mammalian animals aged one or more' (Regan, 1988, p. 81). However, both theories do raise the spectre of 'speciesism' – discrimination on the grounds of species alone – and ask us whether such discrimination can be rationally justified. Rationalist approaches to a properly *environmental* ethic proceed along similar lines, with ethicists seeking less restrictive attributes for non-human entities than either sentience or a degree of mental complexity.

Lawrence Johnson, for example, argues that organisms and collections of organisms (including species and ecosystems) have well-being needs, and therefore an interest in having them met. This 'well-being interest' is the attribute, according to Johnson, which accords moral significance to those entities said to possess it (Johnson, 1991). This is an environmental ethic in two senses: first, it may be argued to apply to the whole environment; and second, it grants moral considerability to 'wholes' (species, ecosystems) as well as to individuals. It therefore covers the ground outlined by Aldo Leopold in his classic statement of the reach of an environmental ethic in *A Sand County Almanac:*

> All ethics so far evolved rest upon a single premise: that the individual is a member of a community of interdependent parts. His instincts prompt him to compete for his place in that community; but his ethics prompt him also to co-operate (perhaps in order that there be a place to compete for).
>
> The land ethic simply enlarges the boundaries of the community to include soils, waters, plants, and animals, or collectively: the land.
>
> (Leopold, 1949, p. 204)

Leopold also provided us with a general rule of thumb for sound environmental action by writing that '[A] thing is right when it tends to preserve the integrity, stability and beauty of the biotic community. It is wrong when it tends otherwise' (Leopold, 1949, pp. 224–5). This has worried subsequent commentators for its apparent implication that *individual* entities can justifiably be sacrificed for the *general* good, thereby bearing out Tom Regan's worries regarding 'environmental fascism' (Regan, 1988, p. 362).

Rationalist seekers after an environmental ethic have responded to this common criticism by advancing the cause of attributes which grant moral considerability to both individuals *and* wholes. Lawrence

Johnson's 'wellbeing interests' are a case in point, as is the attribute of 'autopoiesis' which Robyn Eckersley describes as the 'characteristic of self-reproduction or self-renewal' (Eckersley, 1992, p. 60), building on Fox's observation that '[L]iving systems ... are not merely *self-organizing* systems, they are self-regenerating or *self-renewing* systems' (Fox, 1990, p. 170). Eckersley continues:

> [A]n autopoietic approach to intrinsic value is not vulnerable to the objections that are associated with either extreme atomism or extreme holism. Whereas atomistic approaches attribute intrinsic value only to individual organisms, and whereas an unqualified holistic approach attributes intrinsic value only to whole eco-systems (or perhaps only the biosphere or ecosphere itself), an autopoietic approach recognizes ... the value not only of individual organisms but also of species, ecosystems, and the ecosphere ('Gaia').
>
> (Eckersley, 1992, p. 61)

Of course, this attribution of moral considerability to wholes as well as parts does not preclude the possibility of clashes between them – in fact, such clashes are inevitable. Attfield has pointed out, while considering the 'Gaian' argument that the biosphere as a whole has moral standing, that 'there can be a conflict between maximising its excellences and maximising the intrinsic value of its components' (Attfield, 1983, p. 159). The difficulties involved in resolving conflicts between the claims of different 'ecological subjects' have proved very awkward, and these problems emerged early on in the history of deep ecology with Naess' 'Principle Two' of deep ecology, described in his seminal 1973 paper. The idea is: 'Biospherical egalitarianism in principle' (Naess, 1973, p. 95). The difficulty with this becomes clear if one focuses on the small-print clause 'in principle' and Naess' own comment upon it: 'The "in principle" clause is inserted because any realistic praxis necessitates some killing, exploitation and suppression' (Naess, 1973, p. 95). This has become a famous phrase in environmental-ethical literature – how much killing, and who or what is to be exploited and suppressed?

The notion of biospherical egalitarianism is evidently problematic. Mary Midgley caustically rejects the principle of an 'equal right to live and blossom' when she says that biospherical egalitarians:

> have ... made things extremely hard for themselves lately by talking in a very wholesale, *a priori* French-revolutionary sort of way about all animals being equal, and denouncing 'speciesism' as

being an irrational form of discrimination, comparable to racism. This way of thinking is hard to apply convincingly to locusts, hookworms and spirochaetes, and was invented without much attention to them.

(Midgley, 1983a, p. 26)

So how are problems of conflict to be resolved? How is the 'in principle' clause to be filled out?

In general terms, environmental ethicists cope with this in the same way as the rest of us: by constructing a *hierarchy* of valued entities and collections of entities. These hierarchies are usually arrived at on the basis of taking the valued attribute in question and arguing that some entities or collections of entities have more of this attribute than others and therefore weigh more heavily in the moral balance. So Lawrence Johnson bases moral considerability on the possession of well-being interest. But it becomes clear that not all entities have the same (kind of) well-being interest: 'certainly it seems that humans are capable of a much higher level of well-being than is the smallpox organism' (Johnson, 1991, p. 261).

Indeed, it is striking how often these intrepid philosophical adventurers return, in a fairly traditional way, to home base. Complexity is a favourite datum around which to construct the requisite hierarchies. Warwick Fox has related value to complexity in the following way:

To the extent that value inheres in complexity of relations, and to the extent that complexity of relations is evidenced in the degree of an organism's central organisation (and therefore for capacity of richness of experience), then organisms are entitled to moral consideration commensurate with their degree of central organisation (or capacity for richness of experience) for the duration of their existence.

(Fox, 1984, p. 199)

He goes on: 'Recognising this, we should be clear that the central intuition of deep ecology does not entail the view that intrinsic value is spread evenly across the membership of the biotic community' (Fox, 1984, p. 199), and that therefore 'these hierarchical conceptions of intrinsic value . . . provide a guide to action in situations where values come into genuine conflict' (Fox, 1990, p. 182).

In this way, attempts to solve the difficulties with Naess' principle have often ended by undermining the principle itself. This is clear evidence of the intractability of the problem – and it is an absolutely practical problem for the politics of the green movement. Anyone who has drowned slugs in a cup of beer to stop them eating the lettuces may be congratulated on a certain ecological sensibility (by not using a chemical pesticide), but was the action environmentally ethical? As Richard Sylvan has commented: 'The guidelines as regards day-to-day living and action for a follower of deep ecology remain unduly and unfortunately obscure' (Sylvan, 1984b, p. 13).

At the root of all of this is the search for a way of investing value in beings other than in human beings such that we cannot legitimately treat them only as means to our ends: 'We need an ethic that recognises the intrinsic value of all aspects of the nonhuman world' (Bunyard and Morgan-Grenville, 1987, p. 284). Thus, it is hoped, an ethical non-anthropocentrism will underpin responsible behaviour towards the non-human natural world.

But what would intrinsic value look like? In a detailed survey, John O'Neill outlines three possibilities. First, '[A]n object has intrinsic value if it is an end in itself [as opposed to] a means to some other end'; second, '[I]intrinsic value is used to refer to the value an object has solely in virtue of its "intrinsic properties" '; and third, '[I]ntrinsic value is used as a synonym for "objective value", i.e. the value that an object possesses independently of the valuation of valuers' (O'Neill, 1993, p. 9). O'Neill concludes that holding an environmental ethic involves holding that 'non-human beings have intrinsic value in the first sense', but that holding a *defensible* environmental ethic might involve commitment to intrinsic value in the second or third senses (ibid., pp. 9–10).

As far as the issue of objective value is concerned, several attempts have been made to counter the subjectivist's objection that value is a quality invested in objects by human beings – in other words, objects do not possess value in their own right, rather we confer it upon them. Often, these attempts amount to an appeal to our intuition. For example, Holmes Rolston writes that 'We can be thrilled by a hawk in a windswept sky, by the rings of Saturn, the falls of Yosemite'. He admits that 'All these experiences are mediated by our cultural education', but asserts that they 'have high elements of giveness, of finding something thrown at us, of successful observation' (Rolston, 1983, p. 144). Similarly, he says that 'we have sometimes found values so intensely delivered that we have saved them wild, as in the Yellowstones, the Sierras and the Smokies' (ibid., p. 156). It is not the demand on our intuition that offends here, but while Rolston might persuade us to agree about the value of nature's 'spectaculars', it might not stretch as far as other offerings such as the anopheles mosquito and the tsetse fly.

Another favourite gambit of the intrinsic valuers is to ask us to conduct a thought experiment so as to test our susceptibility to their suggestions. The experiment can take many forms but the general idea is always the same. Consider, for example, Robin Attfield's version. Attfield asks us to think of the last surviving human being of a nuclear holocaust confronted by the last surviving elm tree. Attfield's question is: Would this human being be doing anything wrong in cutting down the elm tree, knowing that she or he would die before the tree? He reports that 'most people who consider this question conclude that his (*sic*) act would be wrong' (Attfield, 1983, p. 155), and that this is evidence of a visceral feeling for intrinsic value. His rationalization of this effect is that trees have a 'good of their own' and 'are thus at least serious candidates for moral standing' (ibid., p. 145).

It will be clear that cashing out all the complexities of intrinsic value involves detailed argumentation – any more of which would be misplaced here. The point at present is to contrast instrumental with non-instrumental value – and to say that although O'Neill (above) talks only of non-human 'beings', environmental ethicists also talk of the 'states, activities and/or experiences' of objects as potential sites of intrinsic value (e.g. Attfield, 1990, p. 63), and *collections* of entities, likewise.

Some ecophilosophers regard the difficulties of extending the work of animal rights theorists and sustaining an 'intrinsic value' position for nature as insurmountable, and have preferred to concentrate on the cultivation of a 'state of being' rather than a 'code of conduct' (Fox, 1986b, p. 4). This approach involves the belief that the development of an ecologically sound ethics is not possible within the current mode of ethical discourse (rights, duties, rational actors, the capacity for pain and suffering, and so on), and that such an ethics can only, and must, emerge from a new world-view. Those who argue from this perspective point out that the current mode of discourse demands that ecologists present reasons why the natural world should *not* be interfered with. What is required, they suggest, is the cultivation of an alternative world-view within which justifications would have to be produced as to why it *should* be interfered with (Fox, 1986a, p. 84). I turn to this now.

Deep ecology: ethics as a state of being

There was a time, then, when deep ecology was associated primarily with the belief that the non-human world could have (and did have) intrinsic value. This appeared to be a radical move within traditional ethical discourse, with far-reaching practical implications for the relationship between human beings and their environment. In ethical terms it was (and is) an attempt to move beyond human-prudential arguments for concern for the biosphere. However, as I have indicated above, a number of deep ecology theorists have balked at the implications of developing a cast-iron intrinsic value theory. This has led them to propose the necessity for an ethics proceeding from a changed state of consciousness, rather than hoping that it might be developed from within the present dominant one.

The 'state of being' position begins from the following sort of premise: that an 'ecological consciousness connects the individual to the larger world' (Bunyard and Morgan-Grenville, 1987, p. 282), and it has been developed in its most sophisticated form by Fox (1990). This 'ecological consciousness' serves as a new foundation on which a different (ecological) ethics and new (ecological) forms of behaviour would be built. The idea involves the cultivation of a sense of self that extends beyond the individual understood in terms of its isolated corporal identity. To this is added the notion that the enrichment of self depends upon the widest possible identification with the non-human world. Naess puts this in the following way:

> Self-realisation cannot develop far without sharing joys and sorrows with others, or more fundamentally, without the development of the narrow ego of the small child into the comprehensive structure of a Self that comprises all human beings. The ecological movement – as many earlier philosophical movements – takes a step further and asks for a development such that there is a deep identification of all individuals with life.
>
> (quoted in Fox, 1986a, p. 5)

Ecological consciousness, then, has to do with our identification with the non-human world, and the understanding that such identification is a premise for our own self-realization. It is not hard to see how an environmentally sound attitude emerges from this. Fox writes:

> For example, when asked why he does not plough the ground, the Nez Percé American Indian Smohalla does not reply with a closely reasoned explanation as to why the ground has intrinsic value but rather with a rhetorical question expressive of a deep identification with the earth: 'Shall I take a knife and tear my mother's breast?'
>
> (Fox, 1986a, p. 76)

In other words, the ethics issues 'naturally' from an alternative vision of reality, and this is the reason for the rejection of the primacy of ethics:

I'm not much interested in ethics and morals, [writes Naess] I'm interested in how we experience the world. . . . If deep ecology is deep it must relate to our fundamental beliefs, not just to ethics. Ethics follows from how we experience the world. If you experience the world so and so then you don't kill.

(quoted in Fox, 1986a, p. 46)

Fox himself observes that his 'transpersonal ecology' sense of self

has the highly interesting, even startling, consequence that ethics (conceived as being concerned with moral 'oughts') is rendered superfluous! The reason for this is that if one has a wide, expansive, or field-like sense of self then (assuming that one is not self-destructive) one will naturally (i.e. spontaneously) protect the nat-ural (spontaneous) unfolding of the expansive self (the ecosphere, the cosmos) in all its aspects.

(Fox, 1990, p. 217)

There are three points to make about this notion of ecological con-sciousness and its implications. In the first place: How far does it involve a reversion to the original sin of anthropocentrism? It seems clear that the principle of self-realization described above, although it generates concern for the non-human world, generates it for human-prudential reasons. To this extent, the development of an ecological consciousness as foundational to an environmental ethics may avoid the problems associated with producing the latter from conventional discourse, but at the cost of diluting the non-anthropocentrism that is held to be central to an ecological perspective.

The second point revolves around the problem of potential conflicts between human interests and the interests of the environment, dis-cussed in the previous section above. One can imagine an immensely wide identification of my self with the non-human world, but still see the survival of my own self as dependent upon a certain amount of 'killing, exploitation and suppression' of that non-human world. Where does that leave the practical implementation of the new ethics that might arise from an 'ecological consciousness'? It certainly seems that Richard Sylvan's demand for 'guidelines as regards day-to-day living' is not satisfied by anything in the ecological consciousness approach. Nor is this a problem confined to some putative 'pre-ecological conscious-ness era'. There is no suggestion made by this set of deep ecologists that, once a general ecological consciousness has been attained, prob-lems of environmental conflict will 'wither away'. Indeed, Warwick Fox recognizes that conflict between human beings and the non-human world is inevitable: 'my "small" self must meet certain vital needs even at the expense of the vital needs of other (relatively autonomous) entities' (1986a, p. 58). No guidelines are produced, however, for deciding between various sets of 'vital needs', or for deciding what they might be.

One possible answer to this objection is that guidance is given via the creation of hierarchies or 'degrees of intrinsic value' (Mathews, 1991, pp. 122–9), like those outlined in the previous section. The location of entities or collections of entities in these hierarchies will determine which of them are more equal than others in the case of a clash of interests. Of course, there are no agreed criteria for the construction of these hierarchies, so the fine print causes much more trouble than the general rules.

Another answer is that deep ecologists argue that they are in the business not of providing a rule-book, but of advancing a consciousness of identification with the non-human world that would markedly alter the conditions within which any rule-book would be written. Fox makes the point cogently:

> in terms of preserving the nonhuman world, the wider identification approach is more advantageous than the environmental axiological approach in a political or strategic sense because it shifts the onus for justification of one's actions from the person who wants to preserve the nonhuman world to the person who wants to disrupt or interfere with it.
>
> (Fox, 1986a, p. 84)

This is a genuinely significant point to make, and it would certainly have an effect on the environmental ethic that might emerge. Problems of conflict would, of course, remain, but the degree of conflict would be considerably reduced. There is no question but that the non-human world would benefit from a general instilling of an 'environmental consciousness', such as Fox and others have described it. Shifting the onus of justification in this way does not absolve us, of course, from drawing lines of legitimate environmental intervention, but it does mean that the lines will be drawn in very different territory from that which emerges if the onus of justification is not shifted. Put differently, if it is preservation of the non-human world that has to be justified, then more environmental intervention is likely to be countenanced than if it is intervention that has to be justified.

However, the next problem – and this is the third point – concerns the generation of this 'wider identification' in people. How are they to be convinced of it? If Robert Aitken is correct when he says that 'Deep ecology . . . requires openness to the black bear, becoming truly intimate with the black bear, so that honey dribbles down your fur coat as you catch the bus to work' (in Fox, 1986a, p. 59), then deep ecology would seem to be in deep trouble. The guffaws that generally greet this kind of statement reveal deep ecology's profound problem of persuasion.

To explain: those who now choose to advance the claims of a 'state of being' over a new 'code of conduct' were forced into this position by what they saw as a sense of realism – it was understood that traditional ethical concepts could not do the environmental work required of them. Put another way, they asked: 'Where does an ethics come from?' and came up with the answer: from a given understanding of the way the world is, a metaphysics. The conclusion was to argue for a change in metaphysical perspective towards that described in the first part of this chapter, on the understanding that the desired environmental ethic would be more likely to flourish in this new climate.

However, the metaphysics advanced by deep ecology is (to say the least) taking its time getting a grip, and the self-identification with the non-human world demanded by it is restricted – in 'advanced industrial countries' at least – to a very small minority of people. Deep ecology has asked: 'Where does the ethics come from?' and has answered: from a metaphysics. But its long-term problem may lie in finding an answer to the question: 'Where does the metaphysics come from?' because here lies the clue to why the advocacy of a change of consciousness, on its own, is not sufficient. Consciousness is not an independent datum isolated from the social conditions that nurture it.

Janna Thompson gets closest to the remark that needs to be made: 'Ethical resolution . . . presupposes social critique: an attempt to show that present social relations and the goals and desires that spring from them, are unsatisfactory, and that new conceptions of self-fulfilment and happiness are desirable' (Thompson, 1983, p. 98). This social critique ought to be part and parcel of the deep-ecological enterprise, but some ecophilosophers write as though the resolution of philosophical problems were enough to bring about the resolution of practical problems, such as pollution, deforestation and acid rain. Sometimes, indeed, the social and political context receives no attention at all. Warwick Fox writes: 'This attempt to shift the *primary* focus of environmental philosophical concern from ethics to ontology clearly constitutes a fundamental or revolutionary challenge to normal environmental philosophy. It is (and should be) deep ecology's guiding star' (Fox, 1984, p. 204; emphasis in original). If deep ecology is content to remain in the territory of theory, then Fox may be right in his identification of its 'guiding star'. But if it is concerned to turn the theory into practice, it will have to present a programme for social change. This it has so far failed to do.

Anthropocentrism

If there is one word that underpins the whole range of radical green philosophical objections to current forms of human behaviour in the world, it is probably 'anthropocentrism': 'the mistake of giving exclusive or arbitrarily preferential consideration to human interests as opposed to the interests of other beings' (Hayward, 1997, p. 51). Concern for ourselves at the expense of concern for the non-human world is held to be a basic cause of environmental degradation and potential disaster (Curry, 2006, pp. 42–4). On the one hand, however, the very centrality of this word to the green cause has led to a muddying of its meaning and to attempts to clear it up (Hayward, 1997), while on the other, the practical issue of getting the green ideology across has led to contradictory messages from its theorists about anthropocentrism.

As regards the first point, there is a strong and a weak meaning of the word – meanings that emerge from a reading of the ecophilosophical literature, but that are rarely formally distinguished. My understanding of the weak meaning is referred to by Warwick Fox as having to do with being 'human-centred' (1986b, p. 1). The strong meaning also comes from Fox, and involves seeing 'the nonhuman world purely as a means to human ends' (1984, p. 198). We might refer to these positions as 'human-centred' and 'human-instrumental', respectively. The first, or weak, sense is more obviously 'neutral' than the second, or strong, sense – and it is truly astonishing how often 'human-centredness' is confused with 'human instrumentalism'. I want to suggest that anthropocentrism in the weak sense is an unavoidable feature of the human condition (as I shall explain below), while the strong sense carries a notion of the injustice and unfairness involved in the instrumental use of the non-human world.

In the literature, one finds the weak and strong meanings of anthropocentrism mixed together – sometimes in the same sentence. Richard Sylvan, for example, defines as anthropocentrism any attitude that 'does not move outside a human-centred framework, which construes nature and the environment instrumentally, that is, simply as a means to human ends and values' (Sylvan, 1984a, p. 5). To my mind, and contrary to Sylvan's implication, a 'human-centred framework' does not necessarily mean that it is 'human-instrumental'. Consider, for example, the following statement from Jonathon Porritt: 'For us, it is not enough to protect animals for practical, self-interested reasons alone; there is also a profoundly moral concern, rooted in our philosophy of respect for all that dwells on the planet' (Porritt, 1984a, p. 184). The first half of the sentence represents a rejection of human instrumentalism, while the second half involves human-centredness ('our philosophy of respect'). There is no contradiction in this, but it does show that there is room for a (weak) form of anthropocentrism in respectable ecological statements.

The reason for this is that weak anthropocentrism is a necessary feature of the human condition. As Tim O'Riordan has pointed out,

> Man's conscious actions are anthropocentric by definition. Whether he seeks to establish a system of biotic rights or to transform a forest into a residential suburb, the act is conceived by man in the context of his social and political culture.
>
> (O'Riordan, 1981, p. 11)

It is this factor that links even the search for intrinsic value with anthropocentrism. The search is a *human* search, and although it may be successful in displacing the human being from centre stage in terms of value, one will always find a human being at the centre of the enterprise, asking the questions. If there were no human beings there would be no such conceptualized thing as intrinsic value, and it is an open question whether there would be any such thing as intrinsic value at all (although see the earlier discussion of value objectivism). In this sense, any human undertaking will be (weakly) anthropocentric, including the green movement itself.

The reason for dwelling on this is that the green movement may be doing itself a disservice by what has been seen as its insistent distancing from the human. In the first place it is self-contradictory. Charlene Spretnak, for example, writes that:

> Green politics rejects the anthropocentric orientation of humanism, a philosophy which posits that humans have the ability to confront and solve the many problems we face by applying human reason and by rearranging the natural world and the interactions of men and women so that human life will prosper.
>
> (Spretnak and Capra, 1985, p. 234)

There is evidently a reasonable green rejection of human instrumentalism here, but also a disturbing hint that human beings should abandon their pretensions to solving the problems they have brought upon themselves. This suspicion is reinforced by comments of the following kind: 'Humans are like any other plague animal. They cannot destroy the Earth, but they can easily wreck the environment that sustains them. The most likely of [James] Lovelock's . . . outcomes is . . . a large-scale decline in human numbers' (Gray, 2002, p. 12). If this is true then there is little point to green politics – or indeed any other sort – at all. Overall, of course, it is the generalized belief in the possibility of change that makes the green movement a properly political movement. Without such a belief, the movement's reason for being would be undermined. From this perspective, the recognition that weak anthropocentrism is unavoidable may act as a useful political corrective to the idea that 'Nature is in control'.

Indeed when it comes to the politics of the green movement as opposed to its philosophy, there is generally little reluctance to indulge in anthropocentrism – even of the strong variety. In *Green Politics*, for example, Spretnak and Capra talk of 'an understanding that we are part of nature, not above it, and that all our massive structures of commerce – and life itself – ultimately depend on wise, respectful interaction with our biosphere'. And if that is not a clear enough expression of a human-prudential argument, the authors add: 'Any government or economic system that ignores that principle is ultimately leading humankind into suicide' (1985, p. 28).

Again, Jonathon Porritt writes that the 'ecological imperative . . . reminds us that the protection of the Earth's natural systems is something we all depend on', and that 'The fact that thousands of species will disappear by the turn of the century is not just an academic irritation: our own survival depends on our understanding of the intricate webs of life in which we're involved' (1984a, pp. 98–9). In fact, Porritt goes so far as to make human instrumentalism the lever for engineering the changes that ecologism recommends: 'A re-interpretation of enlightened self-interest is . . . the key to any radical transformation' (ibid., p. 117).

The same strong anthropocentric message comes through loud and clear in Green Party manifestos. The German Greens' seminal 1983 manifesto stated that:

> Encroachment on natural habitats and the extermination of animal and plant species is destroying the balance of nature *and along with it the basis of our own life*. It is necessary to maintain or restore a biologically intact environment, *in order to ensure the humane survival of future generations*.
>
> (*German Green Party Manifesto*, 1983, p. 29; emphasis added)

And on the next page we find a perfect expression of the strong anthropocentric principle: 'We must stop the violation of nature in order to survive in it' (*German Green Party Manifesto*, 1983, p. 30).

The list of examples could be endless, and they all demonstrate the same point: that the politics of ecology do not follow the same ground rules as the radical forms of its philosophy. I suggested earlier in this chapter that, for ecophilosophers, the reasons for the care of the non-human world are at least as important as the care itself. For ecophilosophers, care should be disinterested. This principle appears to be abandoned (or at least suspended) when it comes to real world politics. Several reasons for this might be advanced, among which is the reason of convenience – i.e. that for the purposes of communicating the basic idea of care for the 'natural' world, short cuts may have to be taken. This is the approach outlined by Warwick Fox in the following lengthy but worthwhile quote:

> Consider the following. If you ask me to try to tell the 'average person' in one sentence why I think we ought to care about some non-human 'being' (whether alive or not), then the simplest thing for me to say, given our present cultural context, is along the lines: 'Because it has all these uses for us'. However, if I wish to get a little closer to what I really want to say, but at the same time take care to speak in terms that others will immediately understand rather than in terms that might sound alien to them (and, hence, alienate them), then I will probably say something along the lines: 'Because it has value in itself. Unless we have a lot more time to talk, the last thing I am going to say *given the present cultural context* is the first thing I want to say: 'Because it is part of my/our wider Self, its diminishment is My/Our diminishment'. In other words, given the constraints of culture, desire to persuade, and limited time in which to try to communicate something clearly, my *popular* statement of 'basic principles' will, while reflecting my deepest views, nevertheless be an unreliable or superficial guide to the way in which I would elaborate these views in formal, philosophical terms.
>
> (Fox, 1986a, pp. 71–2; emphasis in original)

On this reading, the purveyors of human-prudential reasons for the care of 'nature' can always say that they do so only for tactical reasons – that the end of persuasion is more important than the means of achieving it. At one level this collapses into an issue of the intellectual consistency of individuals, but at another, a profoundly important political question is raised: 'Will human-prudential reasons do the job for the environment that is required of them?' Put another way, does the use of human-prudential reasons (as means) endanger the desired end of a hands-off approach to the environment?

Presumably the answer of 'ecological consciousness' supporters to these questions would be, respectively: no and yes. The whole point of developing a perspective which goes beyond (what I have defined as) a strong anthropocentric principle is that such a principle only serves to reinforce the attitude which radical greens are concerned to invalidate – that which has the universe revolving around the human being. Warwick Fox's argument is that only the development of an ecological consciousness will turn the tables in favour of the environment, such that the onus of persuasion is on those who want to destroy, rather than on those who want to preserve. The best that may be said of human-prudentialists, from the point of view of the deep ecologists, is that they will get some of if not the entire job done. I shall return to these important strategic issues in the Conclusion to this book.

Earth First! and social ecology

One danger with the whole anti-anthropocentrism stance is that it may be interpreted as a form of misanthropism (hatred of humankind). This danger has become clear in the theoretical stances and political activities of the North American group Earth First!, a group that has been referred to as 'deep ecology's political action wing' (Reed, 1988, p. 21), and 'the cutting edge of environmentalism' in the American West (Tokar, 1988, p. 134). One article in an Earth First! journal (engagingly signed Miss Ann Thropy) stated that:

> If radical environmentalists were to invent a disease to bring human population back to sanity, it would probably be something like AIDS . . . the possible benefits of this to the environment are staggering . . . just as the Plague contributed to the demise of feudalism, AIDS has the potential to end industrialism.
>
> (quoted in Reed, 1988, p. 21)

Some time ago, Earth First! took to driving nails into the trunks of Californian redwood trees to deter loggers from cutting them down, and at least one lumberjack has been badly injured by his chainsaw kicking out of the trunk and into his neck. I shall have more to say on Earth First! in Chapter 4.

Perhaps the most committed and principled critic (within the ecology movement, broadly defined) of the excesses to which (what he refers to as) biocentrism can lead is Murray Bookchin, from the perspective of what he calls 'social ecology':

> Whatever its merits, [he writes] the fact is that deep ecology, more than any other 'radical' ecological perspective, blames 'Humanity' as such for the ecological crisis – especially ordinary 'consumers' and 'breeders of children' – while largely ignoring the corporate interests that are really plundering the planet.
>
> (Bookchin, 1991, p. 123)

Bookchin has drawn constant attention to the misanthropic potential within deep ecology and was importantly instrumental in encouraging Dave Foreman – co-founder of Earth First! – to retract some particularly divisive remarks regarding immigration from Mexico to the USA (Foreman, 1991, p. 108; and see Chapter 3).

Social ecology's position on anthropocentrism and biocentrism is to refuse to choose between the two: 'An "anthropocentrism" that is based on the religious principle that the Earth was "made" to be dominated by "Humanity" is as remote from my thinking as a "biocentrism" that turns human society into just another community of animals' (Bookchin, 1991, p. 128). Bookchin prefers to speak of a 'first' and a 'second' nature, with 'first nature' being 'prehuman' (1989, p. 201) and 'second nature' evolving from first nature in the form of the human species. Second nature (humanity) is:

> a product of evolution that has the fullness of mind, of extraordinary communicative abilities, of conscious association, and the ability knowingly to alter itself and the natural world. To deny these extraordinary human attributes which manifest themselves in real life, to submerge them in notions like a 'biocentric democracy' that renders human beings and snails 'equal' in terms of their 'intrinsic worth' (whatever that phrase may mean) is simply frivolous.
>
> (Bookchin, 1989, p. 201)

By now it will be clear that while deep ecologists profess a 'biospherical egalitarianism' in principle, most of them find ways of producing a hierarchy of value so as to cope with clashes of interest between species (for instance). Indeed, it will be remembered that biospherical egalitarians often organize these hierarchies around the datum of complexity – one of the features that distinguishes first from second nature in Bookchin's description. In this respect Bookchin and his opponents may not be so far apart.

What finally sets them apart, though, and what makes it hard to regard social ecology as part of a radical *ecocentric* programme (this is not, of course, to deny its radicalism in its own terms) is Bookchin's view that humanity represents a qualitative improvement so far as natural evolution is concerned. 'Selfhood, consciousness, and the bases for freedom' are only dimly visible (if at all) in 'first nature' (Bookchin, 1989, p. 201). Potentially, on the other hand,

> an emancipated humanity will become the voice, indeed the expression, of a natural evolution rendered self-conscious, caring and sympathetic to the pain, suffering and incoherent aspects of an evolution left to its own, often wayward, unfolding. Nature, due to human rational intervention, will thence acquire the intentionality, power of developing more complex life-forms, and capacity to differentiate itself.
>
> (Bookchin, 1989, p. 203)

Robyn Eckersley has referred to this as Bookchin's 'evolutionary stewardship thesis' (Eckersley, 1992, p. 154) and she suggests two reasons why this thesis offends ecocentric sensibilities. First, the very idea that nature's unfolding might be 'wayward' does not square with the general ecocentric injunction to 'allow all beings (human and non-human) to unfold in their own way' (Eckersley, 1992, p. 156); and the second (connected) reason is that ecocentrics do not purport to know what the direction of evolution is:

> From an ecocentric perspective, it is both arrogant and self serving to make, as Bookchin does, the unverifiable claim that first nature is striving to achieve something (namely, greater subjectivity, awareness, or 'selfhood') that 'just happens' to have reached its most developed form in *us* – second nature.
>
> (Eckersley, 1992, p. 156)

Although Eckersley may overstate somewhat the teleological dimension of Bookchin's thought, it is hard to deny the sense of 'steering' that he gives to humanity's relationship with non-human nature – not that any of this bothers Bookchin too much: '[I]f this [social ecology] be humanism – more precisely ecological humanism,' he writes, 'the current crop of antihumanists and misanthropes are welcome to make the most of it' (Bookchin, 1989, p. 36).

Bookchin aside (if that does not seem too peremptory for a person who has had such a profound influence on North American environmentalism; Bookchin, 1995; Light, 1998), it would be a mistake to think that deep ecology necessarily leads to Earth First!-type activities and so to reject it on that basis. Chris Reed's assertion (in an article referred to above) that 'Descent into irrationality has badly damaged American feminism', and that 'The present uproar among environmentalists seems only too likely to repeat the feminists' mistake' (Reed, 1988, p. 21) is not only misguidedly offensive to radical feminism but is also a one-sided reading of the implications of deep ecology. For example, shifting the onus of justification from those who would preserve the non-human world to those who would intervene in it (presented above as implied by deep ecology) hardly justifies the kind of disciplinary violence practised by some members of Earth First! – and nor need it necessarily lead to anti-humanism and misanthropism, despite what Bookchin, and Bramwell, might say (1994, p. 161).

Hybridity

Both the 'code of conduct' and 'state of being' approaches to going beyond anthropocentrism have their problems. Theorists in the former camp have difficulty with deciding just where to draw the boundary of moral concern, and with articulating a convincing intrinsic value case for 'nature' as well as for individual parts of it. State of being theorists, meanwhile, are confronted with the challenge of persuading people to change nothing less than their entire world-view.

Given these difficulties, there has been a tendency in recent theorizing to try to bypass the impasse by looking at the humanity/nature problem from a rather different point of view. Environmental philosopher and feminist theorist Val Plumwood calls this point of view 'hybridity' (Plumwood, 2006, p. 52). 'Hybridity,' she writes, 'clarifies the range of theoretical options and can *shift the problem focus* in helpful ways that dislodge blockages' (ibid.; emphasis in the original). The 'blockages' she has in mind are those we identified in the 'code of conduct' and 'state of being' approaches to moving beyond anthropocentric politics. The key to the hybrid approach is to recognize the 'links between human and non-human concerns' (ibid.), rather than seeing them as two separate spheres.

Plumwood points out how 'Many, perhaps most, environmental issues involve both humans and non-humans, often in connected ways that are hard to disentangle', so that, 'In a small community, the people who demonstrate about penguins are often the same ones who demonstrate about traffic pollution' (Plumwood, 2006, p. 59). She remarks that 'Although mixing is the norm at the level of activism, at the level of theory there is a puzzling segregation', and it is clear that she has the theories we have been discussing in this chapter in mind when she writes that 'Many theories create a choice between human and non-human issues and forms of concern, or try to privilege one kind over the other in some universalizing, context-insensitive way (for example, as "deep" versus "shallow")' (ibid.). From this point of view the attempt to bridge the gap between the human and non-human spheres which characterizes the philosophy described thus far in this chapter starts off on the wrong foot. It fails to take into account the way in which 'environmental issues involve both humans and non-humans', in Plumwood's words. From the hybridity point of view deep ecology fails because while it 'promotes valuing non-humans for their own sake . . . [it] makes notably poor connections with human ecological issues' (ibid., p. 60). In this sense, deep ecology achieves no more than a '*reverse reduction to non-human issues*' (ibid.; emphasis in the original) and is thus an incomplete account of human and non-human emancipation.

Hybridity involves refiguring the deep/shallow distinction that drives much deep ecological thinking. It involves seeing how the deep/shallow metaphor *cuts across* the human/nature boundary. Plumwood's view is that 'Some non-human concerns can be decidedly "shallow", for example those that automatically privilege human pets like cats or dogs over other animals, or which treat pets as the paradigm of animality' (Plumwood, 2006, p. 63). By the same token, some human concerns may be seen as 'deep'. Another key theorist of hybridity (although he doesn't use the word) is Bruno Latour. In stark contrast to much of the thinking which we have analysed in this chapter, Latour wants the ecology movement to 'let go of nature' (Latour, 2004, p. 11) rather than base its politics on it. This seems profoundly counter-intuitive from a green point of view. Hybridity, though, is not only aimed at the liberation of nature, but of humans and nature together. Latour says that there is 'nothing more political' than the activity of getting things and people to speak. To date, politics has been about getting people to speak, so the circle of legitimate political beings has (on one typical account) been progressively widened to include those previously excluded: people of colour, women and so on. Latour's position is that 'deepness' – if it is to mean anything at all – is about spreading the capacity to speak across the human and non-human realms, and – crucially – about realizing that that capacity is spread unevenly *within* those realms as well as *across* them.

This might seem odd – how can the capacity to speak be spread unevenly within the realm of nature? It doesn't 'speak' at all, does it? Latour will agree that it doesn't speak, but he will point out that it has its 'spokespersons' (Latour, 2004, p. 56), and these spokespersons ensure that some parts of nature speak very loudly indeed. This point of view has it that the so-called 'charismatic megafauna' such as whales, polar bears and orang-utans have very loud voices in that they are spoken for by large and influential organizations such as the Worldwide Fund for Nature and Save the Whale campaigns. Critically, the hybridity perspective invites us to see that in some cases charismatic megafauna have louder voices than some human beings. From this point of view, the important cleavage is not that between humans and nature, but between those who have loud voices and those who do not. The 'noisy/quiet' distinction cuts across the 'humans/nature' distinction, and it provides an alternative basis for connecting humans and nature in an alternative politics. The point is to give voice to the silent – both human and non-human. This determination to avoid the humanity/nature split is characteristic of the contemporary French contribution to political ecology, and stands in contrast to the Anglo-Saxon tradition we have discussed in this chapter (Whiteside, 2002, p. 223). There are signs that this latter tradition is moving in the French direction, so to speak, motivated by the intellectual and practical difficulties that the humanity/nature distinction has caused. Earlier in this chapter I described this as a move from a nature-inclusive 'ethics' to a nature-inclusive 'democracy', and Latour is one of the most distinctive and articulate exponents of this move.

In the round, indeed, the growing importance of environmental justice and environmental democracy in the make-up of the green movement has served to displace ecocentrism somewhat from its central role in the intellectual architecture of the ideology of ecologism. Brian Doherty is right to say that 'Greens share a commitment to ecological rationality, egalitarianism and grassroots democracy' and that 'none of these three commitments has a priori privileged status in relation to the others and greens seek to achieve a balance between all three' (Doherty, 2002, p. 67). In terms of identifying ecologism's ideological distinctiveness, though, it is important to remember that the ecological rationality term is the crucial one. Other ideologies share ecologism's commitment to egalitarianism and grassroots democracy, but none of them can lay claim to prior ownership of the idea of ecological rationality. This remains ecologism's distinctive and unique ideological feature.

Conclusion

Perhaps the most striking feature of environmental philosophy is its failure to make itself practical (Light and De Shalit, 2003) – a fault which the hybridity position tries to rectify. I do not mean that the recommendations of ecophilosophy are impractical or Utopian but that not enough attention has been paid to the practical relations among people, and between people and their environment, that make its recommendations impractical. In his *Eighth Thesis on Feuerbach* Karl Marx wrote that 'Social life is essentially *practical*. All mysteries which mislead theory to mysticism find their rational solution in human practice and in the comprehension of this practice' (in Feuer, 1976, p. 285; emphasis in original).

While not wanting to endorse everything Marx has to say, I think that here he points us in the right direction. The idea is that there are things about the world that are hard to understand ('mysteries'), and that their resolution can take on an inadequate theoretical form ('mysticism'). In our present context, we might say that the environmental crisis is the 'mystery' and that ecophilosophy – in all its various forms – is the 'mysticism'. Marx's thesis goes on to point out that adequate understanding lies in the comprehension of the social life and its practices that give rise to the problem, or 'mystery'. Further, that the tendency towards 'mystical' solutions is a function of those very forms of social life (i.e. the current ones), and thus that both the avoidance of 'mysticism' and the final resolution of the 'mystery' will depend upon changes in social practice. If this is correct, and if I am justified in interpreting ecophilosophy in this light, then ecophilosophy's failure to address the issue of social practice will disqualify it from ever formulating a satisfactory solution to the problems that have given rise to it.

This is what I meant when I said above that environmental philosophy has failed to make itself practical. This is not to say that ecophilosophy's embracing of the practical would immediately resolve all conflicts of theory or practice, but it would make radical disagreements over strategy less likely. The reason is that a practical philosophy would have a strategy for social change built into it, a programme around which activists could work and within which disagreements would be over tactics and not over strategy.

The 'changes in social practice' to which I have just referred are very much conceived of within the ecology movement to be the concern of its political rather than its philosophical 'wing'. It is this tendency towards the separation of the theoretical from the practical – or better, the refusal explicitly to link them – that I would criticize in ecophilosophy. However, if it is also true to say that successful practical resolutions are associated with successful theoretical resolutions, then the lacunae in ecophilosophy will have profound practical (political) ramifications. Discussion of this point will take us both further into this book (see Chapter 4), and towards the heart of ecologism as a political ideology.

3   The sustainable society

Limits to growth

Amid the welter of enthusiasm for lead-free petrol and green consumerism it is often forgotten that a foundation-stone of radical green politics is the belief that our finite Earth places limits on industrial growth. This finitude, and the scarcity it implies, is an article of faith for green ideologues, and it provides the fundamental framework within which any putative picture of a green society must be drawn. The guiding principle of such a society is that of 'sustainability' (now one of the most contested words in the political vocabulary; Dobson, 1998, ch. 2), and the stress on finitude and the careful negotiation of Utopia that it seems to demand forces political ecologists to call into question green consumerist-type strategies for environmental responsibility (Seyfang, 2005). In this respect it is the limits to growth thesis, together with the ethical conclusions to be drawn from ecocentrism and hybridity discussed in the previous chapter, that divides light-green from dark-green politics.

Much has already been written on the limits to growth issue, and I do not see it as my task here to rehearse all of the arguments to which the notion has given rise. I do think it important, though, to stress its centrality to the green position I am describing and to take this opportunity to point out the features of the limits to growth thesis that are most often referred to in green discussions. Greens have all along been confronted with rebuffs to their belief in limits to growth, and as their responses to these criticisms have developed it has become easier to identify what they are prepared to jettison in the thesis and what they feel the need to defend.

There are three principal aspects of the limits to growth thesis that have come to be of prime importance to the radical green position. They are, first, that technological solutions (broadly understood; i.e. solutions formulated within the bounds of present economic, social and political practices) will not in themselves bring about a sustainable society; second, that the rapid rates of growth aimed for (and often achieved) by industrialized and industrializing societies have an exponential character, which means that dangers stored up over a relatively long period of time can very suddenly have a catastrophic effect; and third, that the *interaction* of problems caused by growth means that such problems cannot be dealt with in isolation – i.e. solving one problem does not solve the rest, and may even exacerbate them. These three notions will be discussed in more detail very shortly, but first the strategy and conclusions of the original *Limits to Growth* report ought briefly to be noted. The description and assessments that follow are primarily based on the 1974 report, although I have included references from the 1992 sequel and the 2005 '30-year update' where appropriate. In one or two of these cases it is the sense of the three reports that is identical, rather than the quoted words.

The researchers pointed to what they described as '5 trends of global concern': 'accelerating industrialisation, rapid population growth, widespread malnutrition, depletion of nonrenewable resources, and a deteriorating environment' (Meadows *et al.*, 1974, p. 21). They then created a computerized world model of the variables associated with these areas of concern (i.e. industrial output per capita, population, food per capita, resources and pollution); and programmed the computer to produce pictures of various future states of affairs given changes in these variables. From the very beginning it was understood that such modelling would be rough and ready, and the Club of Rome (the name given to the informal association of scientists, researchers, industrialists and so on who, carried out the research) anticipated later criticisms of inaccuracy and incompleteness by admitting that the model was 'imperfect, oversimplified and unfinished' (Meadows *et al.*, 1974, p. 21; 1992, p. 105). From our perspective, the important point to make is that greens have generally been unperturbed by criticisms of the detail of the various limits to growth reports, and have rather relied upon the general principles and conclusions of these reports.

The first computer run, then, assumed 'no major change in the physical, economic, or social relationships that have historically governed the development of the world system' (Meadows *et al.*, 1974, p. 124; 1992, p. 132; 2005, p. 169). This, in other words, was a run in which business carried on as usual. In this case the limits to growth were reached 'because of nonrenewable resource depletion' (Meadows *et al.*, 1974, p. 125; 1992, p. 132; 2005, p. 168). Next, the group programmed a run in which the resource depletion problem was 'solved' by assuming a doubling in the amount of resources economically available. In this case collapse occurred again, but this time because of the pollution brought about by the spurt in industrialization caused by the availability of new resources. The group concluded that 'Apparently the economic impetus such resource availability provides must be accompanied by curbs on pollution if a collapse of the world system is to be avoided' (Meadows *et al.*, 1974, p. 133; 1992, p. 134; 2005, pp. 172–3). Consequently, the next computer run involved not only a doubling of resources but also a series of technological strategies to reduce the level of pollution to a quarter of its pre-1970 level (Meadows *et al.*, 1974, p. 136; 1992, p. 168; 2005, p. 211). This time the limits to growth are reached because of a food shortage produced by pressure on arable land owing to its being taken for 'urban-industrial use' (Meadows *et al.*, 1974, p. 137; 1992, p. 168; 2005, p. 210).

And so the experiment progresses, with the world model programmed each time to deal with the immediate cause of the previous collapse. Eventually all sectors have technological responses filled in:

> The model system is producing nuclear power, recycling resources, and mining the most remote reserves; withholding as many pollutants as possible; pushing yields from the land to undreamed-of heights; and producing only children who are actively wanted by their parents.
>
> (Meadows *et al.*, 1974, p. 141; 1992, p. 174; 2005, p. 218)

Even this does not solve the problem of overshoot and collapse:

> The result is still an end to growth before the year 2100 [2050 in the 1992 report, p. 174]. In this case growth is stopped by three simultaneous crises. Overuse of land leads to erosion, and food production drops. Resources are severely depleted by a prosperous world population (but not as prosperous as the present [1970] US population). Pollution rises, drops then rises again dramatically, causing a further decrease in food production and a sudden rise in the death rate.
>
> (Meadows *et al.*, 1974, p. 141)

The next sentence of the group's conclusion on the computer's final run helps distance environmentalism from ecologism and provides the intellectual springboard for radical green political strategy: 'The application of technological solutions alone has prolonged the period of population and industrial growth, but it has not removed the ultimate limits to that growth' (Meadows *et al.*, 1974, p. 141).

This, then, brings us to the first of the three notions associated with the limits to growth thesis that I suggested above are essential to the theory and practice of political ecology: that technological solutions cannot provide a way out of the impasse of the impossibility of aspiring to infinite growth in a finite system. Irvine and Ponton point out that:

> technological gadgets merely shift the problem around, often at the expense of more energy and material inputs and therefore more pollution. Favourite devices such as refuse incineration, sulphur extractors in power stations and catalytic converters in cars cost money and energy while at the same time generating new pollutants.
>
> (Irvine and Ponton, 1988, p. 36)

This will most likely appear heretical to those familiar with light-green, environmental politics, which bases itself precisely upon this sort of strategy, but it is at just these points that ecologism distinguishes itself most clearly from environmentalism. The issues at stake here come sharply into view in the context of energy provision, for example. Supporters of the limits to growth thesis will feel themselves vindicated by the constant price rises in non-renewable sources of energy such as gas. They will acknowledge that some of these cost increases have 'non-environmental' causes, such as geopolitical tensions, but will insist that as finite resources run out, their price is bound to increase. The question then is: Can other technologies fill the gap? The range of long-term options seems to have narrowed because we now know that energy based on fossil fuels is a major cause of climate change, or 'global warming'. In this context, some technology enthusiasts will look to already-existing, supposedly carbon-neutral technologies such as nuclear fission to supply us with the energy we are used to. Others will put their faith in commercially untried and untested technologies such as nuclear fusion. Greens are suspicious of nuclear technology for a number of reasons. They point out that it is costly, potentially dangerous, that there are problems dealing with and siting waste, and that future generations are left with a legacy they will not appreciate. They will also point out that uranium is itself a non-renewable resource, due to run out well before the end of this century. So even if it were to be cost-effective, safe, and harmless to future generations, nuclear energy is not a long-term solution to humanity's energy problems. This leaves us with either some as yet undiscovered technology, or the successful commercialization of an existing yet untried one, or the basket of renewable energy possibilities based on wind, solar or hydro sources.

The trouble with this last option is that by all accounts it is unlikely to supply so-called advanced industrial countries with the quantities of energy to which they have become accustomed. This is what leads greens to focus unfashionably on the *demand* side of the energy equation rather than just the *supply* side. Of course mainstream discourse occasionally strays into demand-side territory too, and so we are asked to lag our lofts better or to install double-glazing so as to consume less energy. But greens will say that even these measures are unlikely to be enough. Experience suggests, they will argue, that every time a saving is made through a technological advance (e.g. more fuel-efficient car engines), the saving is soon negated by pressures in other parts of society that drive up demand (e.g. the need, or the willingness, to travel further to work). This suggests that technological advances, on their own, are not a complete answer to the problem of sustainability.

So if the sustainable society is not, on the face of it, (only) going to be full of environment-friendly technological wizardry, what *will* it be like? Part of the answer is provided by Garrett Hardin's definition of a 'technological solution': 'one that requires only a change in the techniques of the natural sciences, demanding little or nothing in the way of change in human values or ideas of morality' (quoted in Meadows *et al.*, 1974, p. 150). It follows that if the green movement believes that technology on its own cannot solve the limits to growth problem, then it will have to argue for more profound changes in social thought and practice – changes in human values, ideas of morality and associated practices. These changes will involve accommodating social practices to the limits that surround them, and abandoning the Promethean (in this context, technological) attempt to overcome them. It is in this kind of respect, once again, that the dark-green sustainable society is different from the environmentalist one, and why the latter can sit only uncomfortably with the former. All of this is a result of the idea that technological solutions can have 'no impact on the *essential* problem, which is exponential growth in a finite and complex system' (Meadows *et al.*, 1974, p. 45).

And this is the second notion that political ecologists have rescued from the debate over limits to growth, making it central to their argument as to why current industrial practices are unsustainable: the idea of exponential growth. Meadows *et al.* claim that all of the five elements in the Club of Rome's world model experience exponential growth, and explain that 'A quantity exhibits *exponential* growth when it increases by a constant percentage of the whole in a constant time period' (Meadows *et al.*, 1974, p. 27; emphasis in original). In quantitative terms this is easily demonstrated by placing rice grains on the squares of a chessboard, with one on the first square, two on the second, four on the third, sixteen on the fourth and so on. The numbers build up very fast, and while the twenty-first square will be covered with over 100,000 grains of rice, the forty-first will require one trillion (Meadows *et al.*, 2005, p. 21).

The central point is that such growth is deceptive in that it produces large numbers very quickly. Translated to the arena of industrial production, resource depletion and pollution, what seems an innocuous rate of use and waste disposal can quickly produce dangerously low quantities of available resources and dangerously high levels of pollution. Greens often point to the staggeringly rapid growth in industrial production this century and ask the (increasingly less rhetorical) question: 'Can this be sustained?' Thus, Irvine and Ponton note that 'In a mere blink on the timescale of human evolution, industrial society has been depleting and impairing Earth's "supply system" at a phenomenal rate,' and that 'Americans, for example, have used more minerals and fossil fuels during the past half-century than all the other peoples of the world throughout human history' (Irvine and Ponton, 1988, pp. 24–5).

Greens believe, simply, that present rates of resource extraction and use – a '3 per cent growth rate implies doubling the rate of production and consumption every twenty-five years' (Ekins, 1986, p. 9) – and the production of waste and pollution necessarily associated with them, are unsustainable. They further believe that the nature of the rate of growth produces a false sense of complacency: what appears to be a safe situation now can very quickly turn into an unsafe one. A relevant French riddle for schoolchildren goes like this:

> Suppose you own a pond on which a water lily is growing. The lily plant doubles in size each day. If the lily were allowed to grow unchecked, it would completely cover the pond in 30 days, choking off the other forms of life in the water. For a long time the lily plant seems small, and so you decide not to worry about cutting it back until it covers half the pond. On what day will that be? On the twenty-ninth day, of course. You have one day to save your pond.
> (Meadows *et al.*, 2005, pp. 21–2)

The 1992 report, indeed, makes much of this effect by running computer scenarios in which the necessary policies for sustainability are implemented in 1975, 1995 and 2015 respectively (Meadows *et al.*, 1992, pp. 202, 198, 204). It will come as no surprise to hear that 1975 would have been best, and that waiting until 2015 will mean a very bumpy first hundred years of the twenty-first century.

The third and final aspect of the limits to growth thesis that has become central to the radical green position is that of the interrelationship of the problems with which we are confronted. It should already have become clear from the description of the Club of Rome's computer runs that solving one problem does not necessarily mean solving the rest, and our refusal to confront the complexity of the global system and to draw the right conclusions for action (or inaction) from it is why most greens believe our attempts to deal with environmental degradation, in particular, to be insensitively inadequate. 'What matters,' write Irvine and Ponton, 'is not any particular limit, which might be overcome, but the total interaction of constraints, and costs' (1988, p. 13). Change in one element means change in the others: nuclear power might result in a temporary drop in climate change emissions from the energy sector, but it will permit greater resource throughput in other parts of the economy, thereby potentially contributing to resource and pollution problems.

In sum, radical greens read off three principal features of the limits to growth message and subscribe to them and their implications wholeheartedly: technological solutions cannot help realize the impossible dream of infinite growth in a finite system; the exponential nature of that growth both underpins its unsustainability and suggests that the limits to growth may become visible rather quicker than we might think; and the immense complexity of the global system leads greens to suggest that our current attempts to deal with environmental problems are both clumsy and superficial.

Linked to all of this is a problem of knowledge, in the context of which green ideologues adopt a predominantly conservative stance:

> One of the worst changes that industrialism has made to pollution is not the addition of individual new pollutants, but their combined effects. . . . Some half a million chemicals are in common use; about another thousand are added each year. Yet we know next to nothing about their interaction and combined effects, and the scale of the problem suggests that we never will.
>
> (Irvine and Ponton, 1988, p. 34)

The implied impossibility of knowing enough is crucial to the green suggestion that we adopt a cautious approach to the environment. If we cannot know the outcome of an intervention in the environment but suspect that it may be dangerous, then we are best advised, from a green point of view, not to intervene at all. This has become known in policy-making circles as the 'precautionary principle' (O'Riordan and

Cameron, 1994). In this respect, green politics opposes drawing-board social design and thus falls into the realm of what is generally considered to be conservative politics – siding with Edmund Burke against Tom Paine, so to speak (see Chapter 5 for more on the relationship between ecologism and conservatism).

At the root of all this, of course, is the most profound belief of all: that there *are* limits to growth. The most common criticism of the *Limits to Growth* report is that its predictions as to the likely exhaustion of raw materials (for example) have been proved wildly wrong. This is a point most famously put by Julian Simon and Herman Kahn in their *The Resourceful Earth* (1984), and then in an engaging debate between Julian Simon and Norman Myers on various aspects of the limits to growth thesis (Myers and Simon, 1994): 'Conventional "green" beliefs are massively contradicted by the scientific evidence' (Simon in Myers and Simon, 1994, pp. xvii–xviii). Bjørn Lomborg has more recently argued much the same thing in his *The Skeptical Environmentalist* (Lomborg, 2001). Lomborg argues that greens have made selective use of data to give the impression that the state of the environment is getting worse whereas in the round it is in fact getting better. To make his point Lomborg asks environmentalists the following question: 'When would you prefer to have been born?' – in the past or in the present? (Lomborg, 2001, p. 351). Environmentalists have responded that Lomborg is asking the wrong question. Given the massive imbalances in political power and the way in which environmental goods and bads are systematically unfairly shared out, the question to ask is not 'When would you rather have been born?', but '*How* would you rather have been born – with power or without it?' There is little doubt that the Queen of Sheba was better-off in her time than the billions of people getting by on less than $5 a day in ours. Lomborg's view that 'things are getting better' (Lomborg, 2001, pp. 3–33) needs to be accompanied by the health warning – 'for some'.

So greens have learned to accept the detail of these criticisms while continuing to subscribe to the general principle of the limits to growth thesis. Thus in his most recent contribution to these debates, the Chair of Prime Minister Tony Blair's Sustainable Development Commission, Jonathon Porritt, writes: 'If we don't learn to live sustainably within the natural systems and limits that provide the foundation for *all* life forms, then we will go the same way as every other life form that failed to adapt to those changing systems and limits' (Porritt, 2005, p. 10).

This is the starting point for thoughts about the sustainable society: that aspirations of ever-increasing growth and consumption cannot be fulfilled because resources are finite, as is the space into which we must throw our waste. Mahatma Gandhi, when asked if, after independence, India would attain British standards of living, commented that 'it took Britain half the resources of the planet to achieve its prosperity; how many planets will a country like India require?' (Enviro Facts, 2006). 'Ecological footprint' analysis gives us some approximate answers to Gandhi's question:

> If just the present [i.e. January 1996] world population of 5.8 billion people were to live at current North American ecological standards (say 4.5 ha/person), a reasonable first approximation of the total productive land requirement would be 26 billion hectares (assuming present technologies). However, there are only just over 13 billion hectares of land on Earth, of which only 8.8 billion are ecologically productive cropland, pasture, or forest (1.5 ha/person). In short, we would need an additional two planet Earths to accommodate the increased ecological load of people alive today. If the population were to stabilise at between 10 and 11 billion sometime in the next century, five additional Earths would be needed, all else being equal – and this just to maintain the present rate of ecological decline.
>
> (Rees, 1996, n.p.)

Thus the concept of scarcity is fundamental because 'every time energy and matter are converted into a different form, their quality is degraded and they become less useful to us' (Porritt, 2005, p. 47). Dark-green politics is based upon a fundamental commitment to the principle of scarcity as an insurmountable fact of life and the consequent limits to growth imposed by a finite system. In this respect, to hint that radical green thinking is damaged by hitching itself to the *Limits to Growth* report – because of its self-fulfilling prophecy of doom, programmed to collapse by dint of Malthusian reasoning – is rather to miss the point. Green thinkers do believe that current industrial practices are programmed to collapse by virtue of their internal logic, and in this respect they are persuaded by the fundamental message of the limits to growth thesis.

It is worth stressing here a point made in the Introduction: that this 'scientific' element in the green position pushes it well beyond a merely romantic response to the trials and tribulations of industrial society. Greens propose a sustainable society not merely because they think, in terms of some bucolic fantasy, that it would be more pleasant to live in. They believe that science is on their side. This has given rise to a radical green economics that was presaged at the beginning of the century by the so-called 'energy economists' – a story told by Anna Bramwell

(1989). She points out that as long ago as 1911 Wilhelm Ostwald wrote that 'the free energy accessible can only decrease, but not increase' (in Bramwell, 1989, p. 64). The most influential contemporary champion of the economics based upon this kind of observation is American economist Herman Daly. Green economics are rooted in our ecological circumstance in a very fundamental way: '[O]ur dependence on the natural world takes two forms – that of a source of low-entropy inputs and that of a sink for high-entropy waste outputs' (Daly, 1992, p. 34).

Daly notes that the first law of thermodynamics states that 'we do not produce or consume anything, we merely rearrange it' – so we cannot produce resources, we can only use them, and they will eventually run out. The second law – that of entropy – has it that 'our rearrangement implies a continual reduction in potential for further use within the system as a whole' (Daly, 1977b, p. 109). This also implies that there is a limit to the use we can make of scarce resources, as well as pointing out that waste (high entropy) is a necessary product of the extraction and use of resources (low entropy). The limits to growth notion is thus the practical reason, as it were, why greens argue for the necessity of a sustainable society. They also present 'social' and 'ethical' reasons (Daly in Ekins, 1986, p. 13), which will be pursued as the chapter progresses. Now, though, we are in a position to outline the parameters within which dark-greens believe any picture of the sustainable society would have to be drawn.

Possible positions

Various responses to the problem of sustainability are possible, both in political-institutional terms and also in terms of the social and ethical practices that a sustainable society would need to follow. By no means all of the 'solutions' that have been presented over the years are green in the sense in which I think we ought to understand the word – i.e. in the sense in which ecologism has become a political ideology in its own right. In drawing the boundaries for ecologism, we find ourselves excluding from its meaning a number of political postures that have been wrongly associated with it. This has the effect, of course, of narrowing down the range of thoughts and practices that we can link with radical green politics, and thus makes clearer the territory within which it most properly moves.

To my mind no one in this context has been able to (or has had to) improve upon the typology provided by Tim O'Riordan in his book *Environmentalism* (1981, p. 307). O'Riordan suggests that in political-institutional terms there are four possible positions. First, there is the possibility of a 'new global order', arranged so as to deal with the problems of global coordination presented by the international nature of the environmental crisis. Supporters of this position typically claim that the nation-state is both too big and too small to deal effectively with global problems and bemoan the lack of efficacy of the United Nations, which, nevertheless, seems to be the kind of organization on which they would base their new global order. O'Riordan refers to people like Barbara Ward and René Dubos (1972) as supporters of this view, to whom we might now add Gro Harlem Brundtland, after her Brundtland Report of 1987. The United Nations Earth Summit of 1992 and its 'Rio+10' successor in South Africa in 2002 have been the most spectacular examples to date of UN-sponsored attempts to deal with global environmental problems, and more governments than ever before were brought together to discuss the issues. Although the 1992 Summit's success was equivocal (Grubb *et al.*, 1993), and environmental movements were critical of the lack of commitment by governments after the 2002 Summit, 'global order' enthusiasts have drawn some succour from the fact that these meetings took place at all.

The second position is described as 'centralized authoritarianism'. This position also takes seriously the existence of an environmental crisis, and its supporters believe that, because no one is likely to succumb voluntarily to the measures needed to deal with it, they will have to be made to do so. The locus of authority is generally seen as the governments of nation-states, and in this respect no major political-institutional changes are held to be necessary. Governments would merely decide upon a course of action leading to sustainability (perhaps protectionism, rationing, population control and restriction of immigration) and put it into effect (for a recent contribution on some of the implications of this approach see Simms, 2006). O'Riordan refers to William Ophuls ('whatever its specific form, the politics of the sustainable society seem likely to move us along the spectrum from libertarianism toward authoritarianism' (Ophuls, 1977, p. 161)) and Garrett Hardin as exemplars of this position.

The third position described by O'Riordan is that of the 'authoritarian commune', which is distinguished from the previous position by the scale on which the sustainable society would operate. Institutional structures would be broken down, the locus of decision-making would (in principle) be devolved, but social structures would, of necessity, remain hierarchical. The model, says O'Riordan, is that of the Chinese commune, and he also refers to Heilbroner's *An Enquiry into the Human Prospect* (1974) as a prototype for this kind of thinking. Some might put Edward Goldsmith, co-author of *A Blueprint for Survival* (1972) and editor *of The Ecologist*, in this bracket, but although he appears traditionally hierarchical in some respects – particularly in the context of relations within the family – his support (for example) for forms of participatory democracy disqualifies him from full membership of the authoritarian commune canon.

The final possibility referred to by O'Riordan in his typology is the 'anarchist solution': 'The classic ecocentric proposal is the self-reliant community modelled on anarchist lines' (1981, p. 307). This shares the commune perspective with the previous position and thus envisages a major shift in the focus of authority and decision-making, but differs from it in adopting a left-liberal stance on relations within the community. In political terms at least (and often in material terms as well), O'Riordan's 'anarchist solution' is fundamentally egalitarian and participatory.

How are we to know which of these possibilities – or which combination of them – is properly descriptive of the political-institutional arrangements associated with ecologism? One approach would be to survey what members of the green movement and sympathetic academic backers have actually said about social arrangements in the sustainable society. Although in the Introduction I dissociated the current description of ecologism from explicit links with any real-life political manifestation of it (party or movement), it is impossible to avoid reference to named individuals, whose perspective is – inevitably – partial and particular. In what follows, then, my discussion of the sustainable society will draw upon views expressed by both activists and academics in and around the green movement.

One common theme in the debate is that there is no one form of society which is singularly appropriate to or suitable for sustainability. Martin Ryle has written importantly that '[E]cological limits may limit political choices, but they do not determine them. . . . A society adapted to ecological constraints . . . could take widely varying forms' (Ryle, 1988, pp. 7–8). This point of view is endorsed by Luke Martell, who writes that:

> while ecology implies some forms of social and political arrangements rather than others it also draws on older traditions to work out which are preferable on these grounds and to answer non-environmental questions to do with issues such as justice and liberty.
>
> (Martell, 1994, p. 159)

(Many greens will of course blench at the suggestion that environmental issues have nothing to do with justice and liberty.)

Although the indeterminacy of ecological criteria for social ones seems to be the dominant opinion at present, there are alternative views. What is crucial for understanding green politics in relation to other forms of political thought is that the non-human natural world always provides the principal context for deciding questions of political-institutional 'design'. Porritt writes that:

> If we can't secure our own biophysical survival, then it is game over for every other noble aspiration or venal self-interest that we may entertain. With great respect to those who assert the so-called 'primacy' of key social and economic goals (such as the elimination of poverty or the attainment of universal human rights), it must be said loud and clear that these are *secondary* goals: all else is conditional upon learning to live sustainably within the Earth's systems and limits. Not only is the pursuit of biophysical sustainability non-negotiable; it's preconditional.
>
> (Porritt, 2005, p. 10)

Robyn Eckersley takes a similar line:

> an ecocentric approach regards the question of our proper place in the rest of nature as logically prior to the question of what are the most appropriate social and political arrangements for human communities. That is, the determination of social and political questions must proceed from, or at least be consistent with, an adequate determination of this most fundamental question.
>
> (Eckersley, 1992, p. 28)

This general statement hides at least three possible types of position, each of which is consistent with Eckersley's lexical ordering. First, social principles are sometimes deduced from those found in 'nature'. There are great difficulties associated with deriving lessons for social design from nature, as John Barry usefully points out: 'non-human nature gives us no determinate prescriptions about how we ought to live, despite the attempts of some deep ecologists and bioregionalists to argue otherwise' (Barry, 1994, p. 383). Second, some radical greens urge us to adapt our social aspirations to the constraints and opportunities provided by a closer relationship with the land of our immediate surroundings – this is a kind of 'materialist ecologism'. I shall have more to say on this shortly under the heading of 'bioregionalism'. Third, there is the view that dealing with the multi-layered and interrelating nature of environmental problems implies that political institutions should somehow 'match' the layers and approximate as far as possible to the interrelations.

Nothing in Eckersley's statement commits her, of course, to deriving social and political arrangements from 'natural' ones (indeed, she explicitly opposes such a position: 1992, pp. 59–60), but there is a suggestion that some arrangements would not be consistent with an appropriate understanding of 'our proper place in the rest of nature'. This seems to imply, in turn, that some social and political arrangements have unsustainability (to use a shorthand description) built into them. If they do, then this also implies that some arrangements could have positive repercussions for sustainability and that, therefore, Ryle is overstating his case in claiming that a society adapted to ecological constraints could take 'widely varying forms'.

In sum, we might say that the political and social options available are narrowed down by recognizing, first, that some ways of life are more sustainable than others, and, second, that some institutional forms are more likely to deal effectively with environmental problems than others. As regards the second, Ryle suggests that it is possible to imagine a sustainable 'authoritarian or post-capitalist society' (Ryle, 1988, p. 7). There is, though, some evidence to suggest that democratic institutions and a 'quite heavily circumscribed market economy that is scaled down in terms of material-energy throughput' (Eckersley, 1992, p. 184) are more conducive to sustainable living than Ryle's putative capitalist authoritarianism. Authoritarianism is found wanting because the information flows needed for effective policy-making are missing, because in the long term, authoritarian regimes lack legitimacy (see e.g. Dryzek, 1987; Paehlke, 1988), and because capitalism needs curbing due to its 'expansionary dynamics' (Eckersley, 1992, p. 121; Kovel, 2002; Porritt, 2005) and the short-termism associated with market logic.

These considerations suggest that there is something about ecologism – despite Martell's objection (1994, p. 159) – that pushes it irrevocably towards the left of the political spectrum, and this view is strengthened if we make a distinction between the *objectives* of ecologism and its informing *principles*. Most of those who argue for a non-determinate relationship between ecology and socio-political form focus upon the objective of sustainability. They then argue that the green stress on this objective leaves them (greens) open to the charge that it (the objective) takes precedence over the means of arriving at it. If it could be shown that authoritarianism was more effective in this sense than democracy, then that would be enough to privilege authoritarianism ahead of democracy.

I have already suggested that the conclusion that authoritarianism is more functional for sustainability than democracy is quite likely wrong, and if we focus, in any case, on principles rather than objectives, then linking ecologism with authoritarianism seems even more implausible. As I pointed out in Chapter 1, Robyn Eckersley argues that ecologism is fundamentally emancipatory in its focus on the self-determination of all entities, including humans (Eckersley, 1992, pp. 53–5). This stress on self-determination rules out authoritarianism as a matter of principle; on this reading it makes no more sense to say that ecologism is a friend of authoritarianism than it would to say that liberalism is a friend of authoritarianism. (I shall say more on the relationship between authoritarianism, democracy and ecologism in Chapter 4.)

In my view, then, there is considerably less room for manoeuvre within ecologism as far as social and political arrangements are concerned than commentators such as Ryle and Martell suggest. This is not to say, though, that the relationship between ecologism and socio-political form is univocal: there is plenty of room within a broadly left-emancipatory framework for disagreement. So much will be clear from what follows.

More problems with growth

'The notion that the living standards of the rich countries are attainable by all countries is pure fantasy,' write Irvine and Ponton (1988, p. 21), thus suggesting that there are physical limits to growth. As noted above, though, greens also typically believe that there are social and ethical limits to growth. It has been argued, by some green economists, for example, that indiscriminate growth exacerbates problems it is intended to solve – particularly in the context of inflation and unemployment. It is suggested that unemployment is significantly the result of techno-logical advances that reduce the labour/output ratio. The traditional idea that rates of unemployment can be brought down only by increased growth is challenged at two levels: first, that further growth and sub-sequent investment in the same direction (i.e. labour-saving technology) can result only in more unemployment, not less; and second, that the rates of necessary growth projected by traditional political interests are unsustainable anyway. Either way, unemployment in a growth-oriented economy at a British (or comparable) level of development is liable to structural increase, despite temporary fluctuations. The social costs of unemployment are unacceptable, say greens, and the aspiration of unlimited growth, being part of the problem, can hardly be a part of the solution.

At the same time, greens argue that the economics of growth are inherently inflationary. In the first place, and building on the position that scarcity is a fundamental and unavoidable datum on a finite planet, they suggest that as resources are depleted there will inevitably be upward pressure on prices. Similarly, the costs of economic growth (some of its 'externalities'), which have, up until now, been largely ignored, will soon have to be taken into account and charged for. This, too, will increase the cost of living. Paul Ekins writes that 'environmental "goods" (e.g. clean air, pure water), which at a lower level of economic activity were effectively "free", will come to have an economic cost, resulting in further inflationary pressure' (1986, p. 11). Indeed, among traditional neoclassical (but pro-environment) economists, the 'internalization of externalities' has come to be seen as the best way forward for environmental protection (see e.g. Pearce *et al.*, 1989).

From a green perspective, then, the problems of inflation and unemployment are (or will be) the products of growth and so cannot be solved by more of it. And the point above about the coming necessity of including the cost of cleaning up dirty water in economic projections also serves to illustrate green concerns about traditional ways of measuring the strength of national economies. An increase, for example, in the Gross National Product (GNP) is invariably seen as a good thing, but, as Jonathon Porritt points out, 'Many of those goods and services [measured by GNP] are not beneficial to people: increased spending on crime, on pollution, on the many human casualties of our society; increased spending because of waste or planned obsolescence; increased spending because of growing bureaucracies' (Porritt, 1984a, p. 121).

More particularly, Paul Ekins (1986, pp. 32–5) points to four reasons why greens (and not a few others) consider GNP to be an inadequate measure of the health of an economy. First, it ignores the production that takes place in the non-monetarized part of the economy – household work, social work such as caring for the old and sick that takes place within the family, home-based production and the myriad networks of production and exchange associated with the underground, or 'black', economy. The value of such informal production in some countries has been calculated at some 60 per cent of GNP (Ekins, 1986, p. 34). Second, GNP calculations give us no idea of the distribution of production or its fruits. Third, they give no indication, either, of the sustainability of the economic practices that contribute to production. For example, the American farming system generates huge profits (for some farmers) but is highly inefficient in terms of the ratio between the energy that is put into the system and the calorific value of the food it produces. Greens would question the wisdom of using economic indicators that pay no mind to the future viability of the system they are measuring. Finally, as pointed out above in the context of the clean water debate, GNP ignores the costs of production – particularly the environmental costs.

In the light of these criticisms, the fact that GNP is still the principal indicator of the health of national economies is, for greens, symptomatic of the myopia induced by what they will see as an obsession with economic growth. In their view, the success of a system of production and exchange can only really be judged once alternative indicators are developed. Victor Anderson has suggested that a start could be made by including 'unpaid domestic labour, non-money transactions outside the household, and environmental deterioration' in the calculation, as well as starting with the Net National Product rather than the Gross National Product – 'i.e. GNP minus capital depreciation' (Anderson, 1991, p. 39). From a green point of view, expenditure on environmental protection and on compensation for environmental damage, the costs of excessive urbanization and centralization (such as travel and trade costs) and the money spent on dealing with what greens see as the problems brought about by 'industrial society' should all be removed from GNP calculations so as to give a measure of the quality of life as well as its quantity.

Even this Adjusted National Product (ANP), though, argues Anderson, would not provide an adequate picture of welfare in any given society due to its one-dimensional concentration on economic factors. He suggests that financial indicators need to be accompanied by two further sets which he calls 'social' and 'environmental' indicators (Anderson, 1991, pp. 55–64, 65–74). The former include factors such as primary school enrolment figures, illiteracy, mortality and unemployment rates, and telephones per thousand people (Anderson, 1991, p. 61). The latter include deforestation and population figures, carbon dioxide emissions and energy consumption data (Anderson, 1991, p. 74). Anderson's own deployment of these indicators across fourteen countries at various stages of development leads him to the following conclusion: '[S]ocial conditions are generally improving, and in the short term this is likely to continue. . . . In the medium term, environmental deterioration threatens to put these social improvements into reverse' (Anderson, 1991, p. 91). All of this has led Jonathon Porritt, in typically epigrammatic style, to say that: 'progress in the future may consist in finding ways of reducing GNP' (Porritt, 1984a, p. 121).

It is in this last respect that the physical, social and ethical objections of greens to the economy and society of indiscriminate growth come together: such an economy and such a society, they say, are not very nice places in which to live. Side-stepping the obvious objection that societies where there is no growth at all are hardly a delight either, greens claim that we are stunted ethically by the growth economy's refusal to take the quality of life of future generations seriously and by its easy preparedness to take the Earth as resource rather than as blessing. We produce indiscriminately and consume voraciously, and our status and aspirations are largely judged and dictated by the wealth at our disposal. Greens believe that lives in the growth economy will tend away from the elegant and towards the grubby and materialistic. Conversely, they suggest that a society orientated around sustainable growth would be a less greedy and more pleasant place in which to live, and if this seems hard to credit, then greens might quote John Stuart Mill as a temporary bulwark against disbelief:

> It is scarcely necessary to remark that a stationary condition of capital and population implies no stationary state of human improvement. There would be as much scope as ever for all kinds of mental culture, and moral and social progress; as much room for improving the Art of Living and much more likelihood of its being improved.
>
> (in Meadows *et al.*, 1974, p. 175)

As pointed out earlier, there are signs that this view is beginning to get a mainstream hearing (Layard, 2003, 2005). As with climate change and other signs of environmental stress, greens will of course take this as confirmation that they were right all along, and that both social and environmental stresses would be less acute if green analyses had been taken seriously – and earlier.

Questioning consumption

Political ecologists argue, then, for a contraction in economic growth or, more accurately, in what economist Herman Daly calls 'throughput' (1992, p. 36). The components of throughput are resource depletion, production, depreciation (involving consumption) and pollution. Of these four components, it is probably production that receives most attention when commentators consider the bases and implications of the sustainable society, but consumption provides the most useful starting point for discussion. In the first place, this is because the other three terms are founded on the existence and persistence of consumption:

consumption implies depletion, which implies production, which implies waste or pollution. And second, the picture of the Good Life that the political ideology of ecologism paints for us is differentiated from most other pictures precisely because of its arguing for less consumption – for some.

An increasingly common way of thinking about our differentiated impact on the environment is through the idea of the 'ecological footprint'. Nicky Chambers, Craig Simmons and Mathis Wackernagel write that:

> Every organism, be it bacterium, whale or person, has an impact on the earth. We all rely on the products and services of nature, both to supply us with raw materials and to assimilate our wastes. The impact we have on our environment is related to the 'quantity' of nature that we use or 'appropriate' to sustain our consumption patterns.
>
> (Chambers *et al.*, 2000, p. xiii)

The 'ecological footprint' is an expression of the quantity of nature we appropriate to sustain our individual and collective lives – a 'time-slice indicator of a human community's metabolistic relationship with the goods and services provided by its natural environment' (Dobson, 2003, p. 100). Every animal, including the human animal, has an ecological footprint, and so there is nothing new – in general – in the idea that humans have ecological footprints. The difference now though, say greens, is that humanity's ecological footprint has become so large that it threatens the continuing provision of nature's goods and services.

The ecological footprint notion focuses our attention on the consumption stage of the reproduction of human life, and it also has the capacity to make us aware of globally unequal shares in nature's goods and services. We could take the example of CO_2 emissions:

> assuming a global target of 11.1 gigatonnes CO_2 emissions is required to maintain climate stability by 2050, and assuming that the global population in 2050 is 9.8 billion, the per capita 'environmental space' for energy is 1.1 tonnes per year. UK per capita production of CO_2 is in the region of 9 tonnes, thus implying a reduction of UK emissions by about 85 per cent.
>
> (Chambers *et al.*, 2000, p. 102)

This kind of analysis implies that some people consume more than their fair share of environmental goods and services, which implies in turn that those people – in the name of fairness – should reduce their consumption of those goods and services.

This view of consumption marks ecologism off from most other political ideologies and it also helps to distinguish it from light-green environmentalism. Jonathon Porritt, for example, writes in dark-green rather than light-green mode when he says that 'A low-energy strategy means a low-consumption economy; we can do more with less, but we'd be better off doing less with less' (1984a, p. 174). In this context, to concentrate on consumption and its implications is both to help mark out ecologism's proper territory and to keep in mind that in this respect at least it comprises 'a sharp break with the principles of the modern era' (Ophuls, 1977, p. 164). One of these principles is that economic growth can go on for ever, and that maximizing individual and collective consumption is the goal of governments around the world.

As with growth, the green questioning of consumption has both a pragmatic and an elegiac content. Irvine and Ponton suggest that 'an attitude of "enough" must replace that of "more" ' (1988, p. 15), not only because they feel that current rates of consumption are physically unsustainable but also because they are unseemly. They balk at the production and purchase of what they consider to be unnecessary items, and press for a life based on 'voluntary simplicity' (Porritt, 1984a, p. 204). The 'middle way between indulgence and poverty' (ibid.), which would be the way of the sustainable society, might be uncomfortable for some: 'Of course people will still have washing-machines (as long as they are energy-efficient). But electric tooth-brushes and carving-knives? That's another matter!' (Bunyard and Morgan-Grenville, 1987, p. 335). Bearing these remarks in mind, ecologism is open to the criticism that it is an ideology for the comfortable middle classes; for those whose lives are secure enough to be able to reduce consumption without an appreciable decline in living standards. This is a potentially significant critique, and I shall say more about the social base of green political movements later.

Essential, then, to ecologism's picture of the sustainable society is reduced consumption (for those with excess-sized ecological footprints), and equally essential is the idea that, while this might involve a reduced material standard of living, such sacrifice will be more than made up for by the benefits to be gained. Greens will always distinguish between quantity and quality: 'in terms of crude material wealth, we're not likely to get any wealthier. But . . . what matters now is the quality of wealth' (Porritt, 1984a, p. 124). In similar vein, Edward Goldsmith reckons that the specious satisfactions of consumption can and should be replaced by 'Satisfactions of a non-material kind . . . social ones' (1988, pp. 197–8), and for Bunyard and Morgan-Grenville (or one of their contributors) the sky is the limit:

> Judged by illusory standards of wealth we might well be 'poorer' in a Green future – but we would, in reality, have a higher standard of living, better food, healthier bodies, rewarding work, good companionship, cleaner air, greater self-reliance, more supportive communities and, above all, a safer world to live in.
>
> (Bunyard and Morgan-Grenville, 1987, p. 335)

Given the centrality of reduced consumption to the dark-green project, for all the reasons given above, it is surprising that so few of ecologism's theorists (as far as I am aware) have paid much serious attention to the role of advertising in reproducing the habits and practices of consumption that they seek to criticize. Irvine and Ponton prove themselves exceptions to this general rule in pointing out that 'Linking mass production and mass consumption is the advertising industry' (1988, p. 62). Greens could perhaps make more of this from the point of view of political strategy – exposure of the social irresponsibility (from the point of view of sustainability) of the advertising industry would be a concrete way of raising the issue of consumption (well beyond, and in opposition to, the phenomenon of green consumerism) and making clearer what a sustainable society might look like. As Irvine and Ponton go on to say:

> Notions such as durability, reduced or shared consumption, or substituting non-material pleasures for the use of objects, conflict with the requirements of mass marketing. Advertising is tied to an expanding economy, the one thing that we, living on a finite planet, must avoid.
>
> (Irvine and Ponton, 1988, p. 63)

In this sense, basic nostrums of the green movement come together in the same place: the finitude of the planet, the need to restrict growth, the consequent need to reduce consumption and the necessity for calling into question the practices (in this case advertising) that help reproduce the growth economy.

Questioning consumption: need

Reducing the material consumption of those who consume too much is an integral part of ecologism's project, and so the green movement has a profound political and intellectual problem on its hands. It is faced, in the first place, with persuading potential supporters that this is a desirable aspiration, and it is saddled with a series of intellectual arguments for its position that currently appear too weak to do the job required. The assertion, noted above, that a society organized around reduced consumption just *would* be more pleasurable to live in seems unlikely – in present circumstances – to cut the necessary ice. Likewise, the most favoured alternative strategy, namely the building of a theory of need, is notoriously difficult to carry out. How did Bunyard and Morgan-Grenville (above) arrive at the conclusion that washing machines are legitimate objects but that electric toothbrushes are not? There is evidently a theory (or more likely an intuition) of need at work here, but how is it to be persuasively expressed? Paul Ekins, for one, thinks that it is important for the green movement to answer this query – 'The question of human needs is of absolutely central significance to the New Economics' (Ekins, 1986, p. 55) – but most expressions of theories of need are far too vague to be of much use: 'needs being those things that are essential to our survival and to civilized human existence, wants being the extras that serve to satisfy our desires' (Porritt, 1984a, p. 196).

The problem with such a formulation is that, while it gives us an idea of the general differences between needs and wants, it does not help us concretely to fill out their content. At the same time, to be able to fill out their content in any universal sense presupposes that 'fundamental human needs are finite, few and classifiable' (Ekins, 1986, p. 49). The obvious objection to this – that needs are historically and culturally mediated – can be partly met by saying that:

> common sense, along with some socio-cultural sensitivity, surely points to the fact that the needs for Subsistence, Protection, Affection, Understanding, Participation, Creation and Leisure have existed since the origins of *homo habilis* and, undoubtedly, since the appearance of *homo sapiens*.
>
> (Max-Neef, 1992, p. 203)

Max-Neef goes on to talk of the distinction between 'needs' and 'satisfiers' – needs are permanent and satisfiers are contingent and therefore open to negotiation (Max-Neef, 1992, pp. 206–7).

But how far does this help? The distinction just pushes the problem back one place. We might all be able to agree on certain 'basic needs' (food, drink, clothing, shelter) but the 'satisfiers' are another matter, and they are precisely what have to be negotiated. As Jonathon Porritt remarks, 'We all need to get from A to B; some people insist they can manage such a feat only in the back of a Rolls Royce' (1984a, p. 196). Just what size car is acceptable? Is a car acceptable at all?

If the needs/wants problem seems currently intractable, it is enough to notice for our purpose – that of identifying the principal features of the radical green sustainable society – that the emphasis on reduced consumption brings up the question sooner or later, and that therefore the distinction between needs and wants is one of the intellectual features of the various pictures of such a society. At the same time, the sense of scarcity that informs the whole discussion also generates another characteristic of the sustainable society to which most of its supporters will subscribe: a tendency towards the egalitarian distribution of the material wealth that is available. Thus, more fully, Irvine and Ponton explain that 'If there are limits to the needs for which society can provide, their fair distribution is even more urgent. . . . Limiting differentials between people is as essential as limiting economic growth and technological innovation' (Irvine and Ponton, 1988, p. 80). We saw a similar point being emphasized in the discussion of the ecological footprint, above. In this respect, the sustainable society of dark-green politics approximates closely to socialistic conceptions of equality in calling for reduced differentials, although it is clear in other respects that the stress on equality of opportunity means that there will be room for differentials, 'fairly' arrived at.

Questioning consumption: population

Thus we can identify a green belief in the benefits and necessity of reducing levels of material consumption, and the problems associated with convincing enough of us (for it to make any appreciable difference) to do so. But greens have another way of reducing consumption – one that does not involve intricate argumentation. Porritt is most clear in this respect: 'In terms of reducing overall consumption, there's nothing more effective than reducing the number of people doing the consuming' (1984a, p. 190). Greens are aware that some people in some countries consume much more than other people in other countries, and that therefore it is far too simplistic to argue for across-the-board reductions: 'Per capita energy consumption in the United States is two and one-half times the European average and thousands of times that of many Third World countries' (Tokar, 1994, pp. 75–6). Nevertheless, the option of population reduction is contentious, constituting as it does a specific aspect of the general green position that even current population levels are unsustainable, let alone projected future levels

(Curry, 2006, pp. 122–36). Experience suggests that this message is a difficult one to swallow for very many people.

The 1999 *Green Party (England and Wales) Manifesto for a Sustainable Society* states that 'growth in human numbers is probably the greatest long-term threat to achieving ecological stability either locally or throughout the world' (1999, p. 100). It is certainly central to most radical green pictures of the sustainable society that population levels would be lower than they are currently, although there is disagreement about what levels would actually be sustainable. Irvine and Ponton put the level for Britain at about 30 million people, which is (as they say) about half its current level (1988, p. 22). Bunyard and Morgan-Grenville, however, suggest that Britain could sustain 55 million people more or less self-reliantly – but only if we could all first be converted to vegetarianism (1987, pp. 94–6). Edward Goldsmith has put the globally sustainable figure at 3,500 million ('and probably a good deal less': 1972, p. 57), which means somehow losing about 1,800 million of the current world population (Lutz, 1994, p. 465).

And, of course, this is exactly the problem: how to 'lose' 1,800 million people. In the furthest reaches of some groups associated with the green movement, draconian measures for solving this problem have been advanced. As we saw in Chapter 2, the Earth First! group in the United States of America has suggested that epidemics such as AIDS should be allowed to run their course so as to help rid us of excess population.

At the same time, the left has been fighting a running battle with Malthus and his supporters ever since 1792 and the publication of *An Essay on the Principle of Population*, and they will generally respond to the green position by arguing that starvation is caused primarily by uneven distribution of resources rather than by their absolute limitation. Greens will take note of this response, but, in the same way in which they will point to the absolute limits on resource extraction despite temporary respites gained by our ingenuity in extracting them, they will also suggest that there are limits to the population that can be sustainably and comfortably maintained on a finite planet.

Despite the contributions of groups such as Earth First!, greens usually suggest that population control and reduction, although considered absolutely necessary, are a matter for negotiation rather than imposition. Thus the *Green Party Manifesto for a Sustainable Society* rejects 'repressive or coercive population control measures' (1999, p. 100), and Arne Naess in his Schumacher Lecture of 1987 recognized that reaching a sustainable population might take hundreds of years, because 'It remains vitally important to reject coercive measures as an unacceptable and morally repugnant infringement of human rights'

(Porritt, 1984a, p. 193). The kinds of tactic that have therefore been suggested within the green movement are summed up by Irvine and Ponton:

> There could be payments for periods of non-pregnancy and non-birth (a kind of no claims bonus); tax benefits for families with fewer than two children; sterilization bonuses; withdrawal of maternity and similar benefits after a second child; larger pensions for people with fewer than two children; free, easily available family planning; more funds for research into means of contraception, especially for men; an end to fertility research and treatment; a more realistic approach to abortion; the banning of surrogate motherhood and similar practices; and the promotion of equal opportunities for women in all areas of life.
>
> (Irvine and Ponton, 1988, p. 23)

With respect to the last point, the authors stress that 'There is a happy correlation between women's liberation and population control' (Irvine and Ponton, 1988, p. 23), and the 1994 World Population Conference in Cairo broadly endorsed such a view. As for the rest, while it is clear that there are sticks as well as carrots at work (and that measures such as 'sterilization bonuses' have often proved unwieldy, offensive and open to abuse), such tactics are a far cry from the culling feared by the greens' opponents and recommended by some deep ecologists.

However, it would be wrong so easily to absolve green strategy with respect to population control from any potential connection with repression. It has been suggested by some of the movement's supporters that communities (whether nation-states or some other political-institutional formation) will need to be protected from population growth by some form of immigration control. This was most notoriously suggested by Garrett Hardin in the wake of his development of the lifeboat ethic, which had it that if there was enough room for only ten people to survive in a lifeboat, then the eleventh (generally read as Third World populations) would have to be thrown out. This is not a standard view in the green movement today, but it has its echoes, I suggest, in some remarks about immigration control.

Dave Foreman, co-founder of Earth First!, has been berated for saying in a notorious interview that 'letting the USA be an overflow valve for problems in Latin America is not solving a thing. It's just putting more pressure on the resources we have in the USA' (in Bookchin and Foreman, 1991, p. 108). Although he has publicly retracted this statement, he still has '[A] little troll in the back of [his] brain [which] keeps whispering nagging questions. Who is really being helped by unlimited immigration? Is it sustainable? Does it actually exacerbate social and ecological problems here and in Latin America?' (in Bookchin and Foreman, 1991, p. 109). In Britain, Jonathon Porritt announced that 'the strictly logical position, as far as ecologists are concerned, is to keep immigration at the lowest possible level while remaining sensitive to the needs of refugees, split families, political exiles etc' (1984a, p. 191), and Edward Goldsmith recommended that 'a community must be relatively closed' (1988, p. 203). The repressive tribalism and exclusion that this could generate is absolutely clear in Goldsmith: 'a certain number of "foreigners" could be allowed to settle but again . . . they would not, thereby, partake in the running of the community until such time as the citizens elected them to be of their number' (1988, p. 203).

These remarks make rather a nonsense of some other green positions, such as that 'Greens celebrate the diversity of culture in a multi-cultural society', and that 'our goal is equality of opportunity for members of all ethnic communities' *(British Green Party Manifesto*, 1987, pp. 14–15). It is hard to see how Porritt could have his way of keeping immigration at the lowest possible level and at the same time argue that this should 'in no way be discriminatory in terms of race or colour' (1984a, p. 191).

Questioning consumption: technology

Quite soon, discussion of the green sustainable society raises the issue of the role and place of technology. To the extent that green politics is a challenge to the norms and practices of contemporary science and society, to the extent that it will blame scientific development (in a certain direction) for many of the ills it believes we now suffer, and to the extent that it attacks the belief that more of the same will cure those ills, technology is always under the critical green microscope. It is this, of course, that has led those outside the movement (and not a few, it has to be said, within it) to view it as anti-technological and therefore as a call to return to a pre-technological age.

This is far too simplistic. The most that can be said, I have concluded, about the green movement's attitude to nineteenth- and twentieth-century technology (which is what I shall principally mean by 'technology' from now on) is that it is ambivalent and that, more specifically, it depends on the kind of technology one is talking about. Rudolf Bahro of Germany, for instance, was (before his death in 1998) opposed to most forms of technology; Jonathon Porritt is in favour of certain sorts, but generally likes to remain agnostic; and Brian Tokar of the

USA is suspicious of it. What may be said is that greens are forever suspicious of the 'technological fix', if this means paying no attention to the political and economic causes of environmental and other social stresses.

This ambivalence towards technology can be instructively expressed by referring to the issue of recycling. Evidently the technology exists to recycle large amounts of 'waste' material (e.g. newspapers, bottles) and make it useful again. This is probably the kind of activity most often associated with green politics, and it is true that members of the green movement will often base their pictures of the sustainable society on such strategies: 'We have already suggested that the key to pollution control is not dispersal but recycling' (Goldsmith, 1972, p. 43).

In the wider context of the green demand for reduced consumption, however, this is clearly not enough, and some greens will be worried that excessive reliance on recycling will shift the onus away from the recognition that more profound changes are required. The emphasis should be on reducing consumption rather than recycling that which has already been consumed. Thus, in a formulation to which I have already referred:

> The fiction of combining present levels of consumption with 'limitless recycling' is more characteristic of the technocratic vision than of an ecological one. Recycling itself uses resources, expends energy, creates thermal pollution; on the bottom line, it's just an industrial activity like all the others. Recycling is both useful and necessary – but it is an illusion to imagine that it provides any basic answers.
>
> (Porritt, 1984a, p. 183)

Greens will insist that in this connection Porritt's basic answers can be provided only by 'A reduction in the total amount of resources we are consuming' (Irvine and Ponton, 1988, p. 28), and by answering the following questions (and particularly the second) from Brian Tokar in the affirmative: 'If something cannot be manufactured, built or grown without causing irreparable ecological damage, can't we strive to create something to take its place, or simply decide to do without it?' (Tokar, 1994, p. 80). The option of doing without things is a direct result of radical greens demanding reduced consumption – a demand that consistently recognizes that even appropriate use of technology is a holding operation rather than an assault on the principal issues.

While there is some ambivalence over the green attitude to technology's capability of dealing with the problem of limited resources, there is even more disagreement over its general role in the sustainable society – we might wonder, for instance, what kinds of technology will be allowed in order to cope with the demands of defending green societies from potential or actual aggressors. Some green thinkers will side-step the issue, of course, by arguing that sustainable societies will be basically peaceful ones anyway. Others will advocate non-violent civil resistance, drawing on practices followed, for example, during the 1980s anti-nuclear actions and demonstrations. This is fine as long as one is not fired upon, or is prepared to die defenceless if one is.

But most green scenarios for defence involve some variation of the 'hedgehog principle' – that the attacked population makes itself as prickly and uncomfortable for the invading forces as possible: 'A high enough level of non-cooperation, civil disobedience and sabotage,' suggests Brian Tokar, 'should be sufficient to make any country ungovernable' (1994, p. 128). This may be true, but civil disobedience and sabotage in the face of an aggressor willing to use force, if they are not to be enormously wasteful of human life, can make high-technology demands. How far would a green society be prepared to go along the road of weapons technology and its associated spin-offs?

Again, it has been suggested more positively that, far from being a *bête noire*, technology can make more palatable the transition to, and practice of, more localized and frugal forms of living. One of the major fears of observers outside the green movement is that its picture of localized politics smacks of petty parochialism, which would be both undesirable and unpleasant to live with. But would not information technology reduce the likelihood of this? Is this not precisely the sort of thing that Edward Goldsmith was thinking of when he wrote about 'the technological infrastructure of a decentralised society' (Goldsmith, 1972, p. 86)? Greens will often be heard contending that one of the beauties of modern technology is that it is ideally suited to decentralized forms of politics. In this respect we would seem entitled to agree with William Ophuls when he suggests that 'The picture of the frugal society that thus emerges resembles something like the city-state form of civilization, but on a much higher and more sophisticated technological base' (1977, p. 168).

Energy

If reduced consumption rather than more technological devices is the answer to the problems raised by the absolute scarcity of resources, then greens will point out that the same must apply to the use of energy. Energy is, of course, a resource, and, to the extent that current global energy policies rely principally on non-renewable sources of energy, it is also a limited resource. Nuclear power itself is produced from the limited resource of uranium and so seems unlikely to solve the problems brought about by resource scarcity. At the same time, while actual resource levels may be quite high, *available* non-renewable energy resource levels will be somewhat lower. This is because, in the first place, the cost of extraction (it is argued by greens) will eventually reach unacceptable heights; and second, there must come a point where, as Herman Daly puts it, it will cost as much energy 'to mine a ton of coal as can be got from a ton of coal' (1977b, p. 111).

Beyond the problem of the limits of non-renewable energy resources, greens are also typically wary of the use of such resources for the environmental damage they can cause. Nuclear energy is potentially highly polluting, the problems of disposing of even low-level waste (often referred to as the nuclear industry's 'Achilles' heel') have not been satisfactorily solved, and nuclear power-stations under normal operating circumstances might just be a source of leukaemia. Likewise, fossil-fuel power-stations notoriously contribute to the greenhouse effect and are one of the causes of acid rain.

In the face of the perceived disadvantages of relying for energy on limited stocks of polluting and dangerous non-renewable resources, greens usually base their energy strategy around renewable sources of energy, the conservation of energy, and reduced consumption, of both energy and the durable objects that it helps us produce. Renewable energy sources are argued to be desirable because they are in principle unlimited (although notoriously difficult to capture and store in any great quantities), they are relatively environmentally benign, and they are suited to the decentralized forms of living often recommended by political ecologists. In all these respects they speak to the basic demands of the green sustainable society. It is worth remarking, however, that in one respect they do not. The technology associated with renewable energy sources (windmills, barrages) is often highly complex and, in the case of the production of solar cells, polluting. Remembering the objections to the technologies associated with recycling and information technology, we can see that the issue of alternative energy sources provides us with yet another specific example of the ambivalence with which greens will view the role of technology.

Few greens pretend, however, that the energy policy referred to above will produce the fantastic quantities of energy currently required, let alone cope with the dizzying projections associated with rapidly developing nations like China and India. This means that demand for energy will have to lessen beyond the reductions brought about by price increases and improved conservation policies. At this point, the green assertion that sustainability will involve reducing material consumption meets the energy problem. Reduced energy use, for dark-greens, involves reduced production, and reduced production involves reduced consumption. They will argue that we can satisfy our needs through renewable energy, but not our greed. Once again the distinction between needs and wants is raised, and once again we see that the green picture of the sustainable society is buttressed by the necessity and desirability of reduced material consumption.

Trade and travel

Consistent with the principles of self-reliance and communitarian decentralization that inform some versions of the sustainable society, greens have unfashionable views on the issues of trade and travel. Before discussing this in a little detail it is important to be clear that self-reliance is not the same as self-sufficiency and that greens go to some lengths to distinguish the two. Despite green politics often being identified with the self-sufficiency commune movement, it is most generally seen to be organized around principles of self-reliance rather than self-sufficiency.

What is the difference? Self-sufficiency may be described as 'a state of absolute economic independence', while self-reliance is best understood as 'a state of relative independence' (Bunyard and Morgan-Grenville, 1987, p. 334). In terms of the importance of the notion of self-reliance to the politics of ecology, Paul Ekins goes so far as to claim that, along with theories of need (already covered) and a reconceptualization of work (see below), it is one of the three pillars of the New Economic framework (1986, p. 97). According to Johan Galtung, the basic rules of self-reliance are:

> produce what you need using your own resources, internalising the challenge this involves, growing with the challenges, neither giving the most challenging tasks' positive externalities to somebody else on whom you become dependent, nor exporting negative externalities to somebody else to whom you do damage and who may become dependent on you.
>
> (in Ekins, 1986, p. 101)

On this reading, trade is something to be carried out as an exception rather than as a rule. There is nothing in the theory of self-reliance that forbids trade, but it certainly aims to shift the onus of justification away from those who would reduce it and on to those who would maximize it. It would be wrong, then, to characterize greens as recommending complete economic independence – they are perfectly aware that 'There are always goods or services that cannot be generated or provided locally, regionally or nationally' (Ekins, 1986, p. 52). The ground rule, however, would be that 'self-reliance starts with the idea of producing things yourself rather than getting them through exchange' (ibid., p. 104). Imagining this rule being followed amounts to imagining an important part of the economic and political framework within which a green sustainable society would operate.

Trade is viewed with suspicion by greens on four grounds. In the first place (not necessarily a green reason), it is a site of the exercise of political and economic power and an easy way to exchange self-determination for dependence; second, it encourages frippery and helps to turn wants into needs (do we need kiwi fruits? but, then, do we need tea?); third, patterns of trade end up being notoriously wasteful of resources, as (for example) tomatoes are grown on the island of Guernsey, exported, and then sometimes shipped back for consumption; and fourth, reliance on one or two products for export can render economies vulnerable to a drop in prices or a general worsening of the terms of trade.

It is this last point that leads Johan Galtung to suggest that, if trade is to take place, 'one field of production – production for basic needs [food, clothing, shelter, energy, health, education, home defence] – should be carried out in such a way that the country is at least potentially self-sufficient, not only self-reliant' (in Ekins, 1986, p. 102). In this way populations would be shielded, at least in terms of necessities, from the vagaries of the market. As a result of these views on trade, green economic practice would be built substantially around protectionism: 'it's clear that selective protection of the domestic economy will be needed to establish its sustainable basis, and to encourage the country to become far more self-sufficient than it is at present' (Porritt, 1984a, p. 135). This puts greens at odds with the overwhelming mainstream view, represented by most governments and organizations such as the World Trade Organisation (WTO) and the World Bank, that trade is the route to development. Often these organizations will see environmental regulation, aimed at protecting environments and practices such as organic farming, as restrictions on trade – just one concrete instance of the tensions between those who advocate free trade and those who advocate sustainability and environmental protection.

Understanding this will help us to understand why much-vaunted 'green' politicians such as Norway's Gro Harlem Brundtland have a long way to go before embracing a radical green programme. In this context she argues that 'protectionism is one of the aspects of confrontation [between nations] which needs to be abolished. . . . The advantages of free trade for the countries of the North and South ought to be evident' (Brundtland, 1989, p. 5). In the current political climate, particularly since the GATT agreement reached in 1994 and despite the ferocious opposition to the World Trade Organisation talks in Seattle in 1999 and at subsequent WTO meetings, this is standard fare, and it provides a further illustration of the way in which political ecology sets its face against dominant paradigms.

Likewise, supporting the green argument for reduced trade we find the central notions of reduced consumption (if you cannot produce it, think about doing without it first, and only trading for it second), and a theory of need which hopes to sustain the view that in many instances the trade to which we have become accustomed is an unwarranted indulgence. If life under these circumstances resembles reproducing the styles of life most often associated with developing countries, then the green position on trade (and not a few of their other recommendations) reflects Rudolf Bahro's view that 'With a pinch of salt one might say . . . the path of reconciliation with the Third World might consist in our becoming Third World ourselves' (1986, p. 88).

Part of the effect of protectionism, of course, would be to throw communities back on to their own resources, and this is entirely in line with the green plan of creating a political life founded upon communitarian decentralization. This plan also affects the green position on travel: one of the characteristics of the radical green sustainable society is that people would travel less. Arne Naess in his 1987 Schumacher Lecture referred to the principle of 'limited mobility', and William Ophuls, too, believes that personal mobility would be limited in such a society (1977, p. 167). In the first place, this is because greens consider present travel practices to be wasteful of resources. The ecological footprint associated with air travel is an increasing worry, even for mainstream politics, as the climate change emissions associated with air travel increase at a faster rate than any other sector of the economy.

Second, and more importantly, greens argue for reduced mobility as a part of their hopes for generating supportive, satisfying relationships in their decentralized, self-reliant communities. From this point of view travel involves dislocation of the ties that hold such communities together, and so endangers the emergence of the 'sense of loyalty and involvement' (Porritt, 1984a, p. 166) that, for greens, will be one of the prime benefits of decentralized communitarian life. The sustainable society is substantially about living 'in place' and developing an intimacy with it and the people who live there; travel, on this reading, is too expansive and too centrifugal an occupation.

Work

Paul Ekins refers to 'a reconceptualisation of the nature and value of work' as one of the principal pillars of the green economic and social framework (1986, p. 97), and it is certainly true that ecologism can be marked off from most other modern political ideologies by its attitude to the subject. Political ecologists have a specific view on the value of work and they also question the dominant tendency to associate work with paid employment. Such an association can lead us to believe that if a person is not in paid employment then they are not working. This, for greens, is simply untrue, and their renegotiation of the meaning of work leads them to suggest ways of 'freeing' it from what they see as restrictions founded on the modern (and archaic) sense that work is just paid employment. This will become clearer shortly, but first a word needs to be said about how greens value work itself.

One of the most common scenarios for advanced industrial societies in this context is the workless future. This is a familiar story – one that begins in automated car factories and suggests that technological advances will eventually enable us to enjoy more or less labourless production across vast swathes of the industrial process. In this future the only problem would be how best to use the increased leisure time created by clean and automated production. Greens have peered into this future and they do not like what they see.

First, they will claim that it is premised upon rates of consumption and production that are called into question by the limits to growth thesis. Second, to the extent that this future is already with us, political ecologists will object to the unemployment that automated production appears to cause, and they typically reject claims that other industries (service, 'sunrise') will take up the employment slack caused by industrial reconversion. Third, such a future (given the present general antipathy to redistribution) would most likely produce a society split between the highly paid monitors of machinery and the recipients of social security payments pitched at a level designed to discourage indolence. Finally, greens look at the burgeoning leisure industry and see its consumer-oriented, environmentally damaging, industrialized and disciplined nature as a threat to the self-reliant, productive practices that the green Good Life holds out for us.

But beyond even all this, greens will be sceptical (at the very least) of the workless future because they believe work is a good thing. In this respect they are part of a tradition which has it that work is a noble occupation, that it uplifts the spirit and helps create and reproduce ties with one's community – even helps to create oneself. This view has it that work is an obligation both to oneself and to one's society, and that this obligation has to be redeemed. The green favouring of work will evidently lead political ecologists – like most other people – to bemoan the existence of unemployment, but greens add a twist to the expected story. They will claim that, while there is clearly unemployment, this does not mean that there is no work being done. At the root of this judgement lies the belief that work should not be seen as synonymous with paid employment. Greens (and, once again, not a few others) point out that enormous amounts of work are done that do not register as work, precisely because the tasks do not take the form of paid employment. Examples of this would be work done by women (mainly) in the home, caring for the sick and elderly outside the institutions of care, and work done in the so-called 'informal' economy.

A concrete example of an attempt to make all this visible is Victor Anderson's suggestion that the 'money value of unpaid domestic labour' and of 'non-money transactions outside the household' should be included in Adjusted National Product (ANP) improvements on Gross National Product (GNP) calculations (1991, p. 39). Greens point out that this distinction between work and paid employment is not merely of semantic importance. The modern tendency to associate reward and status with paid employment results in employers and potential employees looking to the sectors of production traditionally associated with paid employment when it comes to strategies for dealing with unemployment. In other words, the unemployed look for work in paid employment and employers try to place them in such employment. The green approach to problems of unemployment, in contrast, is to concentrate on those areas where work has always been done, but where it is frowned upon, if not actually criminalized. Nothing, evidently, is solved by semantically collapsing the distinction between work and paid employment, but greens argue for a series of policies that would practise such a collapse.

Most generally, the green argument is prefaced by the belief that traditional solutions to the problems of unemployment (like more growth) are doomed to failure either because of the context of a finite planet or because the technological infrastructure that has been built up is actually designed to reduce places of paid employment. Irvine and Ponton are clear about the implications: 'In these circumstances slogans about "No Return to the 30s" and "Jobs for All" are irrelevant if not downright reactionary' (1988, pp. 66–7). Political ecologists will go on to say that work which is done in the informal economy must be liberated and decriminalized, and that policies currently designed to prevent people from working in the informal economy should be abandoned and replaced by policies that will encourage them to work there. In this sense, collapsing the distinction between work and paid employment means collapsing the distinction between the formal and the informal economy.

Greens argue that current systems of social security and the assumptions that inform them prevent the potential of the informal economy from being fully realized. They point out that most social security systems deter people from doing work on a part-time, irregular basis (i.e. just when it 'shows up') because benefits are likely to be withdrawn – in other words, it is not always financially worthwhile to work. Second, rises in income can also lead to the withdrawal of benefits, leading to what has been called the 'poverty trap'. Thus work in the informal economy, the conditions of which bear little relation to the rigid structures of paid employment, is effectively discouraged. Furthermore, most social security systems (and certainly Britain's, based on Beveridge's 1942 proposal) have been designed around the assumptions of a growth economy and a system of reward based on the existence of practically universal paid employment. Once those assumptions no longer hold (and greens believe that they do not), the social security system based upon them must come into question too.

Beyond these points, greens are often critical of the means-testing that is part and parcel of current social security strategies and, associated with this, they are offended by the conditionality of awards and the repercussions this has: 'There are far more unclaimed benefits than illegal claims, though we have not seen many teams of investigators seeking out nonclaimants' (Irvine and Ponton, 1988, p. 84). The solution most often canvassed in green literature to the problems associated with current social security systems, and particularly the way in which they help marginalize the informal economy, is a Minimum Income Scheme (MIS) or guaranteed Basic Income Scheme (GBIS).

The general form of the GBIS is simply expressed. According to the 1999 *Manifesto for a Sustainable Society* of the England and Wales Green Party, it would be 'sufficient to cover basic needs . . . [and] be paid to all adult citizens and will not be withdrawn as income rises. Those payments due to children under school leaving age will be payable to a parent or legal guardian' (1999, EC 750, 752). Likewise, Anne Miller writes that:

A Basic Income Scheme would aim to guarantee each man, woman and child the unconditional right to an independent income sufficient to meet basic living costs. Its main purpose would be the prevention of poverty, as opposed to mere poverty relief.

(quoted in Ekins, 1986, p. 226)

Advocates of the GBIS claim that it has distinct advantages with respect to the drawbacks and anomalies of standard social security systems. First, people will not be discouraged from taking part-time, irregular work because no drop in benefit will be involved; second, small rises in income will not affect benefit payments either; and third, the system would be much simpler to administer than most current ones. More generally, flexible working patterns would be encouraged, leading (it is hoped) to the liberation of the informal economy and its recognition as a site of respectable employment. At the same time, greens hope that the GBIS would help to break down what they consider to be an insidious distinction in status between those employed and those unemployed.

Ever since their inception (and greens are not the only ones to have argued for guaranteed basic income schemes – they have supporters right across the political spectrum) such schemes have been highly controversial. In the first place, people ask how much the weekly or monthly payment would actually be. Some on the left have criticized GBIS proposals on the grounds that payments would likely be so low as to further institutionalize poverty rather than relieve it. But even if greens accept that payments might not be as high as some would like, they will maintain that the GBIS's effect of opening up the informal economy and allowing for flexible patterns of work would mean that very few people would remain at GBIS levels of income – and that, if they did, it could be more meaningfully called a voluntary decision than is currently the case.

The third standard criticism of all guaranteed basic income schemes is that they would be too expensive to put into operation. In response, advocates of such schemes usually take the redistributive bull by the horns and admit that high earners would be expected to finance the GBIS through paying high taxes: one is faced with a graduated income tax system of the type that is currently so out of favour, at least in liberal democratic polities. At the same time, greens can point to all sorts of other taxes that would be levied in the sustainable society: taxes on inputs to the production process, taxes on outputs, resource taxes, consumption taxes, taxes on aviation – all of which they claim would help raise sufficient revenue for the GBIS. Then they will refer to the savings made in administering such a simple system in comparison with the sums spent on current systems, and finally they will suggest that tax revenues would increase anyway given the increase in earnings created by more people working.

Two further issues related to the GBIS remain to be raised, both of which bear on the question of how much such schemes have to do with the green sustainable society anyway. Readers who have taken in the rest of this chapter may feel that the GBIS sits unhappily with the rather radical picture painted up until now of the sustainable society. The GBIS is radical in the sense that it would be a far-reaching extension of current practices, but the point of the green sustainable society as I have been led to see it is that it constitutes a substantial break with current practices. On this reading, we might suggest that there is too much in the GBIS that is 'of this world' to see it as part of a deep-green solution to sustainability.

Boris Frankel (1987) sounds the first alarm in this regard when he asks what political structures greens advocate for administering the GBIS. He argues that the centralized nature of such structures stands in tension with the decentralist impulse of many green programmes. He implies, in other words, that decentralist greens want it both ways – they seek decentralized forms of political life on the one hand and, on the other, they want to institutionalize social practices that are only possible through a high degree of planning and the centralization that this implies. Greens might reply that the administration of (and revenue-raising for) the GBIS will have to be carried out centrally, but that this does not negate the principle that 'nothing should be done at a higher level that can be done at a lower' (Porritt, 1984a, p. 166). GBIS administration, on this view, does have to be carried out at a 'high level', and that is that. How far one considers this to be a heresy within the green canon will depend on how strict one is in one's interpretation of the meaning of decentralization in the green political programme. I shall return to this point below.

More serious in this respect, perhaps, is the objection that the productive system on which the GBIS depends to produce the fabulous amounts of wealth needed to fund it (i.e. the current productive system) is described elsewhere by greens as being in decline and is unsustainable anyway – that is where green politics begins, in fact. Put more bluntly: as productivity declines and tax revenues dwindle, where will the money to pay for the GBIS come from? From this perspective the GBIS resembles a social-democratic measure grafted unsustainably on to the ailing post-industrial body politic, rather than a radically green measure in the spirit of solutions to the problems of sustainability raised by the spectre of limits to growth. At the very least, greens will find themselves back with the problem of negotiating the redistribution of decreasing amounts of material wealth.

At the beginning of this chapter I suggested that the limits to growth notion represents the starting point for radical green politics. The notion is indispensable for understanding ecologism, if only because it points us in the direction – at the outset – of the radical prescriptions for political and social life that the green sustainable society involves. If it were simply a question of eating healthy food, living in a lead-free environment or using biodegradable detergent, then environmentalist strategies such as green consumerism would probably do the job. But greens suggest that green consumerism is no more sustainable – in the long run – than grey consumerism: both are subject to limits to growth (Seyfang, 2005). This state of affairs needs to be addressed by a specifically different set of habits and practices from those that we currently follow, and green consumerism is too tied in to current rates of depletion, production, depreciation (involving consumption) and pollution to constitute the new set of habits and practices that dark-greens say we need.

I also suggested that of these four terms – collected together under Herman Daly's umbrella term 'throughput' – consumption was the one on which to focus attention in order best to see from where green prescriptions take off. The urge to reduce consumption as a response to the limits to growth thesis leads to the development of theories of need, the recommendation to reduce population levels, the questioning of the 'technological fix', the support for sustainable sources of energy – and all this is underpinned by the proposal for a self-reliant society, the ground rule for which is provided by Porritt: 'All economic growth in the future must be sustainable: that is to say it must operate within and not beyond the finite limits of the planet' (1984a, p. 120). The focus on consumption is also of a piece with the green determination to look at the *demand* as well as the *supply* side of dealing with environmental problems. Having outlined the most important features of one way of life of the sustainable society, from a radical green point of view we are now in a position to consider the (broadly speaking) political-institutional characteristics of such a society. What will it look like?

Bioregionalism

When I considered the possible responses to the limits to growth thesis nearer the beginning of this chapter, I proposed that we accept Tim O'Riordan's fourfold classification: the 'new global order', the idea of 'centralized authoritarianism', the 'authoritarian commune' and the 'anarchist solution'. I resisted the temptation of saying that one or another of these possibilities came closest to describing what a green sustainable society would look like, and limited myself to arguing – more generally – that sustainable societies cannot take just any form, and that unregulated markets and authoritarian regimes were likely to be dysfunctional for sustainability as well as contradictory of a basic green principle regarding the autonomous development of self-renewing systems. There have been attempts, though, to articulate more determinate visions of a green society, and one such vision goes by the name of 'bioregionalism' (McGinnis, 1999).

The general principles of what Kirkpatrick Sale has called the 'bioregional paradigm' (Sale, 1985, pp. 41–132) are simply expressed:

> We must get to know the land around us, learn its lore and its potential, and live with it and not against it. We must see that living with the land means living in, and according to the ways and rhythms of, its natural regions – its bioregions.
>
> (Sale, 1985, p. 56)

There are 'ecoregions' of 'perhaps several hundred thousand square miles' (ibid.), smaller 'georegions' of a few tens of thousands of square miles, and 'morphoregions' (he has also called these 'vitaregions' (Sale, 1984, p. 227)) of 'several thousand square miles' (Sale, 1985, p. 58). Living bioregionally involves identifying bioregional boundaries and living (for the most part) with what those territories provide in the way of, for example, 'given ores and minerals, woods and leathers, cloths and yarns' (ibid., p. 75). Bioregionalists have done some work on identifying these regions and have names for them: there is a land along the California coast, for example, known as Shasta (Tokar, 1994, p. 73).

Within these bioregions people would live in communities, because 'If one were to look for the single basic building block of the ecological world, it would be the community' (Sale, 1985, p. 62). Sale suggests that the 'human animal' has historically favoured communities of 500 to 1,000 people for face-to-face contact and 5,000 to 10,000 'for the larger tribal association or extended community' (ibid., p. 64). Communities much bigger than this are regarded as undesirable because they cannot be sustained on their own resources.

The bioregional community would seek to 'minimise resource-use, emphasise conservation and recycling, [and] avoid pollution and waste' (Sale, 1984, p. 230), and all of this would be aimed at achieving sustainability through what Sale calls self-sufficiency. The bioregionalist is likely to be even less keen on trade than the advocate of self-reliance, and Sale himself sees self-sufficiency as centred on a 'full-scale morphoregion' so as to ensure 'a wide range of food, some choice in necessities and some sophistication in luxuries, [and] the population to sustain a university and large hospital and a symphony orchestra' (1985, pp. 74–5). We would, however, be likely to do without some things:

'some bioregions would have to steel themselves for significant changes from their omnivorous and gluttonous habits of the present: noncitrus regions would need to look to other sources of vitamin C, for example' (ibid., p. 75). In general, bioregionalists will claim that the oft-cited problems associated with the unequal endowment of regions with natural resources simply do not, in fact, arise: 'there is not a single bioregion in this country [the United States of America] that would not . . . be able to provide its residents with sufficient food, energy, shelter, and clothing, their own health care and education and arts, their own manufactures and crafts' (ibid.).

Bioregionalists will usually insist that land be communally owned because the fruits of nature are fruits for everyone, and they will urge that polities follow the natural world's example and abhor systems of centralized control. Consequently, they advocate 'the spreading of power to small and widely dispersed units' (Sale, 1985, p. 91). Associated with this is the idea that nature's lesson as far as social relations are concerned is one of equality, or what Sale calls 'complementarity' (ibid., p. 101). The claim is that 'stratification and hierarchy within specific sub-groups in the animal world is extremely rare' (ibid., p. 98), and that, on the basis that what is good for the 'natural' world is good for us as a part of it, hierarchy should not be institutionalized in politics either. One further principle of bioregionalism, that of diversity, will be treated below; it has destabilizing possibilities for the picture presented thus far.

The guiding principle of bioregionalism, then, is that the 'natural' world should determine the political, economic and social life of communities, and that the messages that nature gives off are best read through ecology rather than, say, through social Darwinism: 'by a diligent study of her [nature] . . . we can guide ourselves in constructing human settlements and systems' (Sale, 1984, p. 225). Sustainability for bioregionalists and those who draw their inspiration from them is seen as presaged upon reducing the spiritual and material distance between us and the land:

> We must somehow live as close to it [the land] as possible, be in touch with its particular soils, its waters, its winds; we must learn its ways, its capacities, its limits; we must make its rhythms our patterns, its laws our guide, its fruits our bounty.
>
> (Sale, 1984, pp. 22–5)

No doubt Kirkpatrick Sale's general picture of bioregionalism and the exhortation quoted above both sound extremely far-fetched, but elements of it survive in many of the positions taken by even the least mystical of greens. In this particular context nearly all of them will bemoan the lack of knowledge of the land so typical of the industrialized human being. They will deplore our ignorance of where our food comes from and how it grows, and suggest that the pre-packaged produce on supermarket shelves is both a symptom and a cause of our dangerous distance from the land. In this sense, both they and the bioregionalists will urge us to 'live in place' – to accommodate our lives to the environment in which we live, rather than resisting it (Goldstein, 1999).

Agriculture

In this respect agriculture will always have a special place in the theory and practice of the green sustainable society. This is so in two ways. First, there is the relatively well-known point that the green movement considers current agricultural practices (what they would call 'industrial agriculture') to be unacceptable because unsustainable. Intensive chemical-based farming is held to pollute watercourses, to encourage erosion, to produce tasteless food of low nutritional value, to bring about salinization of the land through irrigation, to upset ecological balances through insensitive pest control, and to bore us with its monocultural panoramas.

But the green point pushes past this rather pragmatic attachment to sustainable agriculture. Jonathon Porritt, for example, suggests that the importance of sound agriculture goes beyond producing healthy food on a sustainable basis. He writes that:

> its implications for a change in the attitude of people to the planet are highly significant. It binds people to the natural processes of the Earth and, with the use of appropriate technology, creates a sense of harmony that is sorely lacking.
>
> (Porritt, 1984a, p. 180)

In this respect, agricultural practices in the green society are charged with the essential task of providing the site at which our rifts with the 'natural' world are to be healed. Spirituality ghosts dark-green politics; green politics is a filling of the spiritual vacuum at the centre of late industrial society, and the land itself is the cathedral at which we are urged to worship. Peter Bunyard's message is instructive: 'The search for self-sufficiency is, I believe, as much spiritual and ideological as it is one of trying to reap the basic necessities of life out of the bare minimum of our surroundings' (in Allaby and Bunyard, 1980, p. 26). In this regard agriculture is where theory becomes practice: the praxis of green politics.

Diversity

One principle of Kirkpatrick Sale's bioregional society has been held over because it is a point at which the wider green movement's notion of the sustainable society will begin to diverge from the bioregional project. The principle is diversity, and the point is that to talk of a generic 'bioregional society' (as I have been doing) is a misrepresentation. More accurately we have to speak of bioregional *societies* – not only in the obvious numerical sense, but also in terms of their informing political, social and economic characteristics.

Sale writes bluntly that it is not necessarily the case that each bioregional society 'will construct itself upon the values of democracy, equality, liberty, freedom, justice, and other suchlike desiderata' (1984, p. 233). This may seem peculiar, given Sale's commitment, expressed above, to the notions of equality and political participation, both derived (in contested fashion) from principles of the science of ecology, but there is evidently a tension between the demands of 'complementarity' and diversity. When diversity is privileged, one is obliged to admit to (and underwrite) the possibility that:

> truly autonomous bioregions will likely go their own separate ways and end up with quite disparate political systems – some democracies, no doubt, some direct, some representative, some federative, but undoubtedly all kinds of aristocracies, oligarchies, theocracies, principalities, margravates, duchies and palatinates as well.
>
> (Sale, 1984, p. 233)

At this point the wider green movement is likely to lose its bioregional nerve. Its members will want to subscribe to Sale's declaration that 'Bioregionalism . . . not merely tolerates but thrives upon the diversities of human behaviour' (ibid., p. 234); but, as images of slavery and sexism come to mind, misty eyes will snap into focus and greens will remember that they are as much the heirs of the Enlightenment tradition as its committed critics. They most certainly believe that 'their model of postindustrialism will maximise democracy, freedom, tolerance, equality and other rationalist values which made their appearance in Europe a few hundred years ago' (Frankel, 1987, p. 180), and in this respect the bioregional imperative of diversity is tempered by the desire to universalize messages most often associated with liberal democracy.

Decentralization and its limits

Many green stories of the sustainable society are written in the language of decentralization, often to the point where the decentralist impetus takes the final form of communal types of living. Rudolf Bahro is probably the person most normally linked with full-blown commune recommendations for the shape of the green society, and the reasons he gives for favouring communes echo those given by Sale. In the first place, communes are not 'economically expansive'; as Edward Goldsmith puts it, 'to deploy a population in small towns and villages is to reduce to the minimum its impact on the environment' (1972, p. 64). Second, they provide an obvious focus for political decentralization. Third, they are what Bahro calls 'anthropologically favourable', i.e. they correspond more 'to human nature, among other things by avoiding both the neuroticmaking family and the alienating big organization' (1986, pp. 87–8). In this respect Goldsmith goes even further: 'it is probable that only in the small community can a man or woman be an individual' (1972, p. 63). Communes therefore provide the site on which personal relationships become fulfilling, and where people will learn to live 'in place' (according to, and not against, their environment).

In this respect, green politics inserts itself into a tradition that is as long as history, and embroils itself in debates that will be most familiar to the modern reader in the context of the theory and practice of communitarian anarchism. Some greens (and particularly bioregionalists) bring a novel perspective to bear on this debate in two respects: first, the idea that communal living is somehow 'read off' from the 'natural' world – that it is a natural way of living, and in this sense responds to the demand for sustainability; second, they are also likely to suggest that something resembling a federation of communes is the only viable political-institutional form for the sustainable society to take.

In this sense they will suggest that other political forms are more susceptible to environmental irresponsibility and that this is therefore a very practical reason (in view of the long-term project of sustainability) for supporting the commune option. This is why Goldsmith claims that decentralization is proposed, not 'because we are sunk in nostalgia for a mythical little England of fetes, olde worlde pubs, and perpetual conversations over garden fences' (1972, pp. 61–2), but for more hardheaded reasons. The idea is that resource problems are best solved by bringing points of production and consumption closer together – we should no longer be talking of producers and consumers but of 'pro-sumers'. It is often argued that greens have no reasons of their own (as opposed to reasons borrowed from other political traditions) for arguing for one particular political form rather than another. This is wrong: all greens of whatever tint will argue that political-institutional design should be guided by environmental and/or ecological realities. In Goldsmith's case there is the suggestion that there are environmental benefits to be derived from political decentralization – a green-sounding argument if ever there was one. From this point of view cities produce too much pollution, degrade neighbouring land through the demands of waste disposal, make 'excessive demands on natural resources' (Stoett, 1994, p. 339), and prevent their inhabitants from acquiring a sense of their dependence on the natural world.

All this, though, is by no means accepted by everyone. It is argued, on the contrary, that essential services can be supplied more cheaply for people living in close proximity, and that environmental degradation can be more effectively dealt with in bounded spaces. Moreover, the Amazonian experience suggests that a rush to the countryside can have devastating consequences under the wrong conditions. Notwith-standing these debates, the other arguments surrounding green com-munitarianism are familiar: 'Is it practical?', 'Would such a life be stultifying?', 'What would the relationships between communes look like?' and so on. Certainly many will feel uncomfortable about the implications of arbitrary justice implied by Edward Goldsmith's sug-gestion that 'crime' be controlled 'through the medium of public opinion' by subjecting the offender to 'ridicule' (1972, p. 135), and will agree with André Gorz that:

> communal autarky always has an impoverishing effect: the more self-sufficient and numerically limited a community is, the smaller the range of activities and choices it can offer to its members. If it has no opening to an area of exogenous activity, knowledge and pro-duction, the community becomes a prison ... only constantly renewed possibilities for discovery, insight, experiment and commu-nication can prevent communal life from becoming impoverished and eventually suffocating.
>
> (quoted in Frankel, 1987, p. 59)

The themes of confinement and surveillance at which Gorz hints haunt some green texts surreptitiously – 'Many in the informal economy who do not now disclose their income ... would find that in the new system the risks of tax evasion outweigh gains', for example (Irvine and

Ponton, 1988, p. 73) – and while this is probably not surprising given the puritanical tenor of much of the green programme, it is an aspect of green politics that (on the face of it) can offend the modern liberal sensibility. I shall say more about the relationship between liberalism and ecologism in Chapter 4.

Many greens will respond to the practical or ethical objections to commune living by falling back on a more loosely conceived notion of political decentralization: the reasons remain the same, but the form is different. The basic rule once the commune option has been set aside, according to the 1999 *Green Party Manifesto for a Sustainable Society*, is that 'nothing should be done centrally if it can be done equally well, or better, locally' (PG 100). This amounts to a call for what Schumacher famously called 'appropriateness', and in green hands often turns into a commitment to local politics and some form of participatory democracy: 'Greens believe that many more decisions should be taken at the local level, encouraging greater participation and accountability', and, in a statement typical of advocates of participatory democracy, 'voting is the beginning and not the end of one's democratic commitment' (Bunyard and Morgan-Grenville, 1987, pp. 319, 320). As far as this last point is concerned, Brian Tokar refers to New England town meetings as the *locus classicus* of face-to-face democracy in action, as well as to 'ancient Greek democracy, the Parisian sections of the French Revolution, pre-revolutionary Boston and the anarchist city of Barcelona during the Spanish Civil War' (Tokar, 1994, p. 105).

This much is clear, and probably familiar. Familiar, too, are the questions normally asked of such a picture, and they have been forcefully put by critics such as Boris Frankel (1987) and Luke Martell (1994). Their principal difficulty with the green decentralist picture revolves around how such a decentralized society is to be co-ordinated, both in the political and the economic spheres. They argue that the green decentralist programme is unrealistic for three reasons. First, not everything that we might reasonably expect from a green society can be produced locally; second, dealing with the environmental problems that the green movement has identified requires the kind of planning and co-ordination that can only be provided by centralized political structures; and third, such structures are needed to organize the redistribution required by the greens' egalitarian project. Greens might respond that they (or rather some of them, depending on what their picture of a sustainable society looks like) are perfectly able to accept these points, within the framework provided by their maxim that no decision should be taken at a higher level that can be taken at a lower level.

With respect to the first issue, Martin Ryle argues that it is not possible to make 'fridges, bicycles [or] kidney dialysis machines' in 'domestic enterprises or craft workshops' (Ryle, 1988, p. 23) – or at least certainly not to the standard required for the safe operating of complex equipment. Chinese experiences of decentralized production during the 'Great Leap Forward' under Mao suggest that even relatively uncomplicated goods are hard to produce adequately.

Second, Ryle points out that 'ecological restructuring' as opposed to 'environmental protection through piecemeal legislation' (Ryle, 1988, p. 63) will involve planning, and concludes that, although one might prefer to have no state:

> If one is honest about the objectives which an ecologically enlightened society would set for itself, it is difficult to avoid concluding that the state, as the agent of collective will, would have to take an active law-making and -enforcing role in imposing a range of environmental and resource constraints.
>
> (Ryle, 1988, p. 60)

On this reading, planning is essential if the green programme is to be realized, and such planning can be devised and carried out only by centralized political structures. Ryle makes the interesting further point that, if it could be successfully argued that environmental problems can be relieved only by intervention, it might be possible more generally to turn the tables on the free marketeers: 'the idea of an ecological transformation of the economy can itself play a part in renewing the legitimacy of political interventions in the market' (Ryle, 1988, p. 66). Boris Frankel adds that redistribution with a view to egalitarianism presupposes centralized structures too:

> Until individuals and groups accept the unpalatable news that stateless, decentralized, moneyless, small-scale communes or other informal alternatives are not viable without the complex administrative and social structures necessary to guarantee democratic, participation, civil rights and egalitarian co-ordination of economic resources, there is not much hope of strong coalitions between labour movements and new social movements.
>
> (Frankel, 1987, p. 270)

Greens might make two responses to these remarks. In the first place, some of them will say that it is a caricature of their position to imply, as do Ryle and Frankel, that they seek entirely stateless societies. They will say that only the bioregionalists and the extreme commune theorists would subscribe to that, and that although they influence the movement's thinking it would be wrong to argue that their position is exhaustively representative of the movement's as a whole. This is not to say that the movement doesn't exhibit confusion on this score, and there are clearly problems associated with the programme of seizing central power and then giving it away again, but this is not the same as suggesting that the green movement is innocent of the need to plan. Robyn Eckersley is a representative ecocentrist who is quite clear about the need for states in bringing about and maintaining a sustainable future (Eckersley, 1992, pp. 183–5).

Decentralist greens, though, might put their same argument a different way. They can also say that, rather than pushing for the abolition of the centralized state, the movement is merely asking that the ground rules for decision-making be changed. Currently, the onus of justification is on those who would have decision-making based locally, and ecologists would like to see this reversed. In other words, the current norm is for decisions to be taken at high levels, while under a green regime decisions would be taken at low levels unless it were expressly necessary for them to be taken higher up. In this context the kinds of decision and the types of production to which Frankel and Ryle refer (income or resource distribution and kidney dialysis machines) are precisely those that would justifiably correspond to higher levels according to the green maxim. In this sense, the socialist critique of green forms of organization enables us to clarify the radical green position rather than undermine it.

We must recognize, of course, that the problems of co-ordination which underpin many of the criticisms of green decentralization do not arise in the most extreme versions of bioregionalism because contact between communities would not be institutionalized. Or rather, different problems would arise, in the sense that relations between and within communities could not legitimately be universalized and regulated. Frankel wonders in this regard whether the relationships between decentralized communes would not simply 'grow into capitalist markets with all the inherent qualities of inequality, exploitation and so forth' (Frankel, 1987, p. 56). But while this could be a problem for Enlightenment enthusiasts, Kirkpatrick Sale and his supporters might consider it merely to be part of life's rich pattern: the outcome of allowing for diversity.

However, if we assume that connections between communes are to be institutionalized, then the relations between local and 'national' levels need to be carefully spelt out. My reading of the green ideologues' approach to this problem (to the extent that they have dealt with it at all) is that they end up where they do not want to be: with a more weighty 'national' framework than some of them would like. Taking the economic arena as an example, greens are typically opposed to the workings of the market as they characterize it. For them, the market unsustainably and therefore irresponsibly encourages consumption, and it is usually prepared to answer only short-term questions (Wall, 2005). This, in the context of limits to growth (which by its nature, according to greens, demands long-term thinking), is unacceptable. The problem in our context is that, if the market is to be fettered, who is to do the fettering? More obviously, if greens demand long-term policies, we might argue that they will have to be planned and co-ordinated. Once again, who is to do the planning and coordinating if not some supra-community political agency (Martell, 1994, pp. 58–62)? As Frankel puts it:

> would a Green post-industrial society minimize or maximize social planning? If it minimized social planning and relied predominantly on market mechanisms, then all the major difficulties of market socialism would appear. If the new society maximized planning, then how would this be possible without national state institutions?
> (Frankel, 1987, p. 55)

In response to these questions, there is a definite trend in green thinking now towards an understanding that environmental problems need to be dealt with at all the levels at which they occur, and that political institutions must both correspond to these levels and integrate between and across them (Paehlke, 2003; Thomashow, 1999). Edward Goldsmith (above) argued that there are good ecological reasons for decentralization; this position recognizes that ecologies are regional, national and international as well as local, and seeks to match this ecological diversity with political-institutional diversity. So Robyn Eckersley writes that 'the ecoanarchist defence of local sovereignty provide[s] no firm institutional recognition of the many different layers of social and ecological community that cohere *beyond* the level of the local community' (Eckersley, 1992, p. 182). From this point of view, the state plays 'a vital role in controlling the operation of market forces and in laying down the framework for a socially just and ecologically sustainable society' (ibid., p. 194). This is all part of the state's rehabilitation in green political thought that has taken place in recent years. From being clearly seen as part of the problem (Carter, 1993, 1999) it is now most commonly regarded as part of the solution (Barry and Eckersley, 2005; De Geus, 2002; Eckersley, 2004).

Indeed, the state has moved from being something of a *bête noire* in green political thought to playing a more positive role in any putative green society's institutional design (Eckersley, 1995). Green state theorists are keen to steer a course between outright endorsement of currently existing states and outright rejection of them. So Eckersley writes that 'By "green state" I do not simply mean a liberal democratic state that is managed by a green party government with a set of programmatic environmental goals. . . . Rather, I mean a democratic state whose regulatory ideals and democratic procedures are informed by *ecological* democracy rather than *liberal* democracy' (Eckersley, 2004, p. 2). Coming at it from the point of view of markets, Bob Paehlke reaches a similar conclusion. He points out the ways in which unfettered markets can result in ecological disaster and that the state can – and should – act as a democratizing force aimed at producing ecological as well as accumulative rationality (Paehlke, 2003, p. 5). So green endorsement of the state seems conditional on its ecological democratization, and this move is best seen as part of a growing tendency towards 'visionary pragmatism' as far as green institutional design is concerned. As Eckersley puts it, 'those concerned about ecological destruction must contend with existing institutions and, where possible, seek to "rebuild the ship while still at sea" ' (Eckersley, 2004, p. 5). As far as democratizing the state is concerned, she writes that 'the regulative ideal or ambit claim of ecological democracy is that all those potentially affected by ecological risks ought to have some meaningful opportunity to participate, or be represented, in the determination of policies or decisions that may generate risks' (Eckersley, 2004, p. 243). There is resonance here with the move from 'ethics' to 'politics' that we saw in the work of hybridity theorists such as Plumwood and Latour near the end of Chapter 2.

States, of course, do no exist in isolation and it is clear that many of the global environmental problems with which we are faced are international in nature. Sometimes these are best dealt with through negotiations between sovereign states, sometimes through international agencies such as the United Nations, and sometimes through supranational bodies with supranational powers such as the European Union. The (tenuous but relevant) relationship between the green statist view and Sale's bioregionalism is that they both seek to match political forms with ecological realities, but the statist view differs in retaining the nation-state as the fundamental political unit, with the authority both to make laws in respect of its own populations and to enter into negotiation with other nation-states in the international arena. Eckersley, in sum, argues that decentralist greens are crucial to the creation of an ecocentric *culture*, but that they have relatively little to contribute to more precise questions of institutional design (1992, p. 182).

Conclusion

In sum, the possible political arrangements in a sustainable society seem to range all the way from radical decentralization to a world government. Ecologism, though, is a transformative political ideology: transformative of people and the way they think about, relate to and act in the non-human natural world. The problems associated with transformative ideologies of any sort were flagged by Jean-Jacques Rousseau as long ago as 1762 when he opened his *The Social Contract* with the words: 'My purpose is to consider if, in political society, there can be any legitimate and sure principle of government, taking men as they are and laws as they might be' (Rousseau, 1762/1968, p. 49). Quite soon he realized that the society he had in mind would not work so long as men remained 'as they are', and so he introduced a *deus ex machina* in the form of a 'Lawgiver' whose job was to 'change human nature' (ibid., p. 84). Transformative greens are in much the same position as Rousseau: the raw material is inadequate to the task at hand. Greens are asked political-institutional questions, and they have to answer them. Taking 'men' (and the societies that have spawned them) as they are, decentralized politics seems ineffective and naive. Taking 'men' (and their modes of production and consumption) as they might be, though, decentralized politics is the preferred radical green form – and for some of these radical greens, indeed, decentralized politics is the ecological equivalent of Rousseau's Lawgiver: the source of the transformation of human nature.

4   Strategies for green change

The Schwarzes ask: 'How do we start? By what imaginable transition can we move from here to a green future? Can the immense gap at least be narrowed, between the Green-thinking dreamers and the present reality?' (Schwarz and Schwarz, 1987, p. 253). Ecologism provides us with a critique of current patterns of production and consumption, and the Schwarzes' 'Green-thinking dreamers' have painted pictures of the sustainable society they would like us to inhabit. Two of the classic requirements of a functional definition of 'ideology' are thus far fulfilled by ecologism: it has a description (which is already an interpretation) of 'political reality', and it has a prescription for the future, which amounts to a description of the Good Life. In the light of the space between the former and the latter, the primary question addressed in this chapter is: 'What is ecologism's strategy for social change?' The subsidiary question posed is: 'Will this strategy (or these strategies) do the job required of them?'

   The first point to note about ecologism and social change is that until recently very little serious thinking had been done about it (Begg, 2000). Boris Frankel once rightly observed that 'one reads very little about how to get there from here' (1987, p. 227), and it is noticeable how many conversations about green politics very soon dry up when the issue of change is broached. There are several reasons for this.

   First, there is the belief that the changes required are so far-reaching that nothing short of an environmental catastrophe could produce the political will needed to bring them about: 'it is quite "unrealistic" to believe that we shall choose simplicity and frugality except under ecological duress' (Daly, 1977a, p. 170). Second, among more optimistic observers there has been a tendency (noted in Chapter 1) to believe that the delivery of the message of impending catastrophe would be enough to generate social change. After all, how could a humanity aware of the threat to its existence fail to act in its own best interests? This certainly seems to have been the line taken in the original *Limits to Growth* report: 'We believe that an unexpectedly large number of men and women of all ages and conditions will readily respond to the challenge and will be eager to discuss not if but how we can create this new future' (Meadows *et al.*, 1974, p. 196). Contrary to its authors' expectations, however, the publication of their report has not of itself produced the changes for which they argue. Indeed, there is a growing consensus that the provision of information, on its own, is not enough to induce behaviour change, either in individuals or collectivities (Kollmuss and Agyeman, 2002). In part this is because 'the environment' amounts to what is known as a collective action problem: individuals can disadvantage themselves by taking the appropriate action if others do not do so at the same time. No matter how well-informed citizens are they may be reluctant to act appropriately if others are likely to 'free-ride' on their behaviour.

Sometimes the immaturity of the ideology is held responsible for its not having got to grips with the issue of social change: green thinkers have had their work cut out simply describing our environmental malaise and convincing us of their arguments. It follows, from this perspective, that the very newness of the ideology is the reason for its current lack of a strategy that might be productive in the light of the ends it proposes. Now that the foundations are more or less in place, it is held, the strategy will follow.

As we think about green transformative strategies we should remember that ecologism proposes a radically different society to the current one. No one would dispute that significant improvements to the environment may be brought about by parliamentary party and pressure group activity – it would be a mistake to underestimate the achievements of groups such as Friends of the Earth and Greenpeace, brought about by high levels of commitment and undeniable expertise. Similarly, most governments are nowadays committed – in principle at least – to sustainable development. However, ecologism's prescriptions for transformation must square with the rather profound political, social and economic changes it envisages. These objectives provide the backdrop for this chapter.

Most of the discussion that follows is organized around the distinction between parliamentary and extra-parliamentary political activity. There is evidently nothing particularly novel about this, although the very fact that this turns out to be the most fruitful way of approaching the issue is symptomatic of the general theme of ecologism and social change: that liberal democratic politics and the spaces in which it allows one to act constitute the parameters for the majority of ecological political action. This mention of liberal democracy allows us to consider, first, the most overarching issue of green social change: the ongoing debate regarding authoritarianism and democracy.

Democracy and authoritarianism

Accusations of authoritarianism are never far from the surface where green social change is concerned. In the early days of the contemporary environmental movement, North American writers such as Heilbroner (1974) and Ophuls (1977) appeared to argue that the environmental crisis was so dire that no one could reasonably be expected to accept voluntarily the kinds of measures that would be needed to deal with it, and that therefore only strong government – even authoritarian government – would do. More recently, as the influence of the catastrophist tendency in green politics has declined, attention has turned to the kinds of values held by political ecologists, and it has been suggested that the political-ecological belief that there is a right way to live the green Good Life is incompatible with the value pluralism normally associated with (liberal) democracy. There are, then, both pragmatic and ethical roots to the palpable tension between radical green objectives and the democratic process. In recent years a great deal of attention has been paid to this tension, and a number of ways of lessening it have been suggested (Mathews, 1995; Doherty and De Geus, 1996a; Lafferty and Meadowcroft, 1996a; Mason, 1999; Smith, 2003). Some have wondered why greens have felt so obliged to defend their democratic credentials – 'greens can ask why they should find new grounds for their adherence to democracy different from those advanced by socialists and liberals' (Barry, 1996, p. 119) – but both the 1970s authoritarian tendency in some environmental political theory and the corrosive association of 'nature politics' with some forms of fascism (Bramwell, 1989) are enough to put both greens and their opponents continually on their democratic guard.

The underpinning source of the tension between radical green objectives and democracy is the apparently *imperative* nature of the former: 'To the extent that the realization of certain green principles – like dealing urgently with over-population – is seen as essential, we are dealing with an imperative that has a no-real-choice quality' (Saward, 1993a, p. 64). This sounds incompatible with the democratic resolution of problems: 'ecological value-sets often contain a considerable tension between advocating certain essential policy outcomes and valuing (direct) democratic procedures' (ibid.). And indeed, some early environmental political theorists, particularly in North America, appeared to eschew democratic processes in favour of the 'right' kinds of ecological outcome. It needs to be said, though, that even the villains of the piece, such as Heilbroner and Ophuls, were never as clear in their rejection of democratic procedures as their detractors have claimed. Two examples from William Ophuls will make this evident.

First, Ophuls does indeed write that 'As the community and its rights are given increasing social priority, we shall necessarily move from liberty toward authority, for the community will have to be able to enforce its demands on individuals' (Ophuls, 1992, p. 285). But he also says that 'this authority need not be remote, arbitrary, and capricious. In a well-ordered and well-designed state, authority could be made constitutional and limited' (ibid., p. 286). Second, Ophuls does seem to endorse 'a movement away from egalitarian democracy toward political competence and status', but he is careful to say that the values which inform competence should be arrived at by 'common consent' (ibid.), and he also writes that 'extreme centralization and interdependence ... should give way to greater decentralization, local autonomy, and local culture' (ibid., p. 291). Ophuls concludes by saying that 'The essential political message of this book is that we must learn ecological self-restraint before it is forced upon us by a potentially monolithic and totalitarian regime or by the brute forces of nature' (ibid., p. 297). A few swallows do not make a summer, of course, but these examples serve to illustrate the care with which we need to treat 'green authoritarian' claims. If indeed, as Saward suggests, 'Ophuls represents the clearest credible example of the authoritarian tendency in green political theory' (Saward, 1993a, p. 71), then the tendency would appear to be equivocal.

We need to be clear, in any case, not to confuse anti-*liberal* elements in green thought with anti-*democratic* ones. The relationship between liberalism and ecologism is discussed in Chapter 5, but it is worth recalling here that a large part of Heilbroner's and Ophuls' prescription for salvation consisted in – as Bob Paehlke puts it – 'a sense of social unity uncharacteristic of liberal, individualistic societies' (Paehlke, 1988, p. 293). The social unity of which they speak is not at all incompatible with democracy, of course, but it may indeed be in tension with the individualism associated with liberalism.

Thus one form of the green imperative is pragmatic, as it were. This is to say that drawing on the dire warnings found in texts such as *The Limits to Growth* (Meadows *et al.*, 1974), some writers reached the conclusion that ecological catastrophe could only be averted by authoritarian means. The other form of green imperative is more ethical, or value-oriented, in origin. Bob Goodin has argued persuasively that what drives environmental political thought and action is the 'green theory of value' to which we referred in Chapter 2. According to this theory, something is 'especially valuable' if it has 'come about through natural rather than through artificial human processes' (Goodin, 1992, p. 30). The task of the political ecologist, then, is to work for the preservation of this 'natural value' through time. Goodin carefully distinguishes between this theory of value and a putative green 'theory of agency', and the crucial issue for us is the relationship between them. Can a particular theory of agency be derived from the green theory of value? No, says Goodin. As we have seen, he argues that what 'lies at the core of green thinking . . . is an abiding concern that natural values be promoted, protected and preserved'. Thus:

> Given that as the logical primitive in their moral system, I think we would have to say . . . that it is more important that the right things be done than that they be done in any particular way or through any particular agency.
>
> (Goodin, 1992, p. 120)

Where there is a clash between green values and any particular way of bringing them about, the former should take precedence:

> In cases of conflict . . . the green theory of value – and the ends that it would have us promote – simply must, within the logic of the greens' own theory, take priority over the green theory of agency, and the principles of right action, agency and structure that that would recommend.
>
> (Goodin, 1992, p. 120)

Goodin himself deploys this distinction to argue against greens endorsing only radical lifestyle change as a means of bringing about green objectives. On Goodin's reading of what green politics is about, the sustaining of natural value is more important than ' "clean hands" principles of personal rectitude' (Goodin, 1992, p. 123), and if this means doing things such as voting for green political parties, then so be it. But his radical distinction between a green theory of value and green theories of agency may be read in more equivocal ways, for if it is true that 'it is more important that the right things be done than that they be done in any particular way or through any particular agency', then *any* form of agency would seem to do, so long as it brings about the right results. As it happens, Goodin himself endorses democratic means of bringing about green ends:

green theory treats individual human beings as agents who naturally are, and morally ought to be, autonomous and self-governing
entities. Politically, that pretty directly implies the central theme of
the green political theory of agency: the importance of the full,
free, active participation by everyone in democratically shaping
their personal and social circumstances.

(Goodin, 1992, p. 124)

But if getting the right thing done is more important than how it
gets done, why should greens not endorse authoritarian means to
green ends? At root, 'the core green concerns are consequentialistic'
(Goodin, 1992, p. 120), and this *consequentialism* is in tension with the
proceduralism of democracy.

As well as the nature of the 'green imperative', two further sources
of the tension between ecological problems and democratic processes
deserve mention – *time* and *space*. We are increasingly aware that policies in the present will have an impact on those in the future – even
those yet to be born. From the point of view of the standard democratic
four- or five-year cycle this is a problem, since governments generally
have an eye on short-term policies for short-term gain. Colin Tudge's
view that 'we cannot claim to be taking our species and our planet
seriously until we acknowledge that a million years is a proper unit
of political time' (Tudge, 1996, p. 371) puts current legislature cycles
around the world into some sort of perspective. Similarly, the dynamics of political accountability cannot easily be made to work in the
environmental context: 'how can politicians be brought to book for
decisions whose consequences will only be fully felt long after the individuals concerned have retired from the political stage?' (Lafferty and
Meadowcroft, 1996b, p. 7).

As for 'space', it is well known that many environmental problems are
of an international character: global warming, by definition, is an issue
that affects many nations rather than only one or two of them. This raises
particular problems for the democratic process because democratic
structures are, almost without exception, based on the nation-state. I
shall say more about these issues of time and space below.

A number of reactions and responses to the authoritarianism/
democracy conundrum have been given in recent years, and in no special
order I outline seven of them in what follows. First, there is the possibility that the distinction drawn between green consequentialism and
democratic proceduralism is too sharp. This is to say that consequences matter for democracy and procedures are important for greens.
Consequences matter for democracy because some consequences may

be inimical to democracy itself. This is sometimes referred to as democracy's 'self-bindingness', according to which democracy 'restricts itself, or proscribes certain types of outcome, in order to preserve itself' (Saward, 1993a, p. 66). The kind of outcome it might proscribe in our context is ecological catastrophe, since that would undermine the conditions for the practice of democracy itself. John Dryzek refers to this as a 'generalizable interest', and remarks that 'The continuing integrity of the ecological systems on which human life depends could perhaps be a generalizable interest par excellence' (Dryzek, 1990, p. 55). If a democratic procedure resulted in an outcome that threatened the integrity of ecological systems, it could legitimately be proscribed for self-binding reasons. I have pointed out elsewhere, though, that this is not a conclusive argument in favour of the compatibility of green objectives and democratic procedures, since 'just as democracy is self-bound not to endorse decisions that endanger the practice of democracy, so is authoritarianism – a sustainable society is as much a generalisable interest for authoritarians as it is for democrats' (Dobson, 1993b, p. 138).

From the other end of the problem, the end according to which procedures must matter for greens, Robyn Eckersley has sought to connect ecologism and democracy in much the same way as liberalism and democracy are connected: through building on the observation that 'liberal support for democracy flows from the liberal principles of autonomy and justice' (Eckersley, 1996, p. 222). In particular, the liberal principle of autonomy 'respects the rights of individuals to determine their own affairs' (ibid.), and if we were to read ecologism not in consequentialist terms but in terms of a 'broader defence of autonomy (let us say, for the moment, the freedom of human and non-human beings to unfold in their own ways and live according to their "species life")', then 'the connection between ecology and democracy would no longer be contingent' (ibid., p. 223). Both the 'preconditional' and the 'principle' approaches, then, call into question the sharp distinction normally drawn between green consequentialism and democratic proceduralism, and show that in this regard, at least, there may be more common ground than is often assumed.

A second argument for bringing ecologism and democracy into line turns on the indeterminacy of green objectives. The 'green theory of value' to which we have had cause to refer takes us some way towards deciding what is important for greens, but calculations of that value in any determinate and final sense are perhaps impossible to make. 'Natural value' and 'sustainability' are both contested ideas, and according to John Barry the achievement of the latter 'makes

democracy a core, non-negotiable, value of green political theory'
(Barry, 1996, p. 117), since due to the 'essential indeterminateness and
normative character of the concept of sustainability . . . it needs to be
understood as a discursively "created" rather than an authoritatively
"given" product' (ibid., p. 116). Michael Jacobs points out that this
creative and open-ended articulation of the meaning of sustainability:

> involves reasoning about other people's interests and values (as
> well as one's own) and the weight which should be given to them;
> about the application of and conflict between ethical principles in
> particular circumstances; and about the nature of the society one
> wishes to create or sustain.
>
> (Jacobs, 1997, p. 219)

For Jacobs,

> This suggests that where public [environmental] goods are at issue,
> the appropriate kind of value-articulating institution is not a pri-
> vate survey, but some kind of public forum in which people are
> brought together to debate before making their judgements. That
> is, the institution should be *deliberative* in character.
>
> (Jacobs, 1997, p. 220)

It is a very short step from here to the idea that the appropriate sorts
of institutions for determining the nature of green objectives and the
means for achieving them are democratic ones. This is the point of
Graham Smith's endorsement of 'deliberative democracy' in connection with the environment, and he discusses a variety of potential institutional designs that would 'promote reflection on and consideration
of the wide range of environmental values that citizens hold' (Smith,
2003, p. 129).

A third, family-related suggestion for bringing green and democratic
thought into alignment relies on an argument from pragmatism regarding the truth: 'democracy can be justified rationally precisely because of
the impossibility of incontrovertible proof of anything' (Saward, 1993a,
p. 76). Given that we can never be certain of anything, the most justifi-
able means of policy- and decision-making is one which takes turns
around a problem and makes provision for reassessing the solution on
a regular basis. With its public debate, accountability and periodic elections, this is democracy in all but name. In our context, Saward points
out that 'Politics without certainty – indeed, politics as a substitute
for certainty – has strong echoes in green political thinking' (Saward,

1993a, p. 77). The 'precautionary principle' (referred to briefly in Chapter 3) has indeed become a byword in green policy-making circles, and while there is no reason why authoritarian regimes could not adopt the precautionary principle of decision-making, the supposedly *provisional* nature of decisions taken in democracies makes them a more appropriate context for the 'epistemological pragmatism' of which we are talking.

The fourth argument takes an alternative view of the truth question. Despite the inherent uncertainty of decision-making, particularly in the environmental context, it may still be argued that some decisions are better – more in line with 'the truth' – than others. The question is: What is the best way of producing these better decisions? John Stuart Mill wrote that 'the opinion which it is attempted to suppress by authority may possibly be true. Those who desire to suppress it, of course deny its truth; but they are not infallible' (Mill, 1859/1972, p. 79). This is an argument for open decision-making of the type normally associated with democratic consultation, and it should perhaps be endorsed by greens – even those with a determinate view of what the truth is:

> To the degree that there is a determinate answer about the 'right' values and the 'right' kind of society in which to live (and greens, in the round, believe that there is), then greens should be committed to democracy as the only form of decision-making that . . . will necessarily produce the answer.
>
> (Dobson, 1996a, p. 139)

A fifth argument derives from the putative environmental benefits of a particular sort of decentralized face-to-face democracy. As Doherty and De Geus point out, and as we had cause to observe in Chapter 3, 'From an ecological standpoint greens view decentralisation as essential because it is less wasteful of resources, giving priority to local production and consumption rather than the production and transport of goods for a global market' (Doherty and De Geus, 1996b, p. 3). In one direction this train of thought actually leads to bioregionalism, and as we saw in Chapter 3, bioregionalism is not necessarily democratic. But there are connections in democratic theory and practice between decentralization and participation, and to this degree there may be quite specific ecological arguments for localized democracy.

Finally, there are two sorts of argument from historical experience. The first of these rests its case on the respective environmental records of 'democratic' and 'authoritarian' societies in the belief that these records count decisively in favour of the former. The empirical strength of this claim cannot be assessed here, and we should certainly enter the caveat that the undoubtedly poor record of those regimes usually referred to as authoritarian in this context (i.e. the Soviet Union and its Eastern European neighbours) may have been due to factors other than their authoritarianism. Nevertheless, Lafferty and Meadowcroft speak for many when they write:

> it may be that acute environmental crises are more readily (or perhaps only) amenable to authoritarian solution. The response here must be that . . . neither theory nor practical experience suggest that authoritarian regimes are likely to best democracies at resolving environmental problems over the long term.
>
> (Lafferty and Meadowcroft, 1996b, p. 3)

The second of these arguments from historical experience picks up on Bob Paehlke's observation that, at precisely the same time as the theoreticians of 'green authoritarianism' such as Heilbroner and Ophuls were peddling their wares, early environmental *activists* were favouring 'openness and participation in environmental administration' (Paehlke, 1988, p. 292). More recently, Doherty and De Geus point out that greens just turn out mostly to have been participatory democrats: 'In their organisation green parties and many grassroots green groups have tried to counter what they see as the dominance of political organisations by bureaucracies and leaders' (Doherty and De Geus, 1996b, p. 5). This defence of the existence of 'green democracy' is sociological rather than political-theoretical, however: a statement of what is (or has been) rather than what ought to be. On this reading, the relationship between ecologism and democracy is contingent rather than necessary, based on the sociological origins of ecologism rather than its theoretical foundations:

> Historically and sociologically the ideas on democracy of most of the Western European green parties developed from the models provided by the New Left in the late 1960s and from the practices of the new social movements in the 1970s and 1980s. The challenge to the bureaucratic character of modern government, and the call for self-management were unifying elements of the discourse of the New Left.
>
> (Doherty and De Geus, 1996b, p. 5)

All of these remarks on the possible connections between green and democratic thinking should be accompanied by the recognition that there are many types of democracy, and the difference this can make to the compatibility question is considerable. For example, Michael Saward points out that the tensions he identifies between green objectives and democratic procedures are most marked in the context of *direct* democracy where the participatory proceduralism of democracy is at its height. In *representative* democracy it is understood that the representative has room for manoeuvre, and is entitled to take decisions on behalf of her or his constituents. Here, says Saward, the 'tensions [between green imperatives and democratic procedures] would be lessened' (Saward, 1993a, p. 70). In other words, the more democracy is understood to be government *for* the people rather than *by* the people, the more compatible with the objective-driven nature of green thinking it becomes.

Similarly, the empirical record suggests that some types of democracy are more amenable to environmental problem articulation than others:

> the link between altruism and environmentalism may explain why the smaller social democracies of northern Europe – Norway, Sweden, the Netherlands – have been more active in promulgating policy discussions about environmental issues which involve regulation of market externalities and making the distributional costs of environmental programmes more transparent.
>
> (Witherspoon, 1996, p. 65)

All of this suggests that a full account of the troubled relationship between ecologism and democracy would require a cross-tabulated assessment of compatibility across *all* possible types of ecologism and *all* possible types of democracy. Such an assessment is beyond the scope of this book (and quite possibly beyond the capabilities of its author, too), but enough has been said to show that any equating of ecologism with authoritarianism needs to be treated with great caution.

One more type of 'green democracy' problem remains to be considered. Environmental problems have brought 'new constituencies' on to the political agenda, constituencies whose interests are affected by environmental change, but which are not easily represented through traditional democratic structures and their boundaries. Such constituencies include 'away country' nationals (e.g. Scandinavians affected by British acid rain), future generations and parts of the non-human natural world. The question is: Assuming that the interests of these constituencies should be represented democratically (a large assumption which is discussed in detail in Dobson (1996b)), how might institutions be appropriately redesigned? This is a question raised, but not answered, by those who see the future of green politics as being about extending democracy into nature (Eckersley, 2004; Latour, 2004; Wenz, 2002).

Two broad, and very different, answers have been given to this question. The first, from Bob Goodin, trades on the possibility of the interests of these constituencies (and particularly those of future generations and non-human nature) being 'encapsulated' in those of current human beings (Goodin, 1996, p. 841) in much the same way as the interests of very small children are regarded as encapsulated in those of their parents. Goodin is aware that this model has a disreputable past: 'Slaves' and servants' interests were, in just such ways, encapsulated within those of their master', he says. Likewise, 'Pre-Edwardian wives, having no independent legal personality apart from that of their husbands, saw their interests incorporated within those of their husbands' (ibid., p. 842). But, he goes on, 'Both in the cases of young children and of future generations, the model of "incorporated interests" seems legitimate largely because it seems inevitable' (ibid., p. 843).

There are three possible problems with Goodin's suggestion for 'enfranchising the earth'. First, and most damaging, it is not democratic: if it was not democratic for Edwardian wives to have their interests incorporated within those of their husbands, then the same must apply to the case of present and future generations. Second, 'encapsulation' is not the only method of representation available to us, and third, there is no guarantee that current people will 'internalize [the] interests' (Goodin, 1996, p. 844) of future generations and of non-human nature in the required way – and if they don't, then encapsulation will not bring about the benefits it promises.

An alternative strategy to Goodin's is to have proxy representatives, elected by proxy constituencies, to represent 'directly' the interests of future generations and non-human nature in national and transnational legislatures:

> The proxy would function in exactly the same way as any democratic electorate. It would, in the first place, 'be' the future generation electorate, and candidates for representing the interests of future generations would be drawn from it. These candidates would fight election campaigns, outlining their objectives as far as furthering the interests of future generations are concerned. . . . The proxy electorate would consider the various candidates' merits and then choose its preferred candidate(s) through a democratic election.

The successful candidates would then sit in the democratic assembly alongside present generation representatives.

(Dobson, 1996b, p. 132)

This form of enfranchisement is not without its difficulties, many of which are discussed elsewhere (Dobson, 1996b; Ekeli, 2005), but such a system would avoid the non-democratic implications of encapsulation, and while it would not quite *guarantee* that the interests of future generations and non-human nature were taken into account, the democratic discipline of accountability – provided by elections, and absent in encapsulation – would help to focus minds appropriately. At present, though, environmentalists and political ecologists have to work with legislatures that are composed in much more traditional ways, and I shall now examine the extent to which they can expect their objectives to be realized through national parliaments.

Action through and around the legislature

Many countries have green parties that seek election to national legislatures. Green movements in all countries that have them see it as at least part of their role to try to influence the legislative process, while policy is being drawn up, while bills are being debated, or during their execution. The principal assumption behind both kinds of activity (broadly speaking, party political activity and pressure group activity) is that the liberal-democratic decision-making process and the economic structures with which it is engaged are sufficiently open to allow the green agenda to be fulfilled through them. It seems to be accepted that even if a green party is not elected to government, then sufficient pressure may be brought to bear on the incumbents to bring about a sustainable society. At one time the question of whether green parties could bring about this kind of change would have been purely theoretical: until the early 1980s there were no Green Party members of Parliament anywhere, and certainly no green parties anywhere near government. Now that has changed. At the time of writing (June 2006), European green parties boast 192 seats in national parliaments, with two ministers in government (in Italy and Latvia) (EFGP, 2006). And until the last election changed the panorama of German politics, the Green Party played a major role in government there, with Green Party member Joschka Fischer holding the key portfolio of Foreign Minister. Thus greens have tasted electoral success within the constraints of the liberal-democratic framework (Müller-Rommel and Poguntke, 2002). The question is whether reliance on this framework is adequate to the task of achieving the radical political and social change that ecologism proposes.

The first problem for any green party (in some countries, and certainly in Britain) is that of getting elected in the first place – by which I mean not necessarily being elected to government but garnering sufficient votes to gain even minimal representation in the legislature. The same list that reveals 192 green party members of European legislatures also shows that seventeen out of thirty-five green parties in Europe have no representation at all (EFGP, 2006). In Britain, the first-past-the-post system, in which the candidate in a given constituency with the most number of votes takes the seat, militates notoriously against small parties. The results of such a system were most obviously on view in the 1989 European elections, when the British Green Party gained 15 per cent of the popular vote and yet won no seats in the Strasbourg Parliament. When a proportional system was introduced for the 1999 elections the Green Party returned two members to the European Parliament with just 5.8 per cent of the vote. Jean Lambert and Caroline Lucas were re-elected in 2004 with a slightly increased share of the vote (EFGP, 2006). It is still extremely hard to imagine the British Parliament with even one green representative, let alone with sufficient members to be able to enter into coalition with one of the major parties. The England and Wales Green Party put a massive effort into its most likely constituency – Brighton Pavilion – in the 2005 General Election. Parliamentary candidate Keith Taylor won by far the biggest ever share of the vote for a green – 22 per cent – but still came third in the constituency.

Of course, not all countries make it so difficult for small parties to taste electoral success, and it is worth looking at the German experience in this regard. In the federal elections of 1983 die Grünen won 5.6 per cent of the vote and entered the Bundestag, increasing their share of the vote to 8.3 per cent in the next election of January 1987. In the 'reunification election' of 1990, the shared East and West German vote plummeted to 1.2 per cent (with the West German party losing all its seats (Jahn, 1994, p. 313)), rising again to 7.3 per cent (forty-nine seats, the third largest party in the Bundestag) in 1994, falling slightly to 6.7 per cent for Bündnis90/die Grünen (forty-seven seats and a share in a coalition government with the Social Democratic Party) in 1998, and rising again to 8.1 per cent (fifty-one seats) in 2005. The last three results, indeed, call the bluff of those who (like Anna Bramwell) had virtually written the party off:

Since 1980 the Green Party [in Germany] has described a parabola.

In the first election after reunification (December 1990) support for the post-unification Greens dropped sharply, and although the Greens retained support in Hesse, there is little doubt that the underlying drive behind their party is diminishing.

(Bramwell, 1994, p. 133)

Subsequent events have rather proved her wrong.

How successful has the German Green Party been, though, in bringing about the radical changes that it called for in its seminal 1983 manifesto? The metaphor of colonization allows us to theorize some of the experiences of Die Grünen since 1983, since in two specific contexts the party seems to have been colonized by the demands and temptations of parliamentary activity. In the first place, enormous amounts of energy have been expended over the issue of whether to make tactical alliances with other political parties so as to influence policy in a more extensive way. From a radical point of view, Petra Kelly's is the crucial observation: 'If the Greens end up becoming merely ecological Social Democrats, then the experiment is finished – it will have become a waste' (in Spretnak and Capra, 1985, p. 152). Any green party operating in the parliamentary sphere will be faced, at some level of administration, with the possibility of coalition, and the German Greens have been increasingly prepared to practise coalition politics (even of the 'traffic-light' variety – red–yellow–green (Poguntke, 1993, p. 398)).

Between 1998 and 2005 this strategy was rewarded with a share of government with the Social Democrats. The Greens had a maximum of three ministers in cabinet during this period, and as I remarked earlier, Joschka Fischer held one of the most important posts – that of Foreign Minister (Rüdig, 2002). Kelly's point is that dealings with other parties are undertaken at the risk of dilution of radical green principles: the demands of parliamentary politics can contribute to a wearing down of the green project and the consequent likelihood of the abandonment of the project as originally conceived. The tremendous tensions within the German Green Party during the 1999 Kosovo crisis are evidence of this. Fischer had to weather a considerable storm from those within his own ranks opposed to NATO intervention in the crisis. Similarly, while he was certainly instrumental in articulating German opposition to the coalition invasion of Iraq, we would be hard pressed to argue that Fischer carved out a distinctively green foreign policy for Germany during his period in office.

Wolfgang Rüdig's assessment of the german experience of greens in government is that 'the Greens lacked the strong constituency, the link to powerful allies and the link to well-established interests within civil society to be able to push for more radical solutions' (Rüdig, 2002, p. 106). Thomas Poguntke summarizes the range of greens in national government experience in similarly measured – even downbeat – terms: 'In the end, Green party power within national coalition governments (and hence their electoral success) rests primarily on the skilful exploitation of a rather limited room for manoeuvre below the threshold of threatening or even exercising the exit option' (Poguntke, 2002). This hardly seems to be an institutional recipe for radical green change.

Robert Goodin has pointed out that 'realist' greens:

> are, as it were, in the same position as the missionary confronting many starving mouths and only a few morsels of food: they would dearly love to satisfy all, but they are only able to satisfy a few: still it is better that few be satisfied than none.
>
> (Goodin, 1992, p. 110)

As we saw above, this follows on from Goodin's (contested) view that the green theory of value is 'distinctively consequentialistic' (Goodin, 1992, p. 111), and that any green theory of political agency should be the servant of the theory of value. The point of green agency, then, is to bring about green consequences, and consequences override agency in the event of conflict. Goodin has been congratulated for sorting out 'woolly green claims about grass-roots democracy and decentralisation' (Saward, 1993b, p. 511), but there remains the worry that too many green good intentions will be given up along the path of compromise. Some radical greens will argue that this is what has happened in a key instance regarding the German greens to which I want to refer: the struggle over the rotation system of delegates elected to the Bundestag. Under the original system, green representatives elected to the Bundestag would serve only two years and then give way for the next two years to understudies who were originally hired as 'legislative assistants' (Spretnak and Capra, 1985, p. 39). The reason given for this principle reflects the fear of colonization: 'Because a person's thinking is affected by the way she or he lives, eight, or even four years in the Bundestag – or a state legislature – machine would be very destructive' (ibid.). At the same time, the rotation system was intended to be a visible sign of green refusal to concentrate political power in the hands of relatively few individuals. Objections to the principle were derived from the demands of working effectively in the Bundestag: rotation was held to prevent the emergence of influential 'personalities', and it reduced expertise.

From 1983, commitment to rotation and the principles it embodies waned and in May 1986 it was formally abandoned. This is not because the principles in themselves were found wanting but because they were unworkable, as originally conceived, in the context of parliamentary politics: 'Under the pressure of political developments, naive notions of rank and file democracy are now a thing of the past' (Hülsberg, 1988, p. 123). In similar vein Spretnak and Capra state that 'the rotation principle for elected officials has proven to be more trouble than it is worth for the Greens in West Germany' (1985, pp. 188–9). The general upshot was that:

> after more than a decade of experience with their experimental attempt at institutionalising direct democratic structures within the framework of representative democracy, the Greens have moved somewhat towards the established parties . . . the structural imperatives of the political system have taken their toll.
>
> (Poguntke, 1993, pp. 395–6)

Of course Parliament is not the only site of green political activity. Most people in the green movement who argue for change through liberal-democratic political structures will also support other forms of action. The rest of this chapter will be taken up with discussing these other options, under the five headings of lifestyle, communities, direct action, class and citizenship.

Lifestyle

The general principle behind both lifestyle and community strategies is that changes of consciousness and changes in behaviour are mutually reinforcing. Lifestyle change concerns changes in the patterns of individual behaviour in daily life. Typical examples of this would be: care with the things you buy, the things you say, where you invest your money, the way you treat people, the transport you use and so on.

Recently there has been a veritable explosion in the popularity of green lifestyle changes in Britain. Home ecology, among certain sections of the community at least, is all the rage. Retailers have picked up and reinforced this trend, and the major supermarket chains fall over themselves to stock their shelves – a few of them anyway – with environmentally friendly goods. Products in green packets sell significantly better than similar products packaged in any other colour. In this context, green has rapidly become the colour of capitalist energy and enterprise. From the point of view of lifestyle changes, the spaces for political action are in principle infinite – even the toilet is a potential locus for radical politics, for as John Seymour and Herbert Girardet inform us: 'A quarter of all domestic water in most countries goes straight down the toilet. Every time somebody flushes the toilet about 20 litres of water are instantly changed from being pure to being polluted' (Seymour and Girardet, 1987, p. 27). They offer concise advice: 'If it's brown wash it down. If it's yellow let it mellow' (Seymour and Girardet, 1987, p. 27). I suppose that's one way to start a revolution.

The lifestyle strategy has been around for a long time in the green movement, and it has spawned an enormous number of books and pamphlets on practical action to avert environmental decay. Back in 1973 E.F. Schumacher wrote, 'Everywhere people ask: "What can I actually do?" The answer is as simple as it is disconcerting: we can, each of us, work to put our own inner house in order' (1976, pp. 249–50). The theme is consistent: that personal transformation leads to altered behaviour; which in turn can be translated into sustainable community living: 'The only possible building blocks of a Greener future are individuals moving towards a Greener way of life *themselves* and joining together with others who are doing the same' (Bunyard and Morgan-Grenville, 1987, p. 336).

The positive aspect of this strategy is that some individuals do indeed end up living sounder, more ecological lives. More bottles and newspapers are recycled, more lead-free petrol is bought, and fewer harmful detergents are washed down the plughole. The disadvantage, though, is that the world around us goes on much as before, ungreened and unsustainable – certainly in terms of a radical overhaul of our habits and practices. In the first place, one has the problem of persuading sufficient numbers of people to lead sustainable lives for it to make a difference to the integrity of the environment. It is evidently hard to predict just how far the message will spread and how many people will act on it, but it seems unlikely that a massive number of individuals will experience the conversion that will lead to the necessary changes in their daily behaviour.

At the same time, many of the proposals for change of this sort ask us to alter our behaviour at particular points in our daily life and then allow us back on the unsustainable rampage. There is nothing inherently green, for example, in green consumerism briefly referred to above. It is true that consumer pressure helped bring about a reduction in the use of CFCs in aerosol sprays. It is true that the Body Shop will supply you with exotic perfumes and shampoos in reusable bottles and that have not been tested on animals. It is true that we can help extend the life of tropical rainforests by resisting the temptation to buy mahogany toilet seats. There is also evidence that consumer resistance in Europe to genetically modified (GM) foods is damaging GM companies, as

Europe's largest bank (Deutsche Bank) advises its major investors to sell their shares in GM companies because consumers do not want to buy their products (*Guardian*, 25 August 1999, p. 1). All of this helps the environment, but none of it – absent other strategies – can bring about the radical changes envisaged by ecologism.

First, it does nothing to confront the central green point that unlimited production and consumption – no matter how environmentally friendly – is impossible to sustain in a limited system. The problem here is not so much to get people to consume soundly but to get them – or at least those living in profligate societies – to consume less. The Body Shop strategy is a hymn to consumption: in their contribution to the Friends of the Earth Green Consumer Week leaflet (12–18 September 1988) they urged people to 'wield their purchasing power responsibly' rather than to wield it less often. It is this that makes green consumerism environmental rather than radically green. So, for example, while the average car does many more miles to the gallon and emits fewer g/km of CO_2 than it used to, transport is still one of the fastest growing sectors so far as CO_2 emissions are concerned. This is because there are now 27 million cars on UK roads – nearly twice as many as twenty-five years ago. It is also because good technologies are misused: there is little advantage in putting a hybrid (electric/petrol) motor in a Sports Utility Vehicle and claiming the virtue – as one manufacturer does – of having reduced SUV emissions to those of the 'average family car'. This manufacturer forgets that the average family car is the problem, not the solution.

Second, it has been pointed out that 'there are masses of people who are disenfranchised from this exercise of power by virtue of not having the money to spend in the first place' (*Green Line*, no. 60, March 1988, p. 12). Third, parts of the green movement feel consumerism to be too grubby and materialistic a means to lead us reliably to the stated end of a society of 'voluntary simplicity'. This is the point behind Porritt and Winner's observation that 'A crude, consumer-driven culture prevails, in which the spirit is denied and the arts are rejected or reduced to a privileged enclave for the few' (Porritt and Winner, 1988, p. 247) and, more generally, that 'it is . . . worth stressing that the underlying aim of this green consumerism is to reform rather than fundamentally restructure our patterns of consumption' (ibid., p. 199). Once more we are forced to recognize the difference between environmentalism and ecologism: the strategy of green consumerism, in its call for change substantially in line with present strategies based on unlimited production and consumption, is a child of the former rather than of the latter.

The strategy of change in individual habits leading to long-term social change takes no account, either, of the problem of political power and resistance to which I referred in the previous section. It is perhaps unrealistic to assume that those forces that would be positively hostile to sustainability will allow current forms of production and consumption to wither away. Of course, this is much less of a problem if the green movement has in mind only some form of attenuated environmentalism, but if (once again) it is serious about the desire to usher in a radically ecocentric society, then it will eventually be forced to confront the issue of massive resistance to change.

What seems common to these lifestyle strategies as I have treated them is that they mostly reject the idea that bringing about change is a properly 'political' affair – they do not hold that green change is principally a matter of occupying positions of political power and shifting the levers in the right direction. In Chapter 1 I noted that spirituality is of greater importance to the green perspective than is probably publicly realized, and this has made a significant impression on some activists in the movement with regard to how change might come about. The general point behind the spiritual approach is that the changes which need to take place are too profound to be dealt with solely in the political arena, and that the psyche is as important as the parliamentary chamber. Jonathon Porritt writes that 'for sustainable development . . . a spiritually inspired work ethic will be an important instrument of change' (Porritt, 2005, p. 144). Marilyn Ferguson has recommended the use of 'psychotechnologies' (Ferguson, 1981) to bring about calmer, gentler, more 'green' states of consciousness, and the Findhorn community in Scotland bases its activities on the belief that this is indeed the right path to change. Such an approach takes seriously the point made above – namely that political opposition to radical green change will be massive – and side-steps it. Bahro talks expressively of needing to take 'a new run-up from so far back that we can't afford to waste our time in the mock battles which are so typical of Green committees' (1986, p. 159), and the change he envisages is the 'metaphysical reconstruction' advocated by Jonathon Porritt and David Winner (1988, pp. 246–9).

This is, of course, in direct opposition to any theory which has it that political and social change is primarily generated through people identifying their immediate material (widely understood) interests and acting to satisfy them. (For an empirically informed assessment of the role of 'psychotechnologies' in social change see Seel, 1999, ch. 6.) I shall consider this kind of approach later in this chapter.

Communities

A general problem with the strategy of lifestyle change is that it is ultimately divorced from where it wants to go, in that it is not obvious how the individualism on which it is based will convert into the communitarianism that is central to most descriptions of the sustainable society. It would appear more sensible to subscribe to forms of political action that are already communitarian, and that are therefore both a practice and an anticipation of the advertised goal. In this sense the future is built into the present, and the programme is more intellectually convincing and practically coherent.

In this context Robyn Eckersley has argued that 'The revolutionary subject is . . . the active, responsible person-in-community, *homo communitas*, if you like' (Eckersley, 1987, p. 19). She goes on to suggest, in a vein referred to above, that this is because 'Perhaps the ultimate principle of ecopraxis is the need to maintain consistency between means and ends' (ibid., p. 21). Consequently, 'the most revolutionary structures are seen to be those that foster the development of self-help, community responsibility and free activity and are consistent with the ecotopian ideal of a loose federation of regions and communes' (ibid., p. 22).

Community strategies might be an improvement on lifestyle strategies, then, because they are already a practice of the future in a more complete sense than that allowed by changes in individual behaviour patterns. They are more clearly an alternative to existing norms and practices, and, to the extent that they work, they show that it is possible to live differently – even sustainably. Rudolf Bahro has expressed it as follows:

> To bring it down to the basic concept, we must build up areas liberated from the industrial system. That means, liberated from nuclear weapons and from supermarkets. What we are talking about is a new social formation and a different civilisation.
>
> (Bahro, 1986, p. 29)

Obviously not just any communities will do. It is not enough to say that 'a major priority for both reds and greens is the campaign to win for communities greater control over their environment' (Weston, 1986, p. 160), without those communities having a clear idea of how they might operate sustainably. In this context, the kinds of communities that represent ecological lifestyles are rural self-sufficiency farms, city farms, some workers' cooperatives, some kinds of squat throughout the cities of Europe, and, more concretely (in Britain), the Centre for Alternative Technology (CAT) at Machynlleth in Wales and the Findhorn community in Scotland: 'The solution, for both Bahro and Findhornians, is to initiate spiritual reconstruction in alternative communities' (Seel, 1999, pp. 262–3). In 1991 David Pepper published the results of a series of interviews with more than eighty commune members from twelve communes in England, Scotland and Wales (Pepper, 1991). Using a measure of 'greenness' revolving around ecologically sound practices such as the sharing of resources, recycling, cutting energy use and so on, Pepper comes to the conclusion that:

> communards [those studied, at least] have a world view that is indeed radically and overwhelmingly green. This view translates rather patchily into individual and group practice, but it is probably true that communes can provide an institutional context which encourages ecologically sound practices.
>
> (Pepper, 1991, p. 156)

The Schwarzes have observed that 'these ventures operate outside and potentially in opposition to, the prevailing culture' (1987, p. 73), and with that they may have put their finger on the necessary defining characteristic of any strategy which hopes to bring about radical change. In the section on parliamentary change, it was suggested that initiatives in and around the legislature were too easily absorbed, and thus neutralized, by their context. Initiatives that live 'outside' the prevailing culture and its diversionary channels have a much brighter chance of remaining oppositional and therefore of bringing about radical change.

However, even this needs to be qualified because 'to be outside' and 'to be oppositional' are not the same thing, and the difference is crucial in terms of understanding the options for green political strategy. This is because it may be argued that the dominant set of modes and practices needs an opposition against which to define itself and with respect to which to judge itself. In this sense the polarity that opposition sets up helps to sustain and reproduce that which it opposes. One can see this phenomenon in operation at the Centre for Alternative Technology (CAT) in Wales. At the outset, the community at the Centre intended to be 'outside' the prevailing culture, independent of the National Electricity Grid and living a daily life organized around radically democratic and sustainable principles: 'low-tech methods, reduced or simplified methods of consumption, job-rotation, personal growth, priority to collective resources, blurring the distinction of work/non-work, a

strong emphasis on community life, and "living the technology" '
(Harper, n.d., p. 4). But, as the same member of the community put
it, 'Gradually the bloom faded. I watched it happen in myself. A combination of hard experience, exhaustion, human frailty, pressures of
family life, a desire to be acceptable to ordinary humanity, ageing . . .
turned me into a reluctant moderate' (ibid., p. 2). One CAT member in
Pepper's commune study argued that the Quarry (the Centre is built
around an old slate quarry) was now a way for people 'already into
social change to renew their batteries. But it's not a way to change
society. I'd like the green movement to promote communes, but it's
more important for it to get political power' (Pepper, 1991, p. 181).

This journey towards moderation must be the story of a thousand
alternative communities which have found that opposition ends up at
incorporation. Now the CAT processes thousands of visitors a year
who come from all over the world and pay money to look in on an
experiment that, by virtue of the visitors themselves, is shown to have
lapsed. Peter Harper writes, 'Sadly, but inevitably, I see a time of
Revisionism ahead. . . . The Quarry will become more efficient, har-
monious, consistent, respectable, and boring. It will be a successful
institution, not a community' (n.d., p. 6). The Centre is now a successful
institution – that which was decolonized has been recolonized, and we
are left to celebrate 'the Quarry's arrival as a respectable and integral
part of British society' (ibid., p. 7). Pepper's study suggests that this
pattern is not unique to the CAT:

> Perhaps the greatest potential barrier to communes acting as
> agents for radical rather than reformist social change towards an
> Ecotopian society is the process whereby they become absorbed
> into conventional society, that culture to which they have previously
> run counter.
>
> (Pepper, 1991, p. 204)

Pepper theorizes this, in conclusion, as a three-stage process: an
attempt to bypass the system; then using it; then becoming part of it
(Pepper, 1991, p. 205). Of course, it might be argued that the respectability produced by becoming part of the system is precisely the
Centre's strongest card in the context of persuading visitors to go
home and practise the kind of lifestyle change described above. Some
might even be so taken by the lifestyle of the community's members
that they go and set up their own communities – and if this were to
happen to sufficient people (although there is no evidence that it has) it
would amount to justification of the strategy of change by example.

The CAT's respectability, it is suggested, makes it a likely source of inspiration in that it is recognizably similar to 'our' society: they have telephones and a restaurant, they care about being warm, and they are surrounded by technology, some of it makeshift but some of it extremely complex (if 'alternative'). The members' daily lives do not appear to revolve around long periods of meditation, shamanistic rituals or talking to lettuces, and so the day visitor is less likely to dismiss the community as irrelevant to her or his own experience. I am sure this is true, but one is still confronted with the distinction between environmental and fully green change. The CAT's success will lie in raising an environmental consciousness rather than in providing a 'liberated zone' (in Rudolf Bahro's evocative phrase) of sustainable living, and this is the distinction Harper was pointing to in describing the Centre as a 'successful institution' rather than a 'community'. Most community initiatives, then, oppose the prevailing culture rather than live outside it. Just what 'living outside' means, and how far it is even possible, will be discussed below, but it seems clear that part of the reason why community initiatives have not brought about the 'fundamental shift' that Jonathon Porritt mentioned at the beginning of this chapter is because their opposition is easily neutralized and, indeed, turns out to be necessary for the very survival and reproduction of that which it opposes.

What I have called 'community strategies' are arguably an improvement on lifestyle change because they make more ready connections between current practice and future aspirations. However, besides easy neutralization, such strategies depend too heavily (as do their lifestyle counterparts) on change by example. They may indeed show us that sustainable styles of life are possible, but as agents for political change they rely entirely on their seductive capacity. The problem is that people refuse to be seduced: rather than producing radical changes in consciousness, sustainable communities perform the role of the surrogate good conscience, and we can go at the weekend to see it operating. Respondents in Pepper's (admittedly restricted) survey were generally downbeat regarding communes forming a vanguard for social change:

> Over six out of ten of our interviewees thought that communes are not important in leading us to a green society, and do not constitute a significant part of the blueprint for survival. Less than three in ten thought that they might be significant, and under one in ten was prepared to be enthusiastic and unconditional in supporting the idea.

(Pepper, 1991, p. 180)

If confrontation appears to result so easily in co-option, then perhaps circumvention is another way forward for the green movement. I have suggested that the principal advantage of community strategies for change is that they anticipate the hoped-for green future, particularly its decentralized communitarian aspects. In this context an interesting practice has recently reappeared, which depends not upon setting up entirely integral communities, but upon allowing communities of work and exchange to 'emerge' through creating a system of what is most generally referred to as 'local money' (Greco, 1994).

Such systems are by no means new, and they have usually appeared when local economies stagnate owing to the flight of capital or the underutilization of local skills and resources. The results of such a situation are familiar:

> When local unemployment rises, for whatever reason, people lose their incomes and have less money in their pockets. They spend less money with local traders, who in turn have less money in their pockets, then the whole local economy takes a downturn and becomes sluggish. Unemployed people sit at home while shopkeepers watch half-empty shops. The economic activity which should be the life spring of an economy begins to dry up.
>
> (Dauncey, 1988, p. 51)

The aim of a local money system is therefore both to return a measure of control of currency to the community and to put dormant skills and resources back into circulation. This happens, in theory, because local currencies 'can be spent only within the limited area of the community . . . [they] can be created locally in accordance with the needs of the local economy, and . . . [they] encourage local people to patronize one another rather than buying from outside the community' (Greco, 1994, p. 46). The results seem sometimes to have been spectacular:

> In the town of Wörgl, Austria, there stands a bridge whose plaque commemorates the fact that it was built by debt-free, locally created money. This was just a small part of a significant experiment that transformed towns and whole areas out of poverty within three months and into prosperity within one year, at a time when there was widespread unemployment in the national economy.
>
> (Weston in Ekins, 1986, p. 199)

This particular experiment took place between about 1929 and 1934 and, significantly, was ended when 200 Austrian mayors met and decided to follow Wörgl's example, whereupon the Austrian National Bank began a long legal battle to have the scheme outlawed. They eventually succeeded and the system was wound up.

One of the best-known contemporary examples of a local money scheme was the Local Employment and Trade System (LETSystem) which ran in the town of Courtenay on Canada's Vancouver Island between 1983 and 1989, and which was the inspiration for 'hundreds of active LETS systems in various stages of development in many countries' (Greco, 1994, p. 88). The general principles of the Courtenay system were as follows:

> A number of people who live locally and who want to trade together get together, agree to the LETSystem rules, and give themselves account numbers. Each person then makes out two lists, one of 'wants' and another of 'offers', with prices attached (following normal market prices). A joint list is made up and circulated to every one. Then the members look down the list, phone whoever has what they want, and start trading. . . . The limits of one-to-one barter are eliminated, as you can now trade with the people in the system as a whole: barter is now a collective proposition.
>
> (Dauncey, 1988, p. 52)

No money changes hands because there is no actual 'money' – credits and debits are recorded on a computer, and the Green dollars in which LETSystem users trade never get beyond being intangible bits of information. If I sell a car for, say, 2000 Green dollars, the computer credits me with those dollars, which I can then use within – and only within – the system. The money thus remains inside the system-community and provides the incentive for people to advertise, sell and buy skills and resources. Shopkeepers may decide to sell their goods wholly or partly in Green dollars, and so benefit from the newly generated buying power of LETSystem users.

This is not the place to go into the details of local money experiments and the problems that can come with them: hoarding, inflation, tax liability, social security implications, defaulting on debits by leaving the 'community' and so on. Likewise, I have mentioned only two of the more obvious advantages of such a system in a run-down local economy: money stays local and incentive is provided to exercise skills that might otherwise remain dormant. LETSystem users have reported other benefits, such as simplicity, the personal nature of transactions and the building of self-confidence that comes with supplying others with the goods and services they require.

My intention here has simply been to show how local money schemes might be considered as one potential strategy for green change – a 'community' strategy in my typology in that they anticipate the decentralized communitarian nature of the sustainable society. At the same time though, the Austrian National Bank's reaction to the Wörgl experiment described above might be taken as a sign of the potentially subversive nature of local money schemes. They appear to be less easily co-opted than other examples of community change, and in this respect have characteristics that might well qualify them as a part-strategy for the possible agents of change discussed further below.

Direct action

So far as individual actors in the green movement are concerned, of course, all the approaches to green change discussed above may be combined. Any one person could be a member of a green party as well as a buyer of Ecover washing-up liquid. She or he may also live in a community which was trying to turn the world green by example. More recently, in Britain at least, she or he may also have been one of the many thousands of people battling it out – sometimes violently, some-times not – with building contractors intent on carrying out the gov-ernment's road-building programme, or the rather smaller – but still effective – number uprooting genetically modified crops in the govern-ment's designated test fields. Direct action to halt what protestors see as environmental degradation has become an increasingly prominent feature of the political scene in recent years, and it is carried out by an apparently disparate collection of people, ranging from middle-class 'NIMBYS' (Not in My Back Yard) through to New Age travellers (Doherty, 2002, pp. 154–82). Disillusionment with mainstream political parties (including the Green Party) and the agendas they promote has given rise to a form of do-it-yourself politics: groups of (mostly) young people organize around a squat, a sound system, a drug, a piece of land, and try to live a self-reliant life:

> Perhaps because of the very feeling of isolation a growing number of what can only be described as 'tribes' have been popping up quietly all over the country. . . . Although they all have different identities and aims, when it comes to their motivation, these groups all speak with one voice. They talk about a resurgence of the free-spirit movement . . . a quiet dignity that refuses to be caught up in the fast-track of winners and losers, fashions and fads. . . . Who knows when this spirit began to speed up from a tricklet to a wave

but certainly in the past few recession-hit years, a network of the
skint but proud has slowly been falling into place.

(Various, 1994, p. 7)

The politics of these groups varies, but a number are moved by concerns that motivate the wider green movement – such as opposition to
the road-building programme (Seel, 1997; North, 1998). Rather than
(or sometimes, in the case of more traditional protestors, as well as)
lobbying their Members of Parliament or joining a mainstream pressure group, activists choose to oppose the roads through direct action.
This usually takes the form of a continuing presence at the site in question (if possible) and non-violent (normally) resistance to contractors
when they appear for work. In international terms the best-known
direct action environmental group is undoubtedly Earth First! (Wall,
1999; Doherty, 2002, pp. 155–68). Earth First! was founded in 1980 by a
group of activists in the United States of America who were concerned
that timid campaigning was doing too little too late to save the planet.
From the outset, Earth First! recommended direct action (or what
they call 'monkeywrenching', after their techniques for disabling bull-
dozers and other heavy machinery) as a strategy for opposing industrialism and preserving wilderness. Their activities have drawn criticism
from both inside and outside the green movement, and they are vari-
ously accused of valuing animals and trees above human beings, of
endangering human life, and of giving the rest of the movement a
bad name.

Monkeywrenching is not unprincipled, however. Dave Foreman – an
erstwhile central figure in Earth First! – and Bill Haywood compiled a
Field Guide to Monkeywrenching (1989), in which the principles of sabotage and its political effectiveness are explained and discussed. Above
all, Foreman writes that monkeywrenching is non-violent in respect of
persons. Earth First! received adverse publicity during its campaign
to spike trees with long nails to prevent them from being cut down,
because of the possibility of injury to loggers from their own saws. The
Field Guide consequently carefully explains that nails should be driven
in high enough up the tree to prevent loggers' access. The intention is
to damage industrial saws in the mill rather than injure the loggers
themselves (Foreman and Haywood, 1989, pp. 1–17).

The political intentions of Earth First! sabotage are to increase the
operating costs of environmentally destructive businesses, to raise public awareness regarding environmental despoliation, and (interestingly)
to increase the respectability of more mainstream environmentalists
(Foreman and Haywood, 1989, pp. 21–3). As Derek Wall remarks:

Environmental pressure groups may be able to frame their demands so as to mobilise financial support or maintain letter-writing campaigns, but seem far less effective in transforming public opinion in a more fundamental way or in promoting the growth of green agency.

(Wall, 1999, p. 191)

Judging the practical effectiveness of direct action is tricky: it is extremely difficult to trace effect back to cause with any degree of certainty. Earth First!'s intentions, outlined above, may be taken as the yardstick by which any direct action group's success should be measured, and I think it would be hard to deny success in these terms to the various groups engaged in the road-building opposition described earlier. One report estimated that the Department of Transport was losing £20,000 per day at the height of the protest, and certainly the protest highlighted the road-building programme in a public and dramatic way. In terms of respectability, one can imagine Friends of the Earth (for example) gaining in credibility when placed alongside Earth First!ers.

On the other hand, direct action protests seem not be connected to a wider movement strategy, and thus run the risk of isolation. As Ben Seel has remarked in connection with the Pollok Free State campaign in Scotland (1994–96):

the core group was not greatly concerned with questions of how different parts of a wider green movement would co-ordinate, nor with the more difficult questions of coalitions with other social movements or the potential role of a political party.

(Seel, 1997, pp. 134–5)

Similarly, the tactical and strategic differences between types of protest can bring about counter-productive conflict. Commenting on the Solsbury Hill protest in the UK, Peter North writes:

On one side were the Dongas, living by their deep ecological values and representing back to society a vision of an alternative; and on the other, S[ave] O[ur] S[olsbury] attempting to mobilise resources to convince the authorities to change their mind and stop building the road.

(North, 1998, p. 20)

He continues:

While debates were at first generally amicable, conflict grew over time as the Dongas attempted to create their own temporary liberated space on the hill, bringing unfavourable publicity and conflict with the landowners which SOS felt mitigated [*sic*] against their claims for legality and respectability.

(ibid., p. 21)

In each of these cases the road or motorway was still completed, even if a little behind schedule. Direct action supporters would no doubt see this as a case of 'lose a battle, win the war', and there was a time when they could point to successive Conservative and Labour ('New' Labour, that is) governments cutting back road-building programmes as evidence of their longer term success (Doherty, 1999, pp. 284–5). Now, though, the wheel has turned full circle as the current administration (2005–present) embarks on a massive road-building programme, which only goes to show that conclusions drawn at any one time about the impact of direct action on environmental policy can only ever be temporary and subject to revision.

Fiscal incentives and ecological citizenship

An increasingly popular way of trying to get people to behave in more sustainable ways is to arrange taxes, charges and benefits in such a way as to encourage them to do so. One example of this is the congestion charges that have sprung up in various cities in Europe and elsewhere. Car drivers in these cities are charged to enter designated zones at certain times of the day, and the hope is that they will be deterred from doing so and use alternative forms of transport instead. Another example is the tax on plastic shopping bags that the Irish government instituted in 2002. Here the idea was to deter people from using new bags each time they went shopping, and to encourage the reuse of bags. The evidence suggests that these schemes work well, at least in their own terms. There are certainly fewer cars in the congestion zone in London – 18 per cent fewer cars entered the zone in the first year of operation, and the numbers have remained stable (Politics.co.uk, 2006). In addition, the Irish government's Plastic Bag Environmental Levy (PBEL) cut the use of bags by more than 90 per cent and removed over one billion bags from circulation in its first year (Dobson and Bell, 2005, p. 2). Thus fiscal incentives of this sort seem to work, and they seem to work quickly.

One potential disadvantage of this approach to changing behaviour, though, is that it may last only as long as the fiscal incentives and disincentives are in place. For example, it is not impossible to imagine the congestion charge in London being repealed by a future Lord Mayor with a different view of things. What would happen then? Would people continue to find other ways of getting into the centre of London, or would they revert to the previous habit of using the car? Much would depend on how far people had been 'converted' to sustainable ways of thinking and behaving by the congestion charge experience. No doubt this in turn would depend on how long the charge had been in place. In the best cases one might imagine people's behaviour becoming habitual, so they unreflectively use alternative transport because that is what they have got used to doing. But one can also imagine them being tempted by the perceived convenience and autonomy associated with car use, and getting back into them at the earliest opportunity. This is what happens in cities which run 'car-free days': on days that people are allowed to use their cars they do so, apparently unchanged by their car-free day experiences.

Another possible difficulty is that this approach takes for granted that people are motivated to do things only (or at least principally) for selfish reasons – to avoid some pain or accrue some reward to themselves. This can have perverse effects. For example, the government might decide to raise a tax on household rubbish in an attempt to encourage people to throw away less and to conserve more. If I, as a householder, am uncommitted to the idea that lies behind the tax (i.e. living less wastefully) I can easily avoid the tax by dumping my rubbish in someone else's backyard. This behaviour is consistent with the model of human motivation that lies behind the tax – the desire on the part of individuals to avoid pain and maximize pleasure – but it does not produce the desired result of more sustainable behaviour.

These potential drawbacks with the fiscal incentive/disincentive route to sustainability have led some commentators to articulate a contrasting notion of environmental or ecological citizenship (Smith 1998; Barry 1999; Light, 2002; Dobson, 2003; Dobson and Bell, 2005; Dobson and Valencia, 2005; MacGregor, 2006). This contested notion draws on various traditions of citizenship to develop a more intersubjective, community-based account of the rights and obligations of individuals in connection with sustainability. Thus liberal citizenship supplies the idea of environmental rights for citizens, such as the right to environmental space. The republican tradition provides an account of the obligations that environmental citizens might have, as well as the idea that citizenship is about contributing to the common good in addition to exercising one's own rights as a citizen. The ancient idea of cosmopolitanism has recently come back into fashion, and sophisticated accounts of cosmopolitan citizenship are part-and-parcel of international relations theorizing nowadays. Environmental citizenship borrows the idea of transnational citizenship from the cosmopolitan tradition.

Thus environmental citizenship speaks the language of obligation, of the common good and of the global reach of citizenship relations. In these respects it takes a rather different view of human motivation to the fiscal incentive strategy. It recognizes (or assumes) that people sometimes act in order to 'do good' as well as to try to ensure some gain for themselves. One of its central ideas is that of the equal right to environmental space for all citizens – that is to say, everyone in the world. Given that environmental space is currently very unevenly shared out, environmental citizens will work towards the redistribution of environmental space – reducing the size of their environmental footprints where appropriate. Thus the environmental citizen is motivated to live sustainably because it is just to do so, not because she or he is prompted to do so by fiscal incentives or disincentives.

These routes to sustainability seem very different, but on the face of it they appear to complement rather than conflict with one another. Does it not seem sensible to combine the insights of both, so far as human motivation is concerned? In that way, fiscal incentives speak to the self-interested side of our motivations, while environmental citizenship draws on the other-oriented aspect of our behaviour. This seems an ideal combination, but it has its drawbacks. Recent research has shown that we need to take account of the ways in which these two approaches to changing behaviour might affect one another. This research suggests that fiscal incentive approaches can 'crowd out' citizenship approaches because those who have citizenly motivations can quickly lose them in an environment where reward and punishment are the key motivating elements (Berglund and Matti, 2006). Similarly, it is hard to sow the seeds of citizenly motivation in a context where self-interest is the norm that informs policy initiatives. So policy-makers may be forced to choose between these two ways of steering behaviour along a more sustainable path, in the knowledge that choosing the fiscal incentive technique may result in relatively quick changes yet shallow commitments, while the citizenship route will take longer, though with potentially deeper commitments as the pay-off.

Class

Despite their differences, citizenship and fiscal dis/incentives share two characteristics: first, they focus on the behaviour of individuals rather than collectives, and second, they seem to assume that changing behaviour is mostly a matter of simply changing people's minds. Greens often speak as though a simple 'change of consciousness' is enough to bring about radical shifts in social and political life. Arnold Toynbee, cited approvingly by Jonathon Porritt, writes:

> The present threat to mankind's survival can be removed only by a revolutionary change of heart in individual human beings. This change of heart must be inspired by religion in order to generate the will power needed for putting arduous new ideals into practice.
> (Porritt, 1984a, p. 211)

This kind of sentiment is often accompanied by an exhortation to education as a necessary preface to conversion. However, as David Pepper has rightly observed, 'people will not change their values just through being "taught" different ones' (Pepper, 1984, p. 224). As we saw earlier, much of the research done in the field of environmental education suggests that the provision of information is not enough, on its own, to stimulate changes in behaviour (Kollmuss and Agyeman, 2002). Most of us are aware of climate change, for example, and most of us have some idea of what causes it and what we could do to mitigate it, but few of us are prepared to take the measures required. Pepper goes on: 'What, then, is the real way forward, if it is not to be solely or even largely through education? It must be through seeking *reform at the material base of society, concurrent with educational change*' (ibid., p. 224; emphasis in original). Quite – but how?

The answer to this question might just turn on initially side-stepping it and asking instead: *Who* is best placed to bring about social change? A central characteristic of green political theory is that it has never consistently asked that question, principally because the answer is held to be obvious: everyone. The general political-ecological position that the environmental crisis will eventually be suffered by everybody on the planet, and that therefore the ideology's appeal is universal, has been perceived as a source of strength for the green movement. What could be better, from the point of view of pressing an idea, than to be able to claim that failure to embrace it may result in a global catastrophe that would leave no one untouched? From the current point of view this may be the movement's basic strategic political error because the universalist appeal is, properly speaking, Utopian. It is simply untrue to say that, given current conditions, it is in everybody's interest to bring about a sustainable and egalitarian society. A significant and influential proportion of society, for example, has a material interest in prolonging the environmental crisis because there is money to be made from managing it. It is Utopian to consider these people to be a part of the engine for profound social change.

Perhaps the most sophisticated expression of the universalist approach comes from Rudolf Bahro:

> If proceeding from these assumptions we are seeking a hegemonic project and want to keep to the level of the overall interest of humanity – which is what Marx had in mind with the world-historic mission of the proletariat – we must go beyond Marx's own concept and direct ourselves to a more general subject than the Western working-class of today. Like the utopian socialists and communists who Marx sought to dispense with, we must once again take the species interest as our fundamental point of reference.
>
> (Bahro, 1982, p. 65)

Bahro's point here, couched in language expressive of his Marxist background, is that the social subject to which we must look in order to bring about change is not this or that social class but the whole human race. Again, he writes that 'From all appearances . . . the organising factors which can bring the alternative forces together and give them a social coordination (as must be desired) will in future not be any particular class interest, but rather a long-term human interest' (Bahro, 1982, p. 115). As I pointed out earlier, Bahro can argue this because it appears transparent that the threatened environmental crisis will not discriminate between classes – the catastrophe, if it is to come, will be visited upon everybody. While this may be true in the long run, it is not necessarily the best point from which to plan immediate political strategy.

In many respects, for instance, one can already see that environmental degradation is not suffered by everyone equally. Organic foods as an alternative to chemical-dosed products, for example, are widely available in principle but their relative expense prevents them from being accessible to all. It is not simply a question of education, then, but of money. Similarly, if one considers the built environment, money makes available green spaces into which to retreat, and satisfying the primal call of the wilderness is an option currently open to only a very few. The influential 'environmental justice' movement in the USA is based on the observation that poor people live in poor environments (Dobson, 1998; Low and Gleeson, 1998; Schlosberg, 1999; Agyeman *et al.*, 2003; Agyeman, 2005; Pellow and Brulle, 2005). Poor people's lack of political voice makes it easier to impose environmental 'bads' such as landfill sites on them, and poor people in developing countries are often forced to degrade their marginal environments in order to survive. The relationship between poverty and environmental degradation is a complex one, and we should not assume that the former always leads to the latter. Indeed, in many cases the poor sustain their environments very effectively out of necessity, and in line with tried and tested methods of living in appropriate balance with their environments. Likewise, we should not forget that it is wealthy societies, not poor ones, that have caused many of the global environmental problems which assail us today – climate change, ozone depletion, waste mountains. Having said that, though, environmental problems are no different from other sources of harm in that they affect the vulnerable disproportionately. This is why Joan Martinez Alier has called for an 'environmentalism of the poor' aimed at securing sustainable environments for the disenfranchised, in distinction to what he regards as middle-class environmentalism organized around preserving 'nature' for its own sake (Martinez-Alier, 2002). Robert Gottlieb makes a similar point on behalf of the disenfranchised poor in so-called developed societies: 'a new framework for social change activity can be identified by reconstructing and linking environmental justice and pollution prevention through a radical, community- and workplace-centred, or production-focused and place-based approach' (Gottlieb, 2001).

More generally, it is simply not in the immediate interests of everybody to usher in a sustainable society. *The Limits to Growth* report remarks that:

> The majority of the world's people are concerned with matters that affect only family or friends over a short period of time. Others look farther ahead in time or over a larger area – a city or a nation. Only a very few people have a global perspective that extends far into the future.
>
> (Meadows *et al.*, 1974, p. 19)

This statement captures the problem of persuasion with which the green movement is confronted. Somehow people are required to begin to think in global terms and with respect to events that might or might not occur generations hence. 'Only a very few people' think like that, and they are precisely the people who already live in sustainable communities, refuse to use chemical pesticides in the garden and flush the toilet only when they really have to. If these people constitute a vanguard, it is hard at present to see how they are going to drag large numbers of people with them. In light of this, class theory has it that radical greens must abandon their Utopian, universalistic strategy, and instead identify and organize a group of people in society whose immediate interests lie in living sustainable lives, with all that this implies.

With respect to everything that has been said so far about green strategies for political change, it is interesting to look at the critique which Marx made about the Utopian socialists of the early nineteenth century (without jumping to the conclusion that this endorses everything Marx had to say or comprises an embryonic Marxist critique of ecologism as a whole). This is what he said of them:

> They want to improve the condition of every member of society, even that of the most favoured. Hence they habitually appeal to society at large, without distinction of class; nay, by preference, to the ruling class. For how can people, when once they understand their system, fail to see in it the best possible plan of the best possible state of society? Hence they reject all political, and especially revolutionary action; they wish to attain their ends by peaceful means, and endeavour, by small experiments, necessarily doomed to failure, and by the force of example, to pave the way for the new social gospel,
> (from *The Manifesto of the Communist Party* [1848] in Feuer, 1976, p. 79)

Word for word, these comments literally describe most present green, as well as Utopian socialist, approaches to political change. Marx makes two principal criticisms here, each of which contributes to his characterization of the type of socialism to which he refers as 'Utopian'. First, that Utopian socialism's appeal was counter-productive: it was objectively impossible to expect all classes to usher in socialism. Second, that its strategy of change through 'small experiments' and 'force of example' was an unfounded attempt to change *people* without changing the *conditions* in which they lived and worked.

Both of these criticisms of Utopian political strategy are relevant to the contemporary green movement. The 'small experimental' nature of much of the movement's practice was made clear above. From the Centre for Alternative Technology in Wales, through any number of pesticide-free vegetable plots, to the New Age community at Findhorn, Scotland, the practice of much green politics takes the form of a series of 'small experiments'. Marx, of course, made clear his recognition of the political value of the Utopian socialists' enterprises for calling into question the accepted truths of early nineteenth-century European society, and any critique of green Utopianism must do the same for the initiatives mentioned above.

It is well known that Marx's solution to the problem posed by the false universal appeal of the Utopian socialists was to recommend the identification and formation of a class in society (given the right historical conditions) whose prime interest lay in changing that society. This is how he put it in his *Toward a Critique of Hegel's Philosophy of Right* of 1844:

> Where is there, then, a *real* possibility of emancipation in Germany? This is our reply. A class must be formed which has *radical chains*, a class in civil society which is not a class of civil society, a class which is the dissolution of all classes, a sphere of society which has a universal character because its sufferings are universal, and which does not claim a *particular redress* because the wrong which is done to it is not a *particular wrong*, but *wrong in general*. There must be formed a sphere of society which claims no traditional status but only a human status, a sphere which is not opposed to particular consequences but is totally opposed to the assumptions of the German political system, a sphere which finally cannot emancipate itself without therefore emancipating all those other spheres, which is, in short, a *total loss* of humanity and which can only redeem itself by a *total redemption of humanity*.
>
> (in Bottomore and Rubel, 1984,
> p. 190; emphasis in original)

According to Marx, then, the basic characteristics of the 'sphere of society' (or 'class') capable of bringing about profound social change were as follows: first, it had to have 'radical chains' such that, second, its emancipation would involve the general emancipation of humanity; and third, it had to be opposed not just to the 'particular consequences' of a political system but also to its general 'assumptions'. For Marx, of course, this class with a universal historical mission was the proletariat. Of course, the proletariat has not proved to be the class that Marx thought it was: its claims were not so radical that it questioned the assumptions of the political system, and its emancipation (while any-way only partial and material) has not led to the emancipation of humanity.

We are left, then, with a critique of Utopian (in Marx's rather special-ized sense) political strategies, and how he considers it possible to transcend them. We have already established that green ideologues are typically averse to class theories of politics because they believe them divisively to undermine the green universal appeal. There has, though, been some discussion about the general issue of agents for change in green literature. Two suggestions may briefly be followed up: that of the middle class as the instigator of change, and the potentially central role of the 'new social movements', such as feminism, the peace movement, gays and so on (Doherty, 2002).

Jonathon Porritt presents a classic formulation of the first position:

> one must of course acknowledge that the post-industrial revolution is likely to be pioneered by middle-class people. The reasons are simple: such people not only have more chance of working out where their own genuine self-interest lies, but they also have the flexibility and security to act upon such insights.
>
> (Porritt, 1984a, p. 116)

Much depends here on what one understands by 'pioneer'. If Porritt means simply the questioning of current social and political practices and the presentation of alternatives, then the middle class clearly has a central role to play. Indeed, there is plenty of sociological evidence to show the influence of the middle classes in the environmental movement. Just why this is the case is hotly disputed, but the debate suggests that throwing one's eggs prematurely into the middle-class basket could be a mistake. The general position combines two suggestions: first, that rises in post-war living standards have shifted political goals (for some) away from material concerns and towards 'quality of life' issues (Inglehart, 1977); and second, that a new middle class of non-marketized professionals (educationalists, health workers) have occupations that are conducive to the generation and pursuance of green values.

Luke Martell, though (for example), has doubts regarding the long-term position of this middle class in radical green politics on the grounds that 'it is difficult to see a basis for economic interest in middle-class concern for the environment' (1994, p. 130). He points out that:

> [R]adical environmentalism argues for slowing down growth and rates of consumption. A comfortable group, but which sees itself to be materially disadvantaged relative to otherwise comparable groups, would not be likely to perceive cuts in growth as in its interest.
>
> (Martell, 1994, p. 130)

This kind of observation renders Porritt's faith in the middle class somewhat problematic – particularly when placed alongside his working hypothesis of self-interest: 'I do not believe that the majority of people will change until they believe it is in their own interests to do so. . . . A reinterpretation of enlightened self-interest is therefore the key to any radical transformation' (Porritt, 1984a, p. 117). One of Porritt's earlier remarks endorses Martell's worries on this score so far as the middle class is concerned:

> one thing is clear: even if we continue to think in terms of working class and middle class, it is not the latter that has the most to worry about in terms of the current crisis. It is the middle classes that have the flexibility to weather traumatic shifts in social and economic patterns; by and large, they are not the ones to suffer most from mindless jobs, dangerous working conditions, a filthy polluted environment, shattered communities, the exploitation of mass culture, the inhumanity of bureaucrats and the mendacity of politicians.
>
> (Porritt, 1984a, p. 116)

On this reading, and taking into account Porritt's self-interest thesis, it is the working class and not the middle class whose interest lies in shifting away from current social practices. Porritt's conclusion in favour of the latter class, despite his own evidence, may be explained only by inserting him into the liberal tradition to which he belongs, and which has always proclaimed the middle classes as the agents of change.

It is this, too, that leads him to make optimistic remarks about 'the role of small businesses' under the general heading 'the agents of change' (Porritt, 1984a, p. 139). He goes on: 'In the kind of long-term economy that we envisage, small businesses would not just be a useful adjunct to the world of corporate big business: they would be the mainstay of all economic activity' (Porritt, 1984a, p. 139). The problem with the notion of small businesses as agents of change is that their success, and even survival, depends on their producing and reproducing the products and values demanded by the system within which they operate. In the name of efficiency, such businesses may 'have to' cut the workforce, deunionize it, hire temporary labour with no security and provide poor conditions of work. There is no guarantee whatsoever that small businesses, far from acting as agents for social change, will not rather be vehicles for the reproduction of the system they seek to overcome. Indeed, in the absence of any strategy for disengaging from the system, the latter is far more likely to be the case.

Beyond the middle class, one sometimes reads that the 'new social movements' represent new forms of political activity that anticipate new forms of society (Doherty, 2002). Fritjof Capra, for example, writes of a 'winning majority' of 'environmentalists, feminists, ethnic minorities etc.', and then that 'the new coalitions should be able to turn the paradigm shift into political reality' (Capra, 1983, p. 465). More explicitly, Murray Bookchin refers to 'the new classes' and argues that they are 'united more by cultural ties than economic ones: ethnics, women, counter-cultural people, environmentalists, the aged, the déclassé, unemployables or unemployed, the "ghetto" people' (Bookchin, 1986, p. 152).

Similarly Jürgen Habermas has theorized a 'new politics' centring on 'the peace movement, the anti-nuclear and environmental movement, minority liberation movements, the movement for alternative lifestyles, the tax protest movement, religious fundamentalist protest groups and, finally, the women's movement' (Roderick, 1986, p. 136). Habermas goes on to make an important distinction that helps us to make some sense of the social pot-pourri offered up by himself, Capra and Bookchin. He argues that not all of these groups have the same emancipatory potential, and suggests that we distinguish between those that seek 'particularistic' change and 'those that seek fundamental change from a universalistic viewpoint' (Roderick, 1986, p. 136). This ought to remind us of the quotation from Marx cited earlier in which he argued that the source of social change must be found in 'a sphere which is not opposed to particular consequences but is totally opposed to the assumptions of the German political system'. Roderick continues:

> For Habermas, at the present time only the women's movement belongs to this latter category to the extent that it seeks not only a formal equality, but also a fundamental change in the social structure and in real concrete life situation.
>
> (Roderick, 1986, p. 136)

This is a very important observation, particularly in the context of the most typical critique of social movements as agents for social change: i.e. that they have no common interest and therefore cannot act coherently. As Boris Frankel has written, for example, 'women, environmentalists, peace activists, gays, etc., do not have a ready formed identity as a social movement' (1987, p. 235). This is undoubtedly true, but with reference to Habermas' distinction it is hardly important. The crucial project would not be to manufacture an identity between heterogeneous groups, but to identify that group (or those groups) whose project most profoundly questions the presuppositions on which current social practices depend. Only such a group can already be in a sufficiently 'disengaged' position to resist the attempts at colonization by the system it seeks to overcome, and even then, of course, success is by no means guaranteed. I shall pick up the suggestion that women may constitute such a vanguard shortly.

The point of all this is to suggest that a possible strategy for the green movement would be to identify and foment a group in society that is not only relatively 'disengaged' from it, but that is also already inclined towards the foundations of sustainable living. This will be the agent for radical green change, and in the spirit of experiment I can now outline what it might look like, beginning with a cursory green materialist analysis of the situation that is producing it.

The green movement will certainly want to argue that the production process is threatened by an actual or potential shortage of raw materials – that is precisely the point of its founding its ideology in the concept of a finite Earth. If this is correct, then production itself will become ever more expensive (even allowing for temporary technological substitutes/ solutions), and the capital required for investment in the process will be ever harder to find. There are two likely responses to this: first, the reduction of the costs of production in ways that will compensate for the increased cost of scarce materials; and second, the encouragement of increased consumption to generate more capital. A serious green materialist analysis would of course need extensive empirical work to back up its own claims.

The point in our context, though, is that the first strategy may come into conflict with the second and generate social tensions (and a social class) that cannot be satisfied within the current scheme of production and consumption. For instance, one of the ways in which the costs of production in the metropolitan countries can be reduced is by employing cheaper labour in other parts of the world. This, naturally, has the effect of increasing unemployment in the metropolitan countries. In turn, the number of people who are marginalized from the second response referred to above – that of encouraging increased consumption – increases. From their perspective, the system is characterized by its failure to fulfil the expectations it generates.

This characteristic is, of course, not new to the general history of the current mode of production, but greens might argue that what is new to our particular period is that the external limits imposed by the Earth circumscribe that system's room for manoeuvre. There is less and less space within which *both* to produce *and* to fulfil the expectations of consumption that the system generates. In other words, it may be argued from a radical green perspective that the external limits imposed on the production process by the Earth itself are beginning to shape a class that is more or less permanently marginalized from the process of consumption. From this point of view it is *the distance from the process of consumption and the degree of permanence of this isolation that currently determine the capacity of any given group in society for radical green social change.*

In Marx's terms such a group would be a class with 'radical chains' – 'a class in civil society which is not a class of civil society'. In other words, it is a class whose daily life sets it apart from all other classes of society. It is a class that does not buy anything and therefore calls into question the production process that fills the shop windows. In this sense, it is a class that is opposed not just to the 'particular consequences' of this particular system, but also to its general 'assumptions'. It is therefore so sufficiently 'disengaged' that it might hope to surmount the problems of colonization and recolonization that we saw dogging the parliamentary, lifestyle and community strategies for change.

Are there any signs that such a class exists in the contemporary world? One place to look might be in the 'developing' world, where large swathes of the population are excluded from enjoying the fruits of free-trade globalization. In a speech in Caracas in 1981, Rudolf Bahro referred to what Arnold Toynbee called 'the external proletariat' and translated it, in general terms, into those who 'are not yet "really subsumed", i.e. the majority of the population who are marginalised to varying degrees and in varying ways' (1982, p. 129). He continued:

> it may well be worthwhile to investigate the connection between the immediate interests of the marginalised sections (and these are growing now also in the metropolises, if on a different scale) and the general interest of a humanity which has reached the earth's limits with its industrial capitalist expansion.
>
> (Bahro, 1982, p. 129)

Bahro is here pointing towards a social subject with similar characteristics to those that I have described (marginalization from the process of production and consumption), but situates it in the so-called Third World. This serves to emphasize the international character of the crisis and the shared interests of the 'metropolitan' and 'peripheral' marginalized, and provides greens with an instance of, and practice for, its slogan: 'act locally think globally'. It also gives concrete content to Jeremy Seabrook's suggestion that 'the most urgent task is to show how and why the poor would be the chief beneficiaries of Green politics' (Seabrook, 1988, p. 166). Seabrook is surely right that:

> Nothing could be more damaging to the Green cause than the perception that it is supported by privileged people who have

enough for their own needs, and are now eager to limit the access of the poor to those benefits of industrial society which they themselves enjoy.

(Seabrook, 1988, p. 166)

As we saw earlier in the context of the environmental justice movement and Martinez-Alier's environmentalism of the poor, some progress is being made in this respect. As Andrew Szasz has written, 'Toxic victims are, typically, poor or working people of modest means. Their environmental problems are inseparable from their economic condition. People are more likely to live near polluted industrial sites if they live in financially strapped communities' (Szasz, 1994, p. 151). In the context of the search for a group coalescing around an issue which has broad social and political implications, it is interesting to read that the hazardous waste movement 'increasingly defines its environmental mission in terms of a larger critique of society . . . [I]t even envisions a future in which grass-roots environmentalism spearheads the reconstitution of a broad social justice movement' (ibid., p. 166).

Throughout this section I have been talking about marginalization in the context of the formal processes of production and consumption. This approach is criticized by ecofeminists – on whom I will have more to say in Chapter 5 – for its lack of attention to the crucial sphere of reproduction. In the hands of materialist ecofeminists this criticism turns into a fully fledged theory of gendered political agency which has women at the forefront of change. Ariel Salleh, for example, remarks that:

> The Green movement must use a materialist analysis. This accords beautifully with an ecofeminist premise for women's historical agency, because on an international scale, undertaking 65 per cent of the world's work for 5 per cent of its pay, effectively are 'the proletariat' . . . women as an economic underclass are astonishingly well placed to bring about the social changes requisite for ecological revolution.

(Salleh, 1997, p. 6)

Marginalized in this way from the formal processes of production and consumption, women also – and critically, for materialist ecofeminists – occupy a critical space in the reproductive process, a space that makes them ideal candidates for bringing about green political objectives. From a materialist ecofeminist point of view, 'humans come to know nature through their bodies and . . . make sense of that experience' (Salleh, 1997, p. 38). Women's 'coming to know' is a specific sort, mediated through pregnancy, childbirth and suckling. Women experience a 'continuity with nature' that men currently lack, and it is this that makes 'Woman' the 'biological and social mediator of Nature for men' (ibid., p. 49). 'Could women, still invisible as the global majority, actually be the missing agents of History, and therefore Nature, in our troubled times?' asks Salleh. For her, the answer is clearly yes.

Materialist ecofeminism has much to recommend it: its insights into the role and consequences of reproduction are absolutely critical, and any green materialism that ignores this will do so at its peril. It is, though, important to strike a balance between production and reproduction. Focus on the latter has the inevitable consequence of putting women in the vanguard of green change, and while this may be desirable for all sorts of reasons, it is not a consequence that can be derived from a fully fledged materialist analysis – one that takes full account of production as well as reproduction. Taking account of production brings marginalized men as well as women into the frame, something which materialist ecofeminism cannot do directly, despite Salleh's remark that 'Under certain circumstances, a man can also feed a child at the breast' (Salleh, 1997, p. 37). It is important that men be brought back into the frame, not just because otherwise the poor things will feel left out, but because a green materialism demands their presence. The slogan for a green materialism might therefore be 'production *and* reproduction' rather than either one or the other.

However one looks at it, though, difficulties with class-based or gender-based strategies for green change remain. Even assuming that the class has been formed or that the gender is conscious of itself as a historical agent, one is left with the problem of how it is going to act. Is it, for example, envisaged as some sort of revolutionary political subject? If so, then the class is confronted with a series of classic problems: the stability of current political systems (in the West at least), the issue of revolutionary organization, and (particularly difficult for non-violent greens) waging the revolutionary struggle.

If, on the other hand, reformist strategies are chosen and the class operates through pressure groups or a parliamentary party, then all of the dilemmas and difficulties referred to in the first part of this chapter resurface: 'How far should compromise be taken?', 'How should elections be contested?', 'Is election a realistic possibility anyway?' Intermediate strategies do present themselves, such as building up green communities through the local money schemes described earlier (perhaps focused on unemployment centres), but all thoughts of green class action seem vitiated by the fact that no unified sense of such a class is currently in sight.

Conclusion

In any discussion of green politics we must distinguish between its dark-green and light-green, or environmental, manifestations. The issue of green social change is no exception. From a light-green point of view, for instance, the reflections which took place under the heading 'class' will probably seem superfluous. It appears self-evident that a parliamentary presence, or pressure through the lobby system, can bring about a cleaner, more sustainable environment. It appears self-evident that we can lead more environment-friendly lives by buying the right things and refusing to buy the wrong ones. It also appears self-evident that sustainable communities are vital as sources of inspiration for the rest of us to live more lightly on the Earth.

But from ecologism's point of view all of these strategies must be measured in terms of the radical green critique of current practices developed in Chapter 3, and the kinds of structures we need to overcome them. Bringing about that kind of sustainable society is an infinitely more difficult task than simply putting environmentalism on the political agenda. So far, that is what the strategies adopted have done, and taking radical green politics seriously – rather than some attenuated environmentalist version of it – may involve a move beyond those strategies.

5 Ecologism and other ideologies

We now have the fundamentals of ecologism in place. We have discussed its critique of contemporary society, we have outlined its proposals for an ecologically sound society, and we have assessed its approach to bringing such a society about. I have claimed that ecologism is a new political ideology, worthy of attention in the new millennium alongside other more familiar ones such as liberalism, conservatism and socialism. If this is correct, then it is only natural to want to compare and contrast this new ideology with those which it seeks to challenge. That is what I propose to do in this chapter. In so doing, it is my intention to deepen our understanding of what marks ecologism off from those other ideologies. I shall be arguing that attempts by liberals, conservatives and socialists to appropriate ecological thought for themselves will founder, since, as I pointed out in the Introduction, ecologism is as different from each of them as they are from each other. The examination carried out in this chapter should drive home this point.

In principle, the list of ideologies with which ecologism could be compared and contrasted is a long one. In choosing to devote attention to just four of them I might be accused of pruning that long list unduly. There are two reasons for doing so, however. The first is that I wanted to give each of these four ideologies a run for its money. Broad comparisons have been helpfully carried out elsewhere (see e.g. Hay, 1988; Martell, 1994, ch. 5; Garner, 2000, ch. 3; Connelly and Smith, 2003, pp. 52–65), but the range of coverage has been bought at the cost of making it rather thin, with typically a page or two devoted to each ideology. Particularly recently, and particularly in the cases of the four ideologies I deal with here, some very interesting comparative work has been done, and it is simply not possible to do this work justice in a short space.

Second, the ideologies I have chosen for assessment might legitimately be regarded as lying at the roots of those I have left out. This is to say that liberalism, conservatism and socialism are widely held to be the most fundamental ideologies of the modern era, and other less fundamental ones can often be read through them (although never wholly reducible to them). I hope, therefore, to have provided an indirect service to those who would want to contrast ecologism with nationalism or with fascism, for example, although I am acutely aware of the breadth I have nevertheless sacrificed. Feminism might not generally be held to be in the same league as liberalism, conservatism and socialism (although I am not so sure myself), but the justification for including a detailed discussion of it here is that it has influenced the development of ecologism in a way unmatched by any other ideology, with the possible exception of socialism. This influence has also, I think, been reciprocal.

For no particular reason, the ideologies with which I compare and contrast ecologism are in the following order: liberalism, conservatism, socialism and feminism.

Liberalism

Ten years ago, Mark Sagoff asked whether environmentalists could be liberals (Sagoff, 1988, pp. 146–70). At the time, the question appeared rather esoteric in that the interesting ideological and theoretical relationships seemed to be between environmentalism (or, as I want to call it here, ecologism) and socialism, or environmentalism and feminism, rather than between environmentalism and liberalism. It is now clear that Sagoff was more perceptive than most of the rest of us, not because ecosocialism and ecofeminism are not interesting – they are – but because the increasing dominance of the liberal world-view in academic and political life has necessarily brought the environmental and liberal agendas into close contact, with the result that some of the most intellectually interesting (if politically questionable) work in environmental political theory is being done in this area.

Thus Robyn Eckersley was able to write in 1992 that:

> Although some emancipatory theorists, such as John Rodman, have noted and discussed these byways in liberal thought [that is, potential compatibilities between liberalism and radical ecology], the general tendency has been to look to other political traditions for the ideals and principles that would underpin an ecologically sustainable *post-liberal* society.
>
> (Eckersley, 1992, pp. 23–4)

Since then a number of theorists (e.g. Hayward, 1995; Eckersley, 1996;

Wissenburg, 1998a, 2006; B. Barry, 1999; Miller, 1999; Hailwood 2004) have sought to demonstrate compatibility between liberal and environmental themes or, more strongly, to show how the ecological political project can be expressed more or less completely in the liberal idiom.

My own view is that the answer to the compatibility question depends entirely on one's terms of reference: environmentalism and liberalism are compatible, but ecologism and liberalism are not. So even if it is true to say that political ecology 'draws on' liberalism, Martell is wrong to jump to the conclusion that this 'shows that green political theory does not stand alone as a new political theory' (Martell, 1994, p. 141). The tensions between liberalism and ecologism are by now well rehearsed. Martell himself points out that:

> there is a lot in liberal political theory that runs counter to radical ecology. Individualism, the pursuit of private gain, limited government and market freedom are contradicted by radical ecology commitments to the resolution of environmental problems as a collective good and to intervention and restrictions on economic and personal freedoms to deal with them.
>
> (Martell, 1994, p. 141)

The issue of liberty is crucial here. As Wissenburg says, 'in no respect can liberal democracy and environmental concerns be so much at odds as where liberty is concerned' (Wissenburg, 1998a, p. 33), and while it would be wrong to regard political ecology as just a series of personal and social prohibitions, there is no doubt that ecologism's stress on 'limits' of all sorts amounts to the potential curtailment of certain taken-for-granted freedoms, particularly in the realms of production, consumption and mobility. It will not be enough for liberals to be told that these restrictions will be offset by hoped-for improvements in the quality of life: liberty is central to the liberal prospectus, and liberals will regard threats to it with great suspicion.

Liberals resist being told what to think as well as what to do. More technically, they regard their felt *preferences* as an accurate indicator of their *interests*, and they will say that attempts by the state to influence tastes and preferences are generally unwarranted. Likewise, liberals do not typically welcome suggestions that people do not know what is in their own best interest. Thus, 'From a liberal perspective, the objection to denying the equation of people's interests with what they think or say they are is that this appears at the same time to be denying basic respect for people's autonomy' (Hayward, 1995, p. 203). The problem from a political-ecological point of view is that this autonomy may clash with ecological objectives: 'Liberal democracy is totally incompatible with attempts to dictate people's tastes and preferences, yet we may reasonably assume that preferences are one of the determining factors of sustainability' (Wissenburg, 1998a, p. 7). Far from regarding people's preferences as sacrosanct, political ecologists seek to influence them all the time, and if we add to this the various potential restrictions on liberty referred to above, then the tensions between liberalism and ecologism become palpable.

Often, autonomy for liberals is understood to mean the freedom to develop and pursue one's own moral goals in life. From this point of view, 'Liberalism is the political theory that holds that many conflicting and even incommensurable conceptions of the good may be fully compatible with free, autonomous, and rational action' (Sagoff, 1988, pp. 150–1), and so, 'The liberal state does not dictate the moral goals its citizens are to achieve; it simply referees the means they use to satisfy their own preferences' (ibid., p. 151). It will be clear from Chapter 2 that political ecologists have a quite distinctive view regarding our moral relationship with the non-human natural world, and this is a view that they will feel bound to encourage the rest of us to endorse. This gives rise, though, to another potential tension between liberalism and ecologism – and to the question from Mark Sagoff that heads this section: 'If the laws and policies supported by the environmental lobby are not neutral among ethical, aesthetic and religious ideals but express a moral conception of people's appropriate relation to nature, can environmentalists be liberals?' (ibid., p. 150).

There are two reasons why Sagoff thinks they can, the first of which has been adopted by many people who would like to press for compatibility between liberalism and ecologism (e.g. Barry, 1995, pp. 145–51). This first reason turns on the common distinction in liberal theory between the structure of institutions and the social policies that emerge from them (Sagoff, 1988, p. 166). Sagoff suggests that while liberals must be neutral in respect of the former (that is, that the institutions be fair between the individuals who participate in them), there is nothing to prevent them from having decided views on social policy – even views that are based upon 'particular ethical, cultural, or aesthetic convictions' (ibid.). Convictions of this sort, of course, amount to convictions regarding the nature of the Good Life about which liberals are traditionally supposed to be neutral. Sagoff squares the circle by making the distinction between institutions and policy, and arguing that liberal neutrality applies only to the former and not necessarily to the latter. Thus Sagoff's 'liberal environmentalist' will argue for neutrality only at the level of institutions, while remaining perfectly free to advance and defend Good Life-type views about the proper relationship between human beings and the non-human natural world.

Sagoff's second reason for believing that environmentalists can be liberals is based on liberalism's 'tolerance for competing views' (Sagoff, 1988, p. 167), and its endorsement of institutions 'in which individuals and groups may argue for the policies they favor and may advocate various conceptions of the good' (ibid.). It is a short step from here to the conclusion that anyone with a conception of the good they wish to advance would be well advised to endorse the liberal project because only in a liberal political environment is there the guarantee of being able to advance it. Nor is it just a question of ideas. Liberal tolerance of competing views and the belief that people should be allowed to choose their own versions of the Good Life raises the issue of the material preconditions for living the Good Life, whatever it may be. It is virtually meaningless to say that people are free to choose lives if the conditions for doing so are not in place. Liberals should surely therefore be committed to wide-ranging protection of the non-human world in case parts of it are fundamental to the Good Lives of current people. This point is perhaps even stronger if we take future people into account. We cannot know what conceptions of the Good Life future people will have, so it is incumbent on the current generation (the argument goes) to pass on as wide a range of possible conditions for living good lives as possible. We need only think of conceptions of the Good Life that are land-based (e.g. animist religions) to see the potential force of this argument. More technically: 'liberals . . . should be in favour of strong sustainability – and not because of any special commitment to "nature", but because a structured bequest package amounts to a wider range of options from which to choose good lives' (Dobson, 2003, p. 168). We might even agree with Sagoff by this point, not only that environmentalists can be liberals, but that they *should* be liberals.

At the same time, some liberals have become less demanding in terms of their views of what 'neutrality' in terms of the Good Life might mean. More accurately, they have come to argue that some 'ecological principles' may be included in 'the set of values on which reasonable individuals should agree'. These values 'make social co-operation possible and at the same time limit the areas in which individuals may disagree on the good life' (Wissenburg, 2006, p. 25). In other words, not all versions of the Good Life are compatible with sustainability, and ones that are not should be ruled out of court – even by liberals.

This second argument, though, merely confirms what we knew already: that liberalism tolerates competing conceptions of the Good Life. What political ecologists will want to know, in addition, is whether liberalism will bring about their objectives. No political system can offer such guarantees, of course, but liberalism's thoroughgoing focus on the *means* rather than the *ends* of political association makes it only problematically compatible than some other political ideologies with an end-orientated conception of political and social life such as ecologism. Thus while it is true that 'Liberal social policy cannot be inferred from liberal political theory' (Sagoff, 1988, p. 166) – i.e. that liberal political theory's neutrality as regards institutions should not be taken to entail morality-free social policy – political ecologists are likely to support institutions and policies that endorse *their* view of what morality should be, rather than 'merely' neutral ones.

Nor may it be so easy for a putative green liberalism to avoid nailing its colours to the mast so far as a moral conception of people's relationship with non-human nature is concerned. As Marcel Wissenburg surveys the likely future relationship between liberalism and ecologism, he writes:

> We may also expect the introduction of the notion of limits to growth and resources, and with it that of sustainability, to lead to questions of a substantive normative nature. A sustainable society need not be one big Yellowstone Park – we can imagine a worldwide version of Holland stuffed with cows, grain and greenhouses, or even a global Manhattan without the Park to be as sustainable and for many among us as pleasant as the first. Hence a greener liberalism will have to define more clearly what kind of sustainability, what kind of world, it aims for.
>
> (Wissenburg, 1998a, p. 81)

If Wissenburg is right about this – and I believe he is – then this 'greener liberalism' will be obliged to develop a moral conception of our relationship with the non-human natural world as a necessary step on the road to deciding what kind of world we want to hand on to future generations. On this reading, environmental sustainability *by definition* raises questions regarding the Good Life, and so if liberalism is to have a 'take' on environmental sustainability then it must also have a definitive moral conception of 'people's appropriate relation to nature' (in Sagoff's words (1988, p. 150)). If this is a pill that liberalism cannot swallow – as I suspect it cannot – then this may be where liberalism and ecologism finally part company.

The history of liberal thought gives some succour to those who seek compatibilities between liberalism and radical ecology. Marcel Wissenburg, among others, has identified two types of liberal legacy, one centred on the work of John Locke and the other on John Stuart Mill and Jeremy Bentham (Wissenburg, 1998a, pp. 74–6), and he (Wissenburg, 2001) and Piers Stephens (2001a, 2001b) have debated the relative merits of these two types of liberalism from the green point of view. The former type, according to most commentators, is broadly inimical to the modern ecological project, while the latter has resources that may be enlisted in favour of some aspects of it. In Lockean times, writes Wissenburg, 'Nature had two roles to play in liberal thought: physically, it was an inexhaustible source of resources; intellectually, it was the incarnation of the laws of nature over which humankind had triumphed, which it had transcended' (Wissenburg, 1998a, p. 74). It will be clear by now that this view of the 'role' of nature is roundly rejected by contemporary political ecologists: the limits to growth thesis suggests that nature's resources are not boundless, and the idea that human beings can 'triumph' over the laws of nature is the hubris that political ecologists blame – in part – for environmental problems surrounding issues such as genetically modified foods (discussion of the possibility of a more ecologically friendly reading of Locke may be found at Hayward (1994, pp. 130–6), and Dobson (1998, pp. 144–8)).

Similarly, Wissenburg refers to 'the crucial role of reason' in classical liberalism (Wissenburg, 1998a, p. 74). The idea, or category, of reason is central to liberalism since the view that all human beings possess reason (even if they do not always use it) constitutes 'the beginning of arguments for the political equality and influence of citizens, for the individual as the source of all political authority, for the priority of private over state interests' (ibid.). The explosive nature of this idea in the late seventeenth century should not be underestimated. But inclusion and exclusion are two sides of the same coin, and just as possessors of reason were drawn into the charmed circle, so those beings lacking it were left outside. As Wissenburg puts it: 'Classical liberalism recognizes only one essential distinction in nature: the line dividing reasonable and unreasonable beings' (Wissenburg, 1998a, p. 75). This is an essential and enduring distinction in one type of liberalism that legitimizes discriminatory treatment between humans and other animals.

The second type of liberalism – that developed through the work of Mill, Bentham and their followers – tells a different story, however. As Bentham famously said, 'The question is not, Can they *reason*? nor, Can they *talk*? but, Can they *suffer*?' (Bentham, 1960: ch. 17, sec. 1). This new category of 'sentience' clearly broadens the community of beings entitled to moral consideration – broadens it sufficiently, indeed, to include some non-human animals. We saw all this in Chapter 2, and we also saw that the game of defining the 'X' in the question 'What faculty, X, must beings possess to be entitled to moral considerability?' can be played interminably. For classical liberalism, 'X' is reason, and this gives one kind of answer to the question. For Bentham (and utilitarians in general), 'X' is sentience, and this gives another kind of answer. Ecocentrics will answer the 'X' question in different ways again; Robyn Eckersley, as we saw (p. 42), refers to the 'characteristic of self-reproduction or self-renewal' (Eckersley, 1992, p. 60). This broadens the community of 'moral patients' beyond anything to be found even in Mill and Bentham, and provides circumstantial evidence that, however hard they try, liberals will not find much in their historical legacy to satisfy ecocentrics.

On the other hand, the idea of *rights* is inseparable from liberalism, and this idea can be – and has been – enlisted in favour of environmental objectives. This appropriation can take the form of piggy-backing such objectives on specifically *human* rights. Tim Hayward points out that the idea of a 'right to . . . an environment of a quality that permits a life of dignity and well-being' was mooted as early as 1972 at the Stockholm UN Conference on the Human Environment. From an environmental point of view, though, there are problems with such a rights strategy. In the first place, as Hayward observes, the problem with the idea of a 'right to an adequate environment' for political ecologists is that 'it does not really go beyond the view that the environment is just a resource which humans have a right to use for their own benefit' (Hayward, 1995, p. 144). Second, the 'limits to growth' thesis suggests that 'natural ecosystems have a limited carrying capacity which simply cannot support all the demands of a growing human population, and so cannot necessarily support all the rights they might want to claim either' (ibid., pp. 144–5).

This second objection points to the need to limit population growth. Such a policy may itself have distinctly non-liberal implications (see Wissenburg, 1998b), but Hayward refers to evidence which suggests that affluence is an effective contraceptive, and he also suggests (along with many others, e.g. B. Barry, 1999) that women's emancipation is the key to reduced birth rates. What should be noted, though, is that the 'affluence' solution both falls foul of the limits to growth thesis and is also the cause of the type of environmental problem associated with wealthy societies. Likewise, the 'emancipation' solution comes from *feminism* not from *liberalism*, so we are perhaps entitled to conclude that liberalism – on its own – lacks the intellectual resources for dealing with the problems associated with piggy-backing environmental objectives on human rights.

Another way in which liberal rights talk can make 'green' sense is in the context of animal rights. A flavour of this move has already been given in Chapter 2, and there is no need to go over the same ground again. Suffice to say that assuming some animals can be regarded as rights-holders (Feinberg, 1981), then rights claims can, in principle, be as politically useful for those animals as they are for human beings. This begs the question, of course, of whether rights claims *are* politically useful, even when social and economic rights are added to the political rights normally associated with the liberal project. Ted Benton, for one, has deployed a Marxist critique of such rights in the context of animals, and he suggests that the discourse of rights will always come up against the practice of exploitation:

> rights are unlikely to be effective in practice unless those who have the power to abuse them are already benevolently disposed to their bearers. . . . Where humans gain their livelihood from a practice which presupposes a 'reification' of animals, or gain pleasure from sports which involve systematic animal suffering, it seems unlikely that a rational argument that this treatment is unjust to the animals concerned would be sufficient to make the humans concerned change their ways.
>
> (Benton, 1993, p. 94)

The crucial thing, he concludes, is to take into account 'the socio-economic and cultural positions and formations of the human agents concerned' (ibid.).

One final and very promising area in which rights have been deployed in the name of environmental objectives is in the context of future generations. It may not be immediately apparent how the rights of future generations and environmental sustainability are connected, but once we realize that 'the environment' is one of the things we hand on to future generations, and if we accept that future generations have a right to a sustainable and satisfying environment, then future generation rights and environmental sustainability may be seen to be intimately linked. As Hayward astutely points out: 'In talking about rights of future generations, one is already addressing matters of environmental concern' (Hayward, 1994, p. 142).

In this context as in many others, the work of the most influential (liberal) theorist of modern times, John Rawls, has proved remarkably fecund. Rawls it was who, in his A *Theory of Justice*, developed a 'savings principle' (Rawls, 1973, p. 287), whereby current generations are enjoined to save for future ones. Much turns on just what form this 'saving' is to take, of course, but if it is understood to include environmental goods and services (understood in the broadest sense), then this liberal theory of justice, at least, appears to be compatible with environmental objectives. Recently, Marcel Wissenburg has argued that this is true of *all* liberal theories of justice: 'liberals in general need to include a savings principle in their respective theories of justice – and . . . (some form of) obligations to future generations is a *conditio sine qua non* of any liberal theory of justice' (Wissenburg, 1998a, p. 134). Once again, the *nature* of these obligations is crucial, but Wissenburg believes it to be entirely compatible with a conditional view of liberal rights that these obligations take the form of what he calls the 'restraint principle':

> no goods shall be destroyed unless unavoidable and unless they are replaced by perfectly identical goods; if that is physically impossible, they should be replaced by equivalent goods resembling the original as closely as possible; and that if this is also impossible, a proper compensation should be provided.
>
> (Wissenburg, 1998a, p. 123)

From an environmental point of view this looks very promising. Yet – as ever – the devil is in the detail: what, precisely, does 'unless unavoidable' mean? Carnivores and vegetarians, for example, will have different answers to this question. More broadly still, the 'unless unavoidable' proviso takes us back full circle to an earlier point: that the idea of environmental sustainability enjoins us, by definition, to have a definitive moral conception of 'people's appropriate relation to nature' – precisely the kind of conception, though, that liberalism eschews.

The liberal language of rights, then, may be deployed in the service of environmental objectives, but not with conclusive success. My own view is that the intentions of ecologism need the idea of *responsibilities* to be added to those of rights because, as Hayward remarks, this:

> seems to capture the key ecological intuition that it is necessary to change our basic attitude to the world from one which considers 'what we can get out of it' to one which considers 'what we can and must do for it'.
>
> (Hayward, 1994, p. 163)

Whether or not animals or future generation human beings have rights, their peculiar vulnerability to our actions 'demands' a responsible attitude of care and concern (Goodin, 1985). Normally, rights and duties are seen as reciprocal – 'rights exist if and only if corresponding duties exist' (Hayward, 1994, p. 169) – and ecologism's contribution (as we saw in the discussion of ecological citizenship in Chapter 4) to this debate lies in severing the connection between rights and duties.

In sum there will always be tensions, to say the least, between liberalism and ecologism. Marcel Wissenburg summarizes the state of play as follows: 'Although liberalism has not been fundamentally changed by its contact with green political thought, it has developed in many important respects. To be more precise, *some* liberals have taken on a shade of green' (Wissenburg, 2006, p. 23). True though this is, pressure points remain. To the oft-remarked differences of opinion over autonomy and individualism we must add ecologism's insistence on a definitive view of the proper moral relationship between human beings and the non-human natural world. We must acknowledge the uses to which rights talk may be put for environmental ends, but also temper this with the recognition that such talk can never fully express the nature of the relationship between human beings and 'nature' that ecologism seeks to establish. Finally, liberalism is firmly located in a tradition of thought and practice that has distinguished sharply between the human and 'natural' realms, both descriptively and prescriptively (but see Wissenburg, 2006, pp. 26–9). Ecologism, by contrast, insists that we are human *animals*, with all the implications that this brings in its train.

Conservatism

In the context of modern political thought, one of ecologism's signal and novel contributions is the idea that our *natural* condition affects and constrains our *political* condition. This is to say that – following on from the last remark in the previous section – our condition as human *animals* constrains us in ways similar to those experienced by all animals. There are differences, of course. Human animals are able to construct plans for life and strategies for realizing them in ways that most, if not all, other animals are incapable of doing. It is this capacity for autonomous thought and action on which liberal thought focuses, as we saw in the previous section, and this view of the human condition dominates contemporary politics.

Political ecologists do not reject this view entirely, but they do recommend that it be tempered by a hard-headed look at our natural circumstances. The lesson of the limits to growth thesis, as we saw in Chapter 3, is that human beings – like any other animal – have to consume natural resources, and that given that these resources are limited, human projects such as open-ended economic growth are impossible to sustain. In this regard, ecologism taps into a tradition that is closer to the conservative than the liberal sensibility. Thomas Malthus, for example, famous for his *An Essay on the Principle of Population* (1792), is widely regarded as contributing to the conservative tradition – largely due to his belief in 'the limits to social progress imposed by man's place in nature' (Wells, 1982, p. 2).

The intellectual history of the past two hundred years is littered with thinkers who have questioned the idea of progress as understood by modernity, but ecologism's reluctance to endorse modernity's notion of progress is not based on 'some view of the cyclic growth and degeneration of civilizations', nor on 'objections based on a philosophical and epistemological opposition to the notion of a "scientific" history' (as in rejections of the Marxist notion of progress), but on a 'particular vision of man's relationship to the physical and biological world: what could be called "the ecological viewpoint" ' (Wells, 1982, p. 3). This viewpoint is animated by the fundamentally conservative thought that 'the basic political question – "what should be done?" – depends on an account of what *can* be done' (ibid., p. 15). Conservatives generally oppose the Enlightenment view that humans can control their environment, and while political ecologists obviously have to believe that a modicum of control is possible, they will probably agree that human beings' determination to 'interfere' with nature is a part cause of our environmental problems. As Gray graphically puts it: 'Most people today think they belong to a species that can be master of its own destiny. This is faith, not science' (Gray, 2002, p. 3).

In ecologism, this account of what can be done turns on an understanding of human beings' place in nature. Moreover, the guiding idea of political ecology is that this is an *ecological* place rather than an *evolutionary* place, with all the implications that this entails. Most particularly, the ecological view talks of 'climax states' of relative stability, while the evolutionists' motif is that of 'progress'. Malthus' ecological view was superseded by that of Darwin and Wallace, whose ideas were grasped with alacrity by progressive thinkers such as Marx, who:

> welcomed the new biological outlook and the support it gave to an evolutionary – and by implication, progressive – view of human society. The idea of general, and perhaps unlimited, progress so strongly attacked by Malthus had been restored as a dominant theme in social and political theory.
>
> (Wells, 1982, p. 12)

With the restoration of the ecological idea in politics, battle with the evolutionary view of political progress has once again been joined.

Luke Martell has summarized the connections between radical green and conservative thinking in the following way:

> Some greens urge humans to be more humble and accommodating before nature, adapting to its laws and rhythms and putting less emphasis on exercising control over their environment and manipulating it to their own advantage. They are often sceptical and critical of Enlightenment ideas about the capacity of human rationality and the commitment to progress and innovation.
>
> (Martell, 1994, p. 140)

These are all recognizably conservative notions, and each one amounts to useful ammunition for those who would claim that ecologism and conservatism are fundamentally similar ideologies.

So similar, indeed, that a sustained attempt has been made by John Gray, sometime supporter of Thatcherite liberal conservatism but now an advocate of a more sceptical conservatism, to appropriate political ecology for the conservative cause (Gray, 1993b). Roger Scruton is another who argues that 'conservatism and environmentalism are natural bedfellows' (Scruton, 2006, p. 8), and he – like Gray – asks us not to equate conservatism with 'the ideology of free enterprise, and free enterprise as an assault on the earth's resources' (Scruton, 2006, p. 7). So, just as there are many liberalisms so there are many conservatisms, and some are more 'compatible' with environmental thought than others. Gray urges us to reject 'the self-image of the Greens as inheritors of the radical protest movements of earlier times, and as making common cause with contemporary radical movements, such as feminism and anti-colonialism' (ibid., p. 124). On the contrary, 'Far from having a natural home on the Left, concern for the integrity of the common environment, human as well as ecological, is most in harmony with the outlook of traditional conservatism of the British and European varieties' (ibid.; and see Scruton, 2006), and:

> Many of the central conceptions of traditional conservatism have a natural congruence with Green concerns: the Burkean idea of the social contract, not as agreement among anonymous ephemeral individuals, but as a compact between the generations of the living, the dead and those yet unborn; Tory scepticism about progress, and awareness of its ironies and illusions; conservative resistance to untried novelty and large-scale social experiments; and, perhaps

most especially, the traditional conservative tenet that individual flourishing can occur only in the context of forms of common life.
(Gray, 1993b, p. 124)

To these similarities, Gray adds the observation that 'both Greens and conservatives consider risk-aversion the path of prudence when new technologies, or new social practices, have consequences that are large and unpredictable, and, most especially, when they [*sic*] are unquantifiable but potentially catastrophic risks associated with intervention' (Gray, 1993b, p. 137). This is the Greens' 'precautionary principle' for decision-making in all but name – widely advocated in recent debates regarding the experimental planting of genetically modified crops, and supported by many political conservatives. Scruton sees a related link between environmental thinking and conservatism in the idea of the 'maintenance of the social ecology' (Scruton, 2006, p. 8). By this he means the duty of the current generation to pass on our social and ecological inheritance – of which we are the 'temporary trustees' (ibid.). He also believes that there is a link between the idea of local loyalties that is present in some conservative thinking, and the localism of much of the green agenda. 'There is no evidence that global political institutions have done anything to limit global entropy', he writes (ibid., p. 16). Thus he finds it surprising that greens have not followed their localism to its logical conclusion: i.e. the conservative view that we 'must retain what we can of the loyalties that attach us to our territory, and make of that territory a home' (ibid.). Conservatives are suspicious of cosmopolitan rootlessness, and suspicious of it when they see it in green globalists such as George Monbiot (2004). Scruton makes the point that rooted localism should appeal to greens on the grounds that it solves the 'motivation problem': that of finding a non-egotistic motive which may be elicited in ordinary members of society and relied upon to serve the long-term ecological goal (Scruton, 2006, p. 13).

The evidence for congruence between radical political ecology and conservatism, then, seems strong, but there are a number of areas where the relationship is severely strained, and others still where it cannot be said to exist at all. We can begin with Gray's 'traditional conservative tenet that individual flourishing can occur only in the context of forms of common life' (Gray, 1993b, p. 124), and that this is an idea shared by 'Green theory' (ibid., p. 136). But just what is this 'common life', and is it the same for political ecologists and for conservatives? From a conservative point of view, Gray says that people's 'deepest need is a home, a network of common practices and inherited traditions that confers on them the blessing of a settled identity' (ibid., p. 125). The common life of which he speaks is therefore defined in primarily *historical* and *cultural* terms as expressed through *tradition*. There are indeed radical greens for whom culture and history are very important. Some of the resistance to road-building programmes, for instance, is based on a belief in the cultural significance of features of the land which are destroyed by building contractors. My own view, though, is that valuing 'nature' in the currency of 'culture' in this way is precisely what distances *conservative* defences of nature from *political-ecological* ones. The political ecologist sees value in nature in itself, and if this value derives from history at all, it is *natural* history that counts, and not *human* history in the form of tradition and culture.

This is as much as to say that the 'common life' of which radical greens speak is an ontological and moral one that crosses species boundaries. It is important for Gray that common cultural, conservative forms:

> cannot be created anew for each generation. We are not like the butterfly, whose generations are unknown to each other; we are a familial and historical species, for whom the past must have authority (that of memory) if we are to have identity.
>
> (Gray, 1993b, p. 124)

But the moral and ontological common life of political ecologists *can* be created anew for each generation through the intellectual effort of grounding inter-species responsibility in a thoroughgoing naturalism that recognizes the implications of our being human *animals*.

Thus the ecocentrism of radical greenery sets it apart from conservatism just as it sets it apart from all other modern political ideologies. The only time Gray mentions anthropocentrism, the *bête noire* of the political ecologist, is in the following context: 'Green theory is an invaluable corrective of the Whiggish, anthropocentric, technological optimism by which all the modernist political religions are animated' (Gray, 1993b, p. 175). There is no evidence adduced, though, to suggest that traditional conservatism is anything other than as irredeemably anthropocentric as other political ideologies. Where conservative defences of the non-human natural world exist, they are usually rooted in romanticism rather than in an appreciation of the independent moral standing of non-human beings that animates much radical green thought.

The second point at which we should interrogate Gray's agenda is on the apparently unassailable point regarding intergenerational relations. It is true that conservatism, unlike any other political ideology with the exception of contemporary liberalism, talks of 'a compact between the generations of the living, the dead and those yet unborn' (Gray, 1993b, p. 124), and that intergenerational responsibility is a crucial feature of the political-ecological agenda. Edmund Burke, the 'father of British conservatism' whom Gray paraphrases here, and whom Roger Scruton also recognizes as a potential source of inspiration for greens (Scruton, 2006, p. 10), puts it like this:

> one of the first and most leading principles on which the common-wealth and the laws are consecrated, is lest the temporary posses-sors and life-renters in it, unmindful of what they have received from their ancestors, or of what is due to their posterity, should act as if they were the entire masters; that they should not think it amongst their rights to cut off the entail, or commit waste on the inheritance, by destroying at their pleasure the whole original fabric of their society; hazarding to leave to those who come after them, a ruin instead of an habitation – and teaching these successors as little to respect their contrivances as they had themselves respected the institutions of their forefathers. By this unprincipled facility of changing the state as often, and as much, and in as many ways as there are floating fancies or fashions, the whole chain and continu-ity of the commonwealth would be broken. No one generation could link with the other. Men would become little better than the flies of a summer.
>
> (Burke, 1790/1982, pp. 192–3)

What is striking about these remarks is that the generations in which Burke is most interested are past generations – those from whom we inherit what we have and to whom we owe some obligation of preserva-tion. The green view of intergenerational obligation is rather different to this: most obviously, the generations that usually interest political ecologists are *future* generations. One thing the current generation can be sure of, they say, is that our actions will affect the conditions under which future people live their lives, and this generates a responsibility for us of which other political ideologies have no conception. Conserva-tism is interested in the conserving and preserving *of the past*; ecologism is interested in conserving and preserving *for the future*. Herein lies a signal difference between the conservative and ecological political imaginations. (Political ecologists might do well to bear in mind, though, Burke's aphoristic warning that 'People will not look forward to posterity, who never look backward to their forefathers' (Burke, 1790/1982, p. 119).)

The third difference between conservatism and ecologism is rooted in disputes about the nature and relevance of 'imperfection'. It is a conservative commonplace that human beings are irredeemably flawed in their nature, and that political aspirations should reflect this. This is to say that political projects aimed at perfecting society will founder on the rock of unalterable human shortcomings and weaknesses. In this regard, political aspirations need to be drawn up within well-defined limits. As we have seen, the language of limits is the language of ecologism as well as of conservatism:

> The earth is finite. Growth of anything physical, including the human population and its cars, buildings and smokestacks, cannot continue forever. . . . The limits to growth are limits to the ability of the planetary *sources* to provide those streams of materials and energy, and limits to the ability of the planetary *sinks* to absorb the pollution and waste.
>
> (Meadows *et al.*, 1992, pp. 8–9)

Gray refers to sentiments of this sort as evidence of an anti-Utopian sensibility that is common to both conservatism and ecologism (Gray, 1993b, p. 127). Burkean conservatism and political ecology (as I have been describing it) seem to be as one in their opposition to the hubristic carelessness expressed in Utopian talk of 'indefinite malleability'. The anti-Utopian's principal target, says Krishan Kumar, is hubris (Kumar, 1987, p. 103), and so is the political ecologist's. If Utopians believe uncompromisingly that '[T]here are no fundamental barriers or obstacles to man's earthly perfection [and that] scarcity can be overcome' (Kumar, 1991, p. 29), then the gap between Utopians and political ecologists is as wide as it can be: scarcity is the most basic and unalterable feature of the human condition so far as political ecologists are concerned (for a full and entertaining analysis of the relationship between Utopianism and political ecology, see De Geus, 1999). So, Utopianism demands malleability, and political ecology's interpretation of the human condition denies its possibility. Does this apparent opposition to Utopianism imply a deep congruence between conservatism and ecologism?

I think not. The crucial and relevant distinction here is between malleability of the human *condition* and the malleability of human *nature*. It is perfectly possible to believe that the human condition is fixed, while human nature is not, and this is indeed what political ecologists believe. Political ecologists do not possess the 'pessimistic and determinist view of human nature' which is common to conservatives and anti-Utopians (Kumar, 1987, p. 100); nor do they believe in 'original sin' (ibid.), if by this we mean unredeemable sin. Tim Hayward believes that 'one cannot reasonably assume that people are generally motivated to do other than what they take to be in their own interest' (Hayward, 1998, p. 7), and proceeds to build his own environmental political theory on the foundations of a reinterpretation of human self-interest that will include respect for '(at least some significant classes of) nonhuman beings' (ibid., p. 118). What makes this an environmental political theory rather than an ecological one is its basis in *human* self-interest, but political ecologists will also refuse the belief that self-interest itself is the only credible, or possible, human motivation. Thus while political ecologists believe that there are (more or less) fixed limits to production, consumption and waste, they have a Utopian sense of what is possible within those limits. Unlike conservatives, radical greens believe that human beings are capable of transformation; that they can, if they wish, abandon the acquisitive, instrumental and use-related relationship with the natural environment that dominates the modern imagination.

Acutely, John Gray observes that what he calls 'green conservatism' is an instance of an:

> ancient paradox, with which the modern world abounds in examples, that conservatives cannot help becoming radicals, when current practice embodies the hubristic and careless projects of recent generations, or has been distorted by technological innovations whose consequences for human well-being have not been weighed.
>
> (Gray, 1993b, p. 128)

In the current environmental climate conservatives may well find themselves opposed to much of the status quo, but radical conservatives are not the same as radical greens, and on at least the three counts discussed above the gap between the conservative and radical green agenda so far as the environment is concerned is wide and deep.

Socialism

In the context of socialism and the largely successful assault launched on it by the right over the past twenty years, the last thing it needed, so the argument goes, was a challenge to its hegemony towards the left of the political spectrum. Early responses to the environmental movement from the socialist left were certainly hostile and often focused on its middle-class nature, either so as to illustrate its marginal relevance to the working class in particular and thus to socialism in general, or, more aggressively, to cast it in the role of a positive distraction from the fundamental battles still to be fought between capital and labour. Either way, the nascent green movement was generally presented as a blip on the screen of radical politics, which would probably soon disappear and which certainly had nothing to say to the left that was worth listening to.

In the pages that follow I shall set out what I consider to be the principal socialist criticisms of green politics, and then show the ways in which socialists sensitive to the ecological position have reinterpreted their own tradition so as to accommodate it. The debate between ecologism and socialism continues to be acrimonious at times and often there is no debate at all. Jonathon Porritt and Nicholas Winner, for example, refer to David Pepper's presentation of the green movement as 'deeply conservative' and 'reactionary', and as 'just so much angry sputtering from worn-out ideologues who have long since lost touch with the real world' (1988, p. 256). Sandy Irvine and Alec Ponton pointedly characterize socialism as 'fair shares in extinction' (1988, p. 142). Elsewhere, though, and particularly in the work of Raymond Williams (n.d.), Boris Frankel (1987), James O'Connor (1996), Peter Dickens (1992) and Ted Benton (1993, 1996), great strides have been taken (on the socialist side at least) to come to terms with the green perspective without abandoning original socialist impulses. It is also true to say that the growing importance of social justice issues in environmental thought and practice – the environmental justice movement in the USA, and the so-called 'environmentalism of the poor' in both developed and developing nations (Martinez-Alier, 2002) – have brought the traditionally leftist issues of distribution and justice much closer to the centre of ecological ground than used to be the case.

The first area of contention between ecologism and socialism is over the source of the ills of contemporary society. Socialists identify capitalism as that source, while political ecologists are much more likely to refer to 'industrialism'. We know by now that one of the reasons why the green movement considers itself to be 'beyond left and right' is because it believes this traditional spectrum of opposition to be inscribed in a more fundamental context of agreement: a 'super-ideology' called 'industrialism'. Greens 'stress the similarities between capitalist and socialist countries' (Porritt and Winner, 1988, p. 256) in that they are both held to believe that the needs of their respective populations are best satisfied by maximizing economic growth. The equating of capitalism with socialism engendered by the identification of 'industrialism' is the aspect of green thinking attacked most often by its socialist critics, and Joe Weston's 'It is time that greens accepted that it is capitalism rather than industrialism *per se* which is at the heart of the problems they address' (1986, p. 5) is a typical refrain.

Socialists make remarks like this, in the first place, not because they don't agree with ecologists that environmental decay is upon us but because they argue that it is capitalism's use of industry to produce for profit and not for need, rather than 'industry' itself, which causes the problems. 'Capitalism,' writes David Pepper, 'is about the accumulation of capital through producing commodities.' The capitalist dynamic involves periodic crises of overproduction which are resolved 'by creating new wants, and by extending the system globally to new consumers in new markets'. This dynamic of production and consumption means that '[C]apitalism *must* inherently if not constantly and explicitly, degrade and destroy that part of its means of production that comes from "nature" ' (Pepper, 1993a, p. 430). This is as much as to say that capitalism is a precondition for the politics of ecology.

James O'Connor also famously argues, like Marx, that capitalism may be digging its own grave, but for reasons that have as much to do with a contradiction between the forces/relations of production and the *conditions* of production as with the time-honoured Marxist contradiction between the forces and relations of production themselves. O'Connor calls this the 'second contradiction' of capitalism, according to which 'the combined power of capitalist production relations and productive forces self-destruct by impairing or destroying rather than reproducing their own conditions' (O'Connor, 1996, p. 206). Examples of such impairment, says O'Connor, are global warming, acid rain, salinization and pesticide poisoning, all of which, he avers, threaten profit-making. This second contradiction, like the first, gives rise to opposition, not this time in the form of the labour movement, but in the form of the new social movements which harbour the potential for transcending the contradictions that give rise to them. The 'second contradiction' thesis has given rise to a great deal of comment, particularly in the journal *Capitalism, Nature, Socialism* (and see Benton (1996, Part 3) for an extended discussion), and in our context it illustrates the yawning gap between greens, who argue that industrialism is the root of environmental degradation, and ecological Marxists, who affirm that capitalism is both the cause of the environmental crisis and the horizon that needs to be transcended if we are to deal with it.

Radical greens will probably accept that a fundamental break with capitalism is indeed a necessary condition for restoring environmental integrity, but they do not see it as a sufficient condition, particularly when they point to former communist countries which had some of the worst environmental records in the entire world. Socialists respond by pointing out that none of these countries were socialist in the sense they want to ascribe to the word (Miliband, 1994), and that this is because they have developed the same 'form of demand for material goods' as the capitalist nations, in competition with them. In this sense, 'capitalism permeates the whole globe' (Weston, 1986, p. 4). As Bahro wrote:

> We have precisely learned that the Russian revolution did not manage to break with the *capitalist horizon of development of productive forces*. We have seen how right round the globe it is one and the same technology that has triumphed.
>
> (Bahro, 1982, p. 131)

In this way socialists side-step the green invitation to consider the environmental problems suffered by socialist countries and to draw the conclusion that there is little to choose between socialist and capitalist management of industry (from the environment's point of view). They then suggest that a truly socialist society would produce for need and not for profit, and that consideration of the environment would be integral to policy formation because the 'traditional humanist concerns of socialism' inevitably involve consideration of human/non-human nature interaction (Pepper, 1993a, p. 438).

However, in one important respect (from a socialist point of view) the issue is not over what a socialist society might or might not do, but that the green refusal to recognize capitalism as the root of the problem renders ecology incapable of fighting its battles in the right places. If from an environmental perspective the socialist view of capitalism is correct, then ecologism's best way forward is to confront the capitalist manifestation of industrialism rather than the many-headed hydra: industrialism itself.

Joe Weston reminds us that this would involve the restatement of traditional socialist principles and practices, on the basis that 'what we find is that behind virtually all environmental problems, both physical and social, is poverty' (1986, p. 4). Pepper makes a similar point: '[A]s the 1992 Earth Summit in Rio showed, the most fundamental issues in global environmental politics revolve around social justice, wealth distribution and ownership and control of the means of production, particularly land' (1993a, p. 429). Many socialists will then analyse phenomena such as deforestation from just this point of view – the fundamental problem is much more one of inequitable land distribution (which produces the slash-and-burn farmers) and structural poverty (which produces periodic but highly damaging jungle gold rushes), than it is one of an insatiable and environmentally insensitive desire to eat hamburgers. From this point of view, environmentalist (or even ecologist) strategies will be found wanting: Weston suggests that:

> Saving hedgerows does not confront capitalism in the same way as do issues relating to poverty; poverty is, after all, of crucial importance to capitalism and has to be maintained in order to preserve the balance of power in market relationships.
>
> (Weston, 1986, p. 156)

Poverty, then, is at the root of most environmental problems and a far-reaching redistribution of wealth is the solution. Crucially, an attack on poverty would constitute an attack on capitalism, and would therefore be a blow against the root cause of environmental decay.

The green question now might be: Why should a redistribution of wealth bring about improvements in the environment? Much evidently turns on just what 'environment' one is talking about, and it is a socialist strategy with respect to ecologism to accuse it of too narrow a definition of the term. It is probably true that radical redistributions of wealth would improve the sanitation, housing and food of millions of dispossessed poor both here and in the so-called Third World, and that this would constitute a significant improvement in their environment. But it is hard to see how a redistribution of wealth on its own would address green warnings about the unsustainability of present industrial practices. One can perfectly well imagine a world in which incomes between and within countries were more or less the same, but which still subscribed to the view that there were no limits to industrial growth. Indeed, this is precisely the world that the dominant themes of socialism have advertised since its inception, and it is the reason why greens are wary of attacks on capitalism that have no ecological content. In this sense, Weston talks past the green movement rather than to it when he says:

> The problems with which most people are now faced are not related to 'nature' at all: they are related to poverty and the transfer of wealth and resources from the poor to an already wealthy minority of the Earth's population.
>
> (Weston, 1986, p. 14)

My own view is that the 'justice' and 'environment' agendas are related in the way that the circles in Venn diagrams are related. That is to say, there are areas of common concern but it is a mistake to regard them as wholly and completely mapping on to one another. The power-ful 'environmental justice' movement in the United States is often deployed as evidence that the environmental and justice movements can sing from the same hymn sheet, but a close examination of the US movement's aspirations shows that it is more concerned with human justice than with environmental protection. Malcolm Dowie, for example, has written that 'The central concern of the new movement is human health' (Dowie, 1995, p. 127), and while there is obviously a link between a healthy environment and human health, concern for the latter will not cover all the objectives of political ecologists. Similarly, Laura Pulido has noted Pezzoli's important observation that 'commu-nities engaged in what appear to be environmentally related struggles at times may not be committed to an environmental agenda' (Pulido, 1996, p. 16). This needs to be taken into account by those who argue that the environmental and justice movements are as one (the issue of the relationship between justice and the environment is addressed in detail in Dobson (1998, 1999)).

A second point of disagreement between socialists and political ecologists concerns 'the environment' itself. It transpired above that Joe Weston's argument that a redistribution of wealth would help solve environmental problems was based upon an interpretation of 'environment' not usually associated with the green movement. In his opinion, greens have policed the word into meaning 'nature': 'the prime concern of the greens is indeed ecology and "nature", which means that other, far more immediate environmental problems are neglected' (Weston, 1986, p. 2). In this context it is indulgent and irresponsible for the green movement to concentrate its 'not inconsiderable resources upon protecting hedgerows, butterflies and bunny rabbits' (ibid., p. 12) while the day-to-day built environments of large numbers of people are in such urgent need of reconstruction.

Sections of the green movement appear to have taken this kind of criticism on board – witness the Friends of the Earth's 'Cities for People' campaign – but there is still a sense in which Weston's critique speaks past the movement rather than to it. Greens have a very good reason for referring so often to the biospherical environment: they are concerned for its survival as a long-term supporter of human and non-human life. From this perspective (eco)socialists are right to ask greens to reassess their understanding of 'the environment', but wrong to ask them to focus on inner city environments if the recipes for them are not placed in the context of the search for a sustainable society.

Socialists (and others) will argue, in any case, that there is no such thing as 'nature' unmediated by human beings, and therefore no great difference between the urban environment and the environment created by farmed land or deforestation: social relations and the capitalist mode of production that underpins them 'produce' the environment. Green exhortations to 'protect' or 'conserve' the environment betray the unfounded impression that there is an 'untouched' nature alongside the areas already corrupted by human beings, and it is this untouched nature that receives the movement's greatest attention. Pepper writes that '[T]here is not a self-contained "humanity" counterposed to and ever battling with a self-contained "non-human" world' but rather each is 'part of a unity that is composed of "contradictory" opposites' (Pepper, 1993a, p. 440), and that the ecocentric view regarding our supposed alienation from nature is internally self-contradictory, since it 'rests on a *dualistic* conception of the human–nature relationship: a conception it is supposed to reject' (ibid., p. 443).

Again, I think that this speaks past the radical green point rather than to it. Both Marxism and deep ecology are types of monism, of course, but all monists separate out parts of the common substance for different purposes. It is no contradiction to hold a monist view regarding the nature of things and to simultaneously distinguish between human and non-human nature (indeed, Pepper himself continually does so). Even Spinoza, perhaps the most thoroughgoing monist of them all, allows for two 'attributes' (thought and extension) of a single 'substance' (Spinoza, 1677/1955). Marxists will make the distinction within *their* monism in order, then, to theorize the dialectical relation between the social and 'natural' (nearly always, for socialists, in inverted commas) worlds. Deep ecologists will distinguish within *their* monism, for example, so as to talk of the ethical relationship which should hold between human and non-human nature.

Socialists, in any case, will argue that an awareness of the social construction of the environment would have three effects: first, it would lead to a healthy widening of green activity; second, it would promote an understanding of the capitalist roots of environmental decay – both in the countryside and in the cities; and third, it would improve the chances of the green movement obtaining a mass following.

This latter point needs some explanation. Joe Weston argues that the green movement as currently constituted is an expression of the ennui of a particular section of the middle classes – the professional, educated section. Green politics is 'an attempt to protect the values – rather than simply the economic privilege – of a social group which rejects the market-orientated politics of capitalism and the materialistic analysis made of it by Marxists' (Weston, 1986, p. 27). These values are reflected, partly, in the 'green' definitions of the environment most often advanced by the movement, referred to above. To the extent that this is 'a political perspective which is specific to a particular social group' (ibid., p. 28) and, moreover, a social group that is of limited size, no mass movement can be formed around it. On this reading ecologism will not progress beyond its minority, subordinate status until it speaks to the kinds of environmental problems suffered by masses of people, and 'that means developing ways to conceptualise and represent ecological issues in ways that speak to the aspirations of the working class movement' (Harvey, 1993, p. 48). This it will never do, suggests Weston, unless it breaks out of its middle-class laager and recognizes that 'rather than conserving the environment in which most people now live, the inner city and the shanty town need destroying' (Weston, 1986, pp. 14–15).

A third faultline between socialists and political ecologists may be found in disputes over the issue of 'limits to growth'. Indeed, the most instructive test to carry out on would-be green socialists is to see how far they have accepted the fundamental green position that there are material limits to productive growth. Some have done so completely, and in the process would appear significantly to have reassessed the content of their socialism. Rudolf Bahro, for example, commented when he was still a socialist that he found it 'quite atrocious that there are Marxists who contest the finite scope of the earth's exploitable crust' (1982, p. 60). We now know that Bahro's dwelling on thoughts like this led him to abandon socialism entirely. Not so Joe Weston and Raymond Williams, but they would probably nevertheless agree with the following remarks:

> I do not believe that anyone can read the extensive literature on the ecology crisis without concluding that its impact will oblige us to make changes in production and consumption of a kind, and on a scale, which will entail a break with the lifestyles and expectations that have become habitual in industrialized countries.
>
> (Ryle, 1988, p. 6)

Joe Weston certainly agrees, up to a point: 'it must be stressed that this rejection of green politics does not mean that we now believe that natural resources are infinite' (Weston, 1986, p. 4), and adds that the left can learn from the greens to call the project of 'perpetual industrial expansion' into question (ibid., p. 5). Raymond Williams, too, accepts the ecological position with respect to 'the central problem of this whole mode and version of production: an effective infinity of expansion in a physically finite world' (Williams, 1986, p. 214), and suggests that 'the orthodox abstraction of indefinitely expanded production – its version of "growth" – has to be considered again, from the beginning' (ibid., p. 215).

Others, though, such as David Pepper, find this sort of thing hard to swallow: Pepper is concerned 'not to abandon humanism by over-pandering to green assumptions about the "natural" limits to the transformation of nature' (Pepper, 1993a, p. 434). While Saral Sarkar, in his extended defence of eco-socialism, calls these 'old illusions' (Sarkar, 1999, p. 197), David Harvey agrees with Pepper that the idea of natural limits is too simplistic and insufficiently dialectical. He suggests that:

> if we view 'natural resources' in the rather traditional geographical manner, as 'cultural, technological and economic appraisals of elements residing in nature and mobilised for particular social ends' . . . then 'ecoscarcity' means that we have not the will, wit or capacity to change our social goals, cultural modes, our technological mixes, or our form of economy and that we are powerless to modify 'nature' according to human requirements.
>
> (Harvey, 1993, p. 39)

Harvey's intention here is to damn political ecologists for their (imputed) belief that human beings are powerless in the face of a hostile natural world characterized by scarcity. Yet the intention is subverted upon the realization that political ecology is actually all about doing what Harvey claims political ecologists think is impossible. Political ecologists *do* think we have the 'will, wit and capacity to change our social goals, cultural modes' and so on. They even think that we have the power to 'modify "nature" according to human requirements' – the question is really over 'How much?', and a significant part of the answer is given, for political ecologists, by the fact that our actions take place under the sign of scarcity. This, in the end, is the 'brute fact' (for political ecologists) which Marxist critics seek to defuse through deployment of the sense of a *dialectical* relationship between human beings and the 'natural' world.

The reconsiderations of socialists like Williams seem to involve them in reconsidering socialism itself. Williams writes that 'any socialist should recognise the certainty that many of the resources at their present levels of use are going to run out' (Williams, n.d., p. 15), and that consequently socialists should rethink their traditional belief that the relief of poverty requires 'production, and more production' (ibid., p. 6). Mary Mellor turns this into an argument which could benefit socialism itself: 'Where resources are limited, the question of who benefits and who loses cannot be passed off as a byproduct of the "hidden hand of the market", or some personal failure of will, risk or effort. It is clearly revealed as a question of moral and political choices, of power relations and social justice' (Mellor, 2006, p. 37). In other words, scarcity puts social justice right at the heart of the debate. Promises of plenty, and the trickle-down of wealth from the rich to the poor, seem less persuasive in a limits to growth context. When the cake is of finite size, the question of how to divide it up fairly cannot be avoided. In this way, suggests Mellor, the green critique of 'growthism' and the socialist critique of social injustice come together productively. Mellor summarizes thus: 'Resources are not infinite; the rich are raising their levels of consumption on things such as sports utility vehicles while the poor are finding it harder to meet their needs' (Mellor, 2006, p. 45).

Of course, socialists have always argued for an equitable distribution of what is produced and in this sense Williams is consistent, but socialism has no dominant tradition of production itself being called into question, and this is what Williams is hinting at here. He appears to be rereading socialism when he refers to 'the pressure point on the whole existing capitalist mode of production' as 'the problem of resources' (n.d., p. 16). We will not find this kind of analysis of the weaknesses of capitalism in any of the dominant sources of socialist thought. To this degree, acceptance of the green position that there are limits to productive growth can have considerable repercussions with respect to the content of the socialism espoused by socialists.

One of the repercussions that stands out is a rethinking of the socialist tradition itself in the sense of emphasizing some aspects of it at the expense of others. Not surprisingly, it is decentralist, non-bureaucratic, non-productivist socialism to which writers like Williams most often refer, and the Utopian socialists and William Morris are those usually resurrected as evidence for its existence (Pepper: 1993a, pp. 431, 447, 449). Thus Rudolf Bahro suggested that 'we shall scarcely come up against any elements that have not already emerged in the writings of one or other of the old socialists, including of course the utopians' (Bahro, 1982, p. 126). By 1994 he was saying: 'If pushed hard I couldn't deny that I am a utopian socialist because so many of the elements of utopian socialism appear in my commune perspective' (1994, p. 235). Martin Ryle echoes this sentiment: 'utopian socialism would seem to be an obvious point of convergence between greens and socialists' (1988, p. 21), while Robin Cook, once Foreign Secretary in one of Tony Blair's governments, is more specific: 'the future of socialism may lie more with William Morris than with Herbert Morrison' (in Gould, 1988, p. 163), as is Raymond Williams: 'The writer who began to unite these diverse traditions, in British social thought, was William Morris' (n.d., p. 9).

From the other side, Jonathon Porritt accepts such genealogies too: 'My own personal points of familiarity and very close connection with the Left come from the early libertarian traditions, William Morris and so on, and from the anarchist tradition of left polities', and he adds a significant point: 'I think that form of decentralised socialism is some-thing that has had a pretty rough time in socialist politics during the course of this century' (Porritt, 1984b, p. 25).

What emerges from these exchanges is evidence for the selective way in which both socialists and ecologists refer to the socialist tradition. Usually, Porritt does not make the distinctions he makes above. He is keen to dissociate ecologism from socialism because he sees the latter as part of the old order, and so usually refers to it in its bureaucratic, productivist guise. To the extent that there is a decentralist tradition within socialism this is a disingenuous move, but it would be equally disingenuous for socialists to respond to the ecologists' challenge by arguing (suddenly) that William Morris is what real socialism is all about.

Sometimes socialists bend over too far backwards in their search for compatible characters. When David Pepper refers, for example, to a 'Kropotkin-Godwin-Owen' tradition (in Weston, 1986, p. 120), one wonders whether we are talking about socialism at all any more. At the very most there is only one socialist among those three, and, although Pepper does cover himself by positing an 'anarchist rather than central-ist' form of socialism (ibid., p. 115), the adjective 'anarchist' has the effect of divesting socialism of much of the resonance usually attrib-uted to it. But there is little to be gained from semantics. The important point is that claims for a convergence between socialism and ecology rest on the resurrection of a subordinate tradition within socialism. To this extent the question of whether or not socialism and political ecology are compatible cannot be answered without first asking: 'What kind of socialism?', and in the end the answer will turn on whether the Utopian/William Morris tradition argues for a sustainable society in anything resembling a modern green sense (Lee, 1989).

In conclusion, some socialists, under pressure from greens, will reassess the traditional goals of production and indiscriminate growth, they will seek to rescue subordinate strains in their political tradition and they may ponder the role of the working class in future political transformations. Greens themselves need to listen to the socialist cri-tique and to think harder about the relationship between capitalism and environmental degradation, about just what 'the environment' is, and about the potential for social change implicit in the identification of a social subject. In the end, Martin Ryle is probably right to identify political ecology and socialism as engaged on a 'converging critique': they both see capitalism as wasteful of resources in terms of production and consumption, and they both criticize it for its inegalitarian outcomes (1988, p. 48).

Feminism

Within feminism generally there is a discussion as to the best way for feminists to proceed: whether to seek equality with men on terms largely offered by men, or whether to focus on the differences between men and women and to seek to re-evaluate upwards the currently suppressed (supposed) characteristics of women. Beyond this distinction, some ecofeminists see ecofeminism as an opportunity to refuse the choice it implies and to opt, instead, for a refigured politics that goes beyond dualism. To the extent that ecofeminists subscribe to the 'difference' strategy, they do so not with a view to liberating women only but also with a view to encouraging men to adopt 'womanly' ways of thinking and acting, thus promoting healthier relationships between people in general, and also between people (but especially men) and the environment. In what follows, I shall take 'difference' ecofeminism to be the discussion's centre of gravity and develop the 'deconstructive' version through a critique of it.

'Difference' ecofeminism is built around three main ideas. In the first place, difference ecofeminists usually argue for the existence of values and ways of behaving that are primarily female in the sense of being more fundamentally possessed or exhibited by women rather than by men. These characteristics may be 'socially' or 'biologically' produced, and considerable importance attached to deciding which view is adopted. First, to the extent that ecofeminists would like to see men taking on these characteristics, they have to believe it is possible for them to do so. In other words, they cannot argue that it is necessary to be a woman to have such characteristics, although they might suggest that men cannot know what they are unless they listen to women telling them. Second, the belief that characteristics are biologically rooted is open to the charge of essentialism, and thereby to the accusation that such characteristics are unalterably attached to one or the other gender. If we then argue that some characteristics are undesirable, then the gender that has them is stuck with them: any possibility of 'progress' is undone. Associated with this belief is the idea that female values have, historically, been undervalued by patriarchy and that it is the 'difference' ecofeminist's task to argue for their positive re-evaluation. Of course, if there are female values and ways of behaving then there are also male values and ways of behaving. In asking that female traits be re-evaluated upwards, these ecofeminists do not necessarily demand that male traits be policed out of existence – rather they are likely to seek a balance of the two.

The second principle of difference ecofeminism is that the domination of nature is related to the domination of women, and that the structures of domination and the reasons for it are similar in both cases: 'The identity and destiny of women and nature are merged', write Andrée Collard and Joyce Contrucci (1988, p. 137). The third idea – related to and tying up the first two – is that women are closer than men to nature and are therefore potentially in the vanguard so far as developing sustainable ways of relating to the environment is concerned – '[E]cofeminists argue that women have a unique standpoint from which to address the ecological crisis' (Mellor, 1992b, p. 236). I shall expand on these three notions and show how some feminists have balked at the ecofeminist programme – and particularly the first point (in its essentialist form, at least) – because of what they believe to be its reactionary implications. In some ('deconstructive') hands this has led to a re(de)fining of ecofeminism; Val Plumwood, for example, argues that what is common to all 'ecological feminisms' is no more than a rejection of the belief in the 'inferiority of the sphere of women and of nature' (1993, p. 33). It is what one does next, having rejected this belief, that distinguishes 'difference' and 'deconstructive' feminism.

With respect to values and behaviour, Ynestra King writes that 'We [i.e. women] learn early to observe, attend and nurture' (1983, p. 12), and Stephanie Leland refers to 'feminine impulses' such as 'belonging, relationship and letting be' (1983, p. 71). These are the kinds of characteristics (sometimes referred to, as I have already remarked, as constitutive of the 'feminine principle') usually ascribed to women by ecofeminists, and, although Val Plumwood rightly suggests that the devaluation of male modes of thought and behaviour does not necessarily entail the affirmation of female traits, my impression is that 'difference' ecofeminists usually do make such affirmations.

In support of her position, Plumwood writes: 'What seems to be involved here is often not so much an affirmation of feminine connectedness with and closeness to nature as distrust and rejection of the masculine character model of disconnectedness from and domination of the natural order' (1988, p. 19). But this appears to be contradicted by, for example, Judith Plant's assertion that 'Women's values, centred around life-giving, must be revalued, elevated from their once subordinate role' (n.d., p. 7), and by Hazel Henderson's advocacy of reassessment:

> Eco-feminism . . . values motherhood and the raising and parenting of children and the maintaining of comfortable habitats and cohesive communities as the most highly productive work of society – rather than the most de-valued, as under patriarchal values and economics where the tasks are ignored and unpaid.
>
> (Henderson, 1983, p. 207)

It is certainly the case that male values – for example, discrimination, domination and hierarchy (Leland, 1983, pp. 68–9), and 'a disregard for the housekeeping requirements of nature' (Freer, 1983, p. 132) – are seen as positively harmful if pursued to the exclusion of other values. In this context Jean Freer scathingly characterizes the space programme as an exercise in which 'Plastic bags full of men's urine were sent to circulate endlessly in the cosmos', and then asks, 'How can they claim to be caring?' (Freer, 1983, p. 132). Ynestra King concludes:

> We see the devastation of the earth and her beings by the corporate warriors, and the threat of nuclear annihilation by the military warriors as feminist concerns. It is the same masculinist mentality which would deny us our right to our own bodies and our own sexuality, and which depends on multiple systems of dominance and state power to have its way.
>
> (King, 1983, p. 10)

There are several difficulties – apart from political-strategic ones – associated with the assertion of female values and the desire to upgrade them. To begin with there is the notorious problem of identifying female traits in the first place: we could only know what a representative sample of 'female' women would look like if we already had some idea of what female traits were, but then the traits would be announced a priori, as it were, rather than deduced through observation. Is it not also true to say that some men exhibit 'female' characteristics and some women 'male' characteristics, in which case such characteristics are not founded in gender as such but in, for example, socialization working on gender?

Next, there is a series of what might be considered negative traits, such as subservience, associated with women by women (including, of course, a large number of feminists). If we are to use woman as the yardstick for valued characteristics we are left with no room to judge what we might suspect to be negative traits in what is regarded as typically female behaviour. We can regard subservience as negative only if we value its opposite positively and this will mean valuing positively a characteristic normally associated with men. In other words, how are we to decide which are positive and which are negative forms of thought or behaviour? We may not want to say that all female characteristics are positive and neither do we want to argue, it seems, that all male traits are negative. However, the generalized assertion that female traits are positive allows us no discriminatory purchase.

A related way of approaching this question may be to ask: 'Given that both male and female characteristics have been developed under patriarchy, what gives us the grounds for suggesting that either form is worthwhile?' The separatist feminist might say that what ecofeminists refer to as healthy traits are as tainted with patriarchy as unhealthy ones, and that the only way to find out what genuine female characteristics are like (if they exist at all) would be to disengage from patriarchy as far as possible, and to let such traits 'emerge'. As Mary Mellor points out: 'Feminists have long argued that until women have control over their own fertility, sexuality and economic circumstances, we will never know what women "really" want or are' (1992b, p. 237).

'Difference' ecofeminists do not usually adopt this strategy: they simply identify some traits that they argue most women already have, they value them positively, and then suggest that both we (all of us) and therefore the planet would be better-off if we adopted such traits:

> Initially it seems obvious that the ecofeminist and peace argument is grounded on accepting a special feminine connectedness with nature or with peaceful characteristics, and then asserting this as a rival ideal of the human (or as part of such an ideal).
>
> (Plumwood, 1988, p. 22)

Plumwood's refusal of the 'obvious' is what sets her and others (see e.g., King, 1989) on the road to 'deconstructive' ecofeminism. She argues against the idea of accepting the feminine and rejecting the masculine (her terms) and goes instead for rejecting them both. This is part of a sophisticated argument locating her feminist strategy within a general attack on dualistic thinking (Plumwood, 1993, 2006). She argues that:

> Women have faced an unacceptable choice within patriarchy with respect to their ancient identity as nature. They either accept it (naturalism) or reject it (and endorse the dominant mastery

model). Attention to the dualistic problematic shows a way of resolving this dilemma. Women must be treated as just as fully human and as fully part of human culture as men. But both men and women must challenge the dualised conception of human identity and develop an alternative culture which fully recognises *human* identity as continuous with, not alien from, nature.

(Plumwood, 1993, p. 36)

In an earlier form this was presented as a 'degendered' model for the human being which:

presupposes that selection of characteristics is made on the basis of independent criteria of worth. Criteria selected will often be associated with one gender rather than another, and perhaps may turn out to resemble more closely the characteristic feminine rather than the characteristic masculine traits. But they're degendered in the sense that they won't be selected because of their connection with one gender rather than the other, but on the basis of independent considerations.

(Plumwood, 1988, p. 23)

This project would be hard to complete and its implications cannot be followed through here; among other things it would have to ask what such 'independent considerations' would look like and what it would mean to be 'fully human'. Suffice to say that Plumwood's feminism:

would represent women's willingness to move to a further stage in their relations with nature, beyond that of powerless inclusion in nature, beyond that of reaction against their old exclusion from culture, and towards an active, deliberate and reflective positioning of themselves *with* nature against a destructive and dualising form of culture.

(Plumwood, 1993, p. 39; emphasis in original)

My principal interest in Plumwood's position here is that it enables us to mark her off from what I understand to be a pair of basic 'difference' ecofeminist principles: that character traits may be identified as either male or female, and that the female traits are those that currently most obviously need to be reasserted, both for our sake and for the planet's. Plumwood herself distances her position from this sort of ecofeminism by referring to her project as a 'critical ecological feminism' (see e.g. Plumwood, 1993, p. 39), or as a theory of 'hybridity' (Plumwood, 2006).

This renaming of positions within or around the ecofeminist project is often a sign of unhappiness with the 'difference' feminist position: Mary Mellor (for example) describes hers as a 'feminist green politics' (1992a, p. 238) rather than an ecofeminism.

It is specific to both ecofeminisms to which I refer here that their advocates see them as good not only for women but also for the non-human natural world. Ecofeminists identify a relationship between the subjection of nature by men and the subjection of women by men. The nature of this link may take two forms: weak and strong. In the weak case, patriarchy is seen as producing and reproducing its domination across a whole range of areas and anything that comes under its gaze will be subjected to it. The link between women and nature in this case is simply that they are two objects for patriarchal domination, without the subjection of one necessarily helping to produce and reproduce the subjection of the other. Thus Christine Thomas quotes Rosemary Radford Reuther: 'Women must see that there can be no liberation for them and no solution to the ecological crisis within a society whose fundamental model of relationships tends to be one of domination' (Thomas, 1983, p. 162).

Judith Plant makes a similar point: 'we are helping to create an awareness of domination at all levels' (Plant, n.d., p. 4), and then continues with a thought that gives a flavour of the strong link sometimes identified between women and nature in the sense of their common subjection: 'Once we understand the historical connections between women and nature and their subsequent oppression, we cannot help but take a stand on war against nature' (ibid.). This latter comment points to connections between the exploitation of women and of nature that go beyond their merely being subject to the generalized gaze of patriarchy.

Plant is suggesting that historical study of their exploitation leads to the conclusion that patriarchy has posited a particular identity between the two that produces and reproduces their common subjection. In this sense, argue the ecofeminists, the struggle for women's liberation must be a struggle for nature as well and, likewise, the despoiling of nature should not be viewed as separate from the exploitation of women. Both have their roots in patriarchy: 'We believe that a culture against nature is a culture against women' (King, 1983, p. 11).

Thus the dualism against which theorists such as Plumwood argue is not only the dualism of men and women but also of humans and nature: 'The dominant position that is deeply entrenched in Western culture constructs a great gulf or dualism between humans on the one side and animals and nature generally on the other' (Plumwood, 2006, p. 56). Plumwood is as critical of deep ecologists who would oppose human beings and nature as she is of essentialist ecofeminists who would oppose men and women on the basis of immutably gendered characteristics. To this degree her theory of 'hybridity' has the same function as the radical democratization of relations between human beings and nature that we saw Bruno Latour arguing for towards the end of Chapter 2. It is wrong, she says, to see concern for human beings as 'shallow' and concern for nature as 'deep' (ibid., p. 62). The problem with deep ecology, she says, is not its focus on nature but 'the way it goes on to marginalize the human side, and the many hybrid forms of environmental activism that are concerned with environmental justice and with situating human life ecologically' (ibid., p. 63). Likewise it would be wrong to think that all concern for non-human life is some-how 'deep': 'Some non-human concerns can be decidedly shallow,' she writes, 'for example those that automatically privilege human pets like cats and dogs over other animals' (ibid.). In sum, the double task of hybridity is, first, to 'ecologize' the human being (to locate human beings in their preconditional ecological context), and second, to resituate human beings in ethical terms (ibid., p. 64).

Those who suggest a strong link argue that patriarchy confers similar characteristics on nature and on women and then systematically devalues them. Thus both are seen as irrational, uncertain, hard to control. Janet Biehl writes:

> In Western culture, men have traditionally justified their domination of women by conceptualising them as 'closer to nature' than them-selves. Women have been ideologically dehumanised and deration-alised by men; called more chaotic, more mysterious in motivation, more emotional, more moist, even more polluted.
>
> (Biehl, 1988, p. 12)

Just when this began to occur is a matter of dispute among ecofemi-nists. Basically, the debate is between two groups – 'those who locate the problem for both women and nature in their place as part of a set of dualisms which have their origin in classical philosophy and which can be traced through a complex history to the present' and those who would rather refer to 'the rise of mechanistic science during the Enlightenment and pre-Enlightenment period' (Plumwood, 1986, p. 121). Indeed, because the first group finds no necessary relationship between the subjection of women and that of nature it is perhaps wrong to refer to them as ecofeminists.

We have already identified the ambiguous relationship that the green movement as a whole has with Enlightenment traditions, and it is entirely consistent that some ecofeminists should see a link between the Baconian impulse to dominate nature and the subjection of women – especially once similar characteristics have been conferred on both. The modern scientific project, which has its roots in Francis Bacon, is held to be a universalizing project of reduction, fragmentation and violent control. 'Difference' ecofeminists will counter this project with the feminine principles of diversity, holism, interconnectedness and non-violence. 'Deconstructive' ecofeminists will argue that the Enlightenment further rigidified a set of dualisms that were in place long before the Enlightenment period began, and which need to be transcended rather than re-evaluated. The problem with the 'difference' position in this context is that its adherents tend to paint too rosy a picture of the pre-Enlightenment period. Organicism may have given way to mechanicism, but the organicists still found reason to persecute witches. It seems that what can be said is that the mechanicist view of nature reinforced the subjection of women, but that this subjection has its roots somewhere else.

Indeed, as Janet Biehl has counterfactually suggested: 'Societies have existed that . . . could revere nature (such as ancient Egypt) and yet this "reverence" did not inhibit the development of full-blown patricentric hierarchy' (1988, p. 13). To this extent men do not need an array of thoughts justifying the subjection of nature in order to dominate women, although it seems likely that such thoughts have been used since the seventeenth century to reinforce that domination. In this way, ecofeminists who link the subjection of women and of nature cannot provide fundamental reasons for the fact of the domination of women by men, but they can point to the way in which, now, women and nature are held to possess similar characteristics and that these characteristics 'just happen' to be undervalued.

In linking the subjection of women and nature (Merchant, 1990), ecofeminists point out that the intellectual structures justifying both are the same. 'Difference' ecofeminists go on to suggest that preventing further destruction of the environment will involve being more 'in tune' with the non-human natural world, that women are habitually closer to nature than men, and that therefore women are best placed to provide role models for environmentally sensitive behaviour.

For some ecofeminists, the basis of this closeness to nature is biology: 'Because of the reproductive cycle it is much harder for women to escape a sense of connection with the natural world', says Elizabeth Dodson Gray (in Plumwood, 1986, p. 125), and Hazel Henderson remarks that 'Biologically, most women in the world do still vividly experience their embeddedness in Nature, and can harbour few illusions concerning their freedom and separatedness from the cycles of birth and death' (1983, p. 207). Maori women bury their afterbirth in the earth as a symbolic representation of the connectedness of women as life-givers, and the Earth as the source and fount of all life. Others, sympathetic to the link between ecology and feminism but not wishing to swallow biological essentialism, will suggest that women's lived experiences give them a head start so far as acquiring an ecological sensibility is concerned:

> so far as political action is concerned, it does not matter whether sexed differences are ontological fact or historical accident. The case for women as historical actors in a time of environmental crisis rests not on universal essences but on how the majority of women actually work and think now.
>
> (Salleh, 1997, p. 6)

Mary Mellor refers to this as 'materialist ecofeminism', the importance of which is that 'it does not rest on psychological or biologically essentialist explanations' (Mellor, 1997, p. 169). Instead, 'Women's identification with the "natural" is not evidence of some timeless unchanging essence, but of the material exploitation of women's work, often without reward' (ibid., p. 189). According to Mellor's version of materialist ecofeminism, women have a special relationship with what she calls 'biological' and 'ecological' time. She defines these as follows: 'Ecological time is the pace of ecological sustainability for non-human nature. Biological time represents the life-cycle and pace of bodily replenishment for human beings' (ibid.). In the biological realm, women undertake usually unacknowledged work related to the reproduction of human life, and in the ecological realm – and particularly in subsistence societies – they are often responsible for nurturing life from the land and for ensuring its sustainability.

For these two *material* reasons, women have a unique standpoint so far as the non-human natural world is concerned, and are exploited in quite specific ways. In particular, women's 'embodiedness and embeddedness' is both the source of a new kind of politics – one which recognizes the unavoidability and crucial nature of being 'encumbered' – and the origins of men's domination over them. As Mellor puts it, women's work in the reproductive and ecologically productive spheres has left 'social space and time largely in the hands of men' (1997, p. 189). They have used this to quite particular effect, to develop a politics and a practice of 'autonomy' which is possible only so long as someone else is doing the 'heteronomous' work involved in reproducing life itself:

The hallmark of modern capitalist patriarchy is its 'autonomy' in biological and ecological terms ... Western 'man' is young, fit, ambitious, mobile and unencumbered by obligations. This is not the world that most women know. Their world is circumscribed by obligated labour performed on the basis of duty, love, violence or fear of loss of economic support.

(Mellor, 1997, p. 189)

This evidently bears upon the green movement's general aspiration to have us living more lightly on the Earth. As we saw in Chapter 2, deep ecologists argue for a change of consciousness with respect to our dealings with the non-human natural world. Warwick Fox wants a shift in priorities such that those who interfere with the environment should have to justify doing so, rather than having the onus of justification rest on the environment's defenders. A precondition for this, he argues, is an awareness of the 'soft' boundaries between ourselves and the non-human natural world. I pointed out at the time that in this connection deep ecologists are presented with a formidable problem of persuasion – most people simply do not think like that, and it is hard to see how they ever will.

Some ecofeminists, though, suggest that there are already millions of people thinking like that, or at least potentially on the brink of doing so – women themselves. On this reading, women's closeness to nature puts them in the green political vanguard, in touch with a world that Judith Plant describes and that many members of the green movement would like to see resurrected – a world in which 'rituals were carried out by miners: offerings to the gods of the soil and the subterranean world, ceremonial sacrifices, sexual abstinence and fasting were conducted and observed before violating what was considered to be the sacred earth' (n.d., p. 3).

One problem ecofeminism needs to confront in the context of the wider aims of the green movement is the reconciliation of the demand for positive evaluation of the activity of childbirth and the need to reduce population levels. Of course, there is no need for such an evaluation to imply a large number of actual births, but a culture that held childbirth in high esteem may find it hard to legitimize population control policies. But again, in the properly functioning sustainable society, people would learn to reach and maintain sustainable reproductive rates, much as members of a number of communities (particularly in Africa and Latin America) already do.

'Difference' ecofeminism, in particular, has not been without its critics and Janet Biehl, for one, believes that the linking of women with nature and the subsequent subordination of both is precisely the reason why it is dangerous to try to use the link for emancipatory purposes:

> [W]hen ecofeminists root women's personality traits in repro-
> ductive and sexual biology, they tend to give acceptance to those
> malecreated images that define women as primarily biological
> beings . . . [this] is to deliver women over to the male stereotypes
> that root women's character structure entirely in their biological
> being.
>
> (Biehl, 1993, p. 55)

Plumwood, too, makes it absolutely clear why this sort of ecofemi-nism is seen in some quarters of the feminist movement as reactionary: The concept of nature . . . has been and remains a major tool in the armoury of conservatives intent on keeping women in their place', and:

> Given this background, it is not surprising that many feminists
> regard with some suspicion a recent view, expressed by a grow-
> ing number of writers in the ecofeminist camp, that there may be
> something to be said in favour of feminine connectedness with
> nature.
>
> (Plumwood, 1988, p. 16; see also 1993, p. 20)

In similar vein, Mary Mellor makes the useful distinction between feminism and feminine values: 'Even where male green thinkers claim that a commitment to feminism is at the centre of their politics, this often slides into a discussion of *feminine values*' (Mellor, 1992b, p. 245; emphasis in original), and while it ought to be pointed out that the evidence in this chapter suggests that there are plenty of female writers who do the same thing, Mellor's general point is well taken: '[T]o espouse a feminine principle without addressing the power relations between men and women is to espouse an ecofeminine rather than an ecofeminist position' (ibid., p. 246).

Janet Biehl's critique is principally aimed at deep ecologists who she sees as engaged on a project that will guarantee the domination of women by men, but her remarks are equally applicable to 'difference' ecofeminism. Women should not be asked, she writes, to 'think like a mountain' – in the context of women's struggle for selfhood, autonomy and acceptance as rational beings, this amounts to 'a blatant slap in the face' (Biehl, 1988, p. 14). She parodies deep ecologists (and 'difference' ecofeminists) who claim that 'male' values and characteristics are worthless: 'Never mind becoming rational; never mind the self; look where it got men, after all; women were better-off than men all along without that tiresome individuality' (Biehl, 1988, p. 13).

The deep-ecological attempt to encourage us to virtues of modesty, passivity and humility with respect to the natural world (and to other human beings), it is argued, can only backfire in the context of women's liberation. From this point of view, the women's movement has precisely been about undoing modesty and humility (and refusing to bear a child every ten or twelve months) because these characteristics have worked in favour of patriarchy. In the context of patriarchy (i.e. now), women cannot afford to follow the deep-ecological programme, and to the degree that ecofeminism subscribes to deep-ecological parameters it does women no favours either: 'it is precisely humility, with its passive and receptive obedience to men, that women are trying to escape today' (Biehl, 1988, p. 14).

These worries seem well founded, in that at one level ecofeminism amounts to asking people in general to adopt 'female' ways of relating to the world in the knowledge that women are more likely to do so than men. If this happens, and if such ways of relating to the world and their devaluation are indeed part of the reason for women's subordination to men, then women's position can only get worse. 'Difference' ecofeminism therefore proposes a dangerous strategy (a strategy Plumwood calls 'uncritical reversal' (1993, p. 31)) – to use ideas that have already been turned against women in the belief that, if they are taken up and lived by everyone, a general improvement in both the human and non-human condition will result. If they are not taken up, then women will have 'sacrificed themselves to the environment', and this is a price some feminists are clearly not prepared to pay: '[In] the absence of a feminist perspective . . . there is a danger that green politics will not even produce a de-gendered proclamation of the "feminine principle" but an overt or covert celebration of the masculine' (Mellor, 1992b, p. 249).

'Deconstructive' ecofeminism, on the other hand, is left with problems of its own. The refusal to choose between the masculine and the feminine has the happy consequence of avoiding the pitfalls associated with basing a transformative politics on the latter, but it leaves the future (arguably) too open-ended. In place of either a masculine or a feminine rationality, Plumwood argues for an ecological rationality that 'recognises and accommodates the denied relationships of dependency and enables us to acknowledge our debt to the sustaining others of the earth' (Plumwood, 1993, p. 196). But what does this mean, and how will it be brought about? Until further work is done, the space beyond dualism is occupied by a fog of indeterminacy – liberating and simultaneously frustrating for its lack of signposts.

Conclusion

I said at the beginning of this chapter that the evidence produced in it should deepen our understanding of the distinctiveness of ecologism as a political ideology. I think it has. Ecologism cannot be 'reduced' to any of the ideologies discussed here, with the faintly possible exception of feminism, and none of these ideologies may be said successfully to have appropriated ecologism for itself. Unlike any other ideology, ecologism is concerned in a foundational way with the relationship between human beings and their natural environment. More specifically, the two principal and distinguishing themes of ecologism, its belief in the limits to material growth and its opposition to anthropocentrism, are nowhere to be found in liberalism, conservatism and socialism – and they are nuanced in ecofeminism, where anthropocentrism is replaced by androcentrism, for example. Our conclusion must be that ecologism is an ideology in its own right, partly because it offers a coherent (if not unassailable) critique of contemporary society and a prescription for improvement, and partly because this critique and prescription differ fundamentally from those offered by other modern political ideologies.

Conclusion

We have established the differences between ecologism and other major political ideologies, and the incompatibility between what I have called environmentalism and ecologism is now clear. Ecologism seeks radically to call into question a whole series of political, economic and social practices in a way that environmentalism does not. Ecologism envisages a post-industrial future quite distinct from that with which we are most generally acquainted. While most post-industrial futures revolve around high-growth, high-technology, expanding services, greater leisure, and satisfaction conceived in material terms, ecologism's post-industrial society questions growth and technology, and suggests that the Good Life will involve more work and fewer material objects. Fundamentally, ecologism takes seriously the universal condition of the finitude of the planet and asks what kinds of political, economic and social practices are (1) possible and (2) desirable within that framework. Environmentalism, typically, does no such thing.

In terms of human relationships with the non-human natural world, ecologism asks that the onus of justification be shifted from those who argue that the non-human natural world should be given political voice to those who think it should not. Environmentalists will usually be concerned about 'nature' only so far as it might affect human beings; ecologists will argue that the strong anthropocentrism this betrays is more a part of our current problems than a solution to them.

Practical considerations of limits to growth and ethical concerns about the non-human natural world combine to produce, in ecologism, a political ideology in its own right. We can call it an ideology (in the functional sense) because it has, first, a description of the political and social world – a pair of green spectacles – which helps us to find our way around it. It also has a programme for political change and, crucially, it has a picture of the kind of society that ecologists think we ought to inhabit – loosely described as the 'sustainable society'. Because the

descriptive and prescriptive elements in the political-ecological programme cannot be accommodated within other political ideologies
(such as socialism) without substantially changing them, we are surely
entitled to set ecologism alongside such ideologies, competing with
them in the late twentieth-century political marketplace. In contrast, I
maintain that the various sorts of environmentalism (conservation, pollution control, waste recycling) can be slotted with relative ease into
more well-known ideological paradigms, and that the way these issues
have been readily taken up right across the political spectrum shows this
co-option at work.

But what of the relationship between ecologism and environmentalism? One obvious answer is to see ecologism as the Utopian picture that
all political movements need if they are to operate effectively. On this
reading, green politics has a reformist as well as a radical wing, with the
latter acting as a kind of puritan policeman, calling the reformists to
order when they stray too far off course during their 'march through
the institutions'. This is as much as to say that questions about whether
or not the dark-green picture as I have described it in this book
is realizable are to miss the point. Indeed, its Utopianism, with the
vision and committed creativity that it can generate, is, on this reading,
ecologism's strongest card.

More positively still, the Utopian vision provides the indispensable
fundamentalist well of inspiration from which green activists, even
the most reformist and respectable, need continually to draw. Green
reformers need a radically alternative picture of post-industrial society,
they need deep-ecological visionaries, they need the phantom studies
of the sustainable society, and they need, paradoxically, occasionally to
be brought down to earth and to be reminded about limits to growth.
Dark-green politics remind reformists of where they want to go even
if they don't really think they can get there. On this view there is
what we might call a 'constructive tension' between ecologism and
environmentalism.

But is it so obvious that the tension is constructive? There are those
who will argue that radical green ideas are wholly counterproductive in
that they 'are beginning to lead the environmental movement toward
self-defeating strategies, preventing society from making the reforms it
so desperately needs' (Lewis, 1992, p. 2). This is an increasingly popular
view among commentators on environmental politics – even among
those who are more sympathetic to its intentions than Lewis. Tim
Hayward (1995, 1998) and John Barry (1999) both endorse it in rather
different ways, for example. Hayward refers to the 'two dogmas' of
ecologism: a belief in intrinsic value and a critique of anthropocentrism

(1998, chs 2 and 3; I discussed Hayward's position on anthropocentrism in Chapter 2), signalling with the word 'dogma' his sense that these foundation stones of green political thought are unexamined and are, in the longer run, a hindrance to the acceptability of environmental politics. Hayward argues that widely held green understandings of these terms are conceptually incoherent *as well as* politically counterproductive. His belief is that an 'enlightened self-interest' is the best way forward, since it is more conceptually coherent than biocentrism or ecocentrism, and because it accords better with basic human motivations.

Similarly, John Barry rejects deep ecology as foundational for green politics for the pragmatic reason that it will not secure widespread support (J. Barry, 1999, pp. 26 and 42). He argues instead for the cultivating of an 'ecological virtue', based on a critical attitude to anthropocentrism, and a stewardship 'ethics of use', which would be practised by green citizens: 'the practice of the "ecological virtues" is constitutive of this green conception of citizenship' (ibid., p. 65). I shall suggest some possible responses to these remarks later in this chapter.

From Lewis' point of view ecoradicalism threatens the environment by 'fuelling the anti-environment countermovement' (Lewis, 1992, p. 6), and he makes it his business, therefore, to dismantle what he sees as the four postulates of 'radical environmentalism' as well as its informing underlying belief: 'that economic growth is by definition unsustainable' (ibid., p. 3). The four postulates are:

> that 'primal' (or 'primitive') peoples exemplify how we can live in harmony with nature (and with each other); that thoroughgoing decentralization, leading to local autarky, is necessary for social and ecological health; that technological advance, if not scientific progress itself, is inherently harmful and dehumanizing; and that the capitalist market system is inescapably destructive and wasteful.
>
> (Lewis, 1992, p. 3)

Lewis considers all these views to be wrong-headed (ibid., p. 9), and he rejects the ecoradical attack on economic growth by arguing that growth in *value* is perfectly compatible with long-term sustainability: '[W]hile the global economy certainly cannot grow indefinitely in *volume* by pouring out an ever mounting cavalcade of consumer disposables, it *can* continue to expand in *value* by producing better goods and services ever more efficiently' (ibid., p. 10; emphasis in original).

Radical greens might respond to the 'four-postulate' criticism by saying that they do not recognize themselves in its composite picture. Lewis appears to have caricatured a caricature of an extreme wing of one sort of West Coast North American environmentalism, and generically dubbed the outcome 'ecoradicalism'. While there is truth in every cartoon, there is plenty of fiction too, and I hope that the rest of this book provides evidence for the undue selectivity of Lewis's artwork. If – as I suspect – Lewis has got the target wrong, then the success of his attack must be equivocal. Radical greens might also say that his knockdown argument regarding economic growth is curious in that it concedes to radical greens just what they want: a recognition that present rates of economic growth *by volume* are unsustainable. I can imagine no green arguing that growth in terms of value is unsustainable (although I can imagine some pretty fierce arguments over how to determine value in the first place).

As far as the strategic question is concerned, radical greens might suggest that their radicalism, far from turning people off green politics altogether, makes ecomoderates seem more respectable than they already are, thereby smoothing their path through the corridors of power. I pointed out in Chapter 4, indeed, that this was a guiding theme of Earth First!'s direct action programme:

> the actions of monkeywrenchers invariably enhance the status and bargaining position of more Reasonable opponents. Industry considers moderate environmentalists to be radical until they get a taste of real radical activism. Suddenly the soft-sell of the Sierra Club and other white-shirt-and-tie eco-bureaucrats becomes much more attractive and worthy of serious negotiation. These moderate environmentalists must condemn monkeywrenching so as to preserve their own image, but they should take full advantage of the credence it lends to their approach.
>
> (Foreman and Haywood, 1989, p. 22)

There are those who will argue, in any case, that Lewis is making a fuss over nothing: that radical green politics is so much in the shadow of its reformist cousin that it is virtually invisible. Ironically, this could be the result of the explosion in the political popularity of environmental issues during the late 1980s. It may seem curious to suggest that radical green politics is the victim of reformist success but, from a point of view which has it that the tension between environmentalism and ecologism is destructive rather than constructive, that may be what has happened. The green movement has spent years trying to get the environment on to the political agenda, and the major political parties have so artfully stitched a green stripe into their respective flags that there seems to be no need for a specifically green (much less *radically* green) politics any longer. As Anna Bramwell has put it: 'What is usable in the Green critique has largely been subsumed by the political system' (Bramwell, 1994, p. 206). On this reading, radical green politics has disappeared behind brighter lights and louder voices, and the call for radical social, political and economic change is muted – if not silent.

Radical greens are evidently in an uncomfortable position. On the one hand they have a message to give, and on the other hand they are confronted by a public and culture they think prevent them from giving it. So they turn reformist in certain public forums either because they think that to be radically green would be to marginalize themselves, or because the discussions in those forums (particularly in television and radio) are weighted towards what already interests the public (polluted rivers, dying seals) rather than what might interest them if they got the chance to hear about it. There is nothing new in all this; it is the typical dilemma of any radical form of politics, and it can produce a burdensome form of political schizophrenia. In this context, Jonathon Porritt once described how being both director of Friends of the Earth and an individual member of the Green Party (in Dodds, 1988, p. 201) pulled him in different directions at the same time.

It works like this: there is a desire to popularize green politics, to 'get the message across', and there is a desire to make sure that the green message is radical rather than merely reformist. But the rub appears to be that in order to get any message across at all it has to be reformist and not radical. Porritt refers, for example, to FoE's highly successful campaign to encourage producers to phase out the use of chlorofluoro-carbons in aerosols. He noted that by the end of 1989 only some 5 or 10 per cent of aerosols would use CFCs, compared with nearly three-quarters just a year or so earlier. This, as he writes, is 'All good stuff – a small, incremental step towards a safer environment'. Then he asks: 'But does it actually bring us anywhere nearer sustainability?' (in Dodds, 1988, pp. 200–1).

Porritt himself observes:

> Various deep Greens (including members of the Green Party) were quick to castigate Friends of the Earth for not campaigning against aerosols in general, inasmuch as they are indisputably unnecessary, wasteful and far from environmentally benign even if they don't use CFCs. Such critics suggested (and who can blame them?) that by campaigning for CFC-free aerosols, we were in fact condoning, if not positively promoting, self-indulgence, vanity, and wholly unsustainable patterns of consumption.
>
> (in Dodds, 1988, p. 201)

This captures the dilemma: if, as the final phrases suggest, environmental campaigns can contribute to unsustainability, then light-green and dark-green politics are in conflict rather than in concert – the notion of 'constructive tension' is called into question. In other words, it is not simply a semantic question about whether or not environmentalism and ecologism are the same thing and, if not, how different they are, but a question that has political-strategic implications. If radical and reformist greens pull in different directions, then this is serious indeed, because the classic defence of the political schizophrenic is that, even if the two positions are in different places, at least they are on the same track. Put differently the light-green will argue that light-green education can lead to dark-green radicalization, that the normal course of things is for the former to evolve into the latter: 'On balance I believe that more good will be done than harm if one sees such an approach as part of a transitional strategy', writes Porritt (in Dodds, 1988, p. 199).

Porritt might even begrudgingly suggest that anything is better than nothing, even if no evolution takes place at all: 'After all, confronted with the choice between green yuppies or naturally nasty yuppies, between mindful green consumers or relatively mindless, old-style consumers, it's your proverbial Hobson's choice' (in Dodds, 1988, p. 199). In these senses radical greens can happily defend the occasional reformist posture because they might thereby green the odd yuppy and improve the Body Shop's annual turnover. But is environmentalist popularity bought at the cost of more radical, mostly private convictions?

A central strategic issue to be confronted by the green movement, then, is whether light-green politics (environmentalism) makes dark-green politics (ecologism) more or less likely. Roughly speaking, it will be held to be more likely if it is believed that both forms of politics are heading in the same direction, even though one might lag slightly behind the other. It will be held to be less likely if it is believed that these forms of politics work more substantially against, rather than with, each other. In this latter case, the conclusion will not be to encourage people to see environmentalism as a 'transitional strategy' for ecologism, but to argue that it is no transitional strategy at all.

There are, of course, arguments for and against both positions, and there are a number of ways of articulating the former (and, it seems, increasingly popular) 'convergence thesis'. The general theme running through these various articulations is that the *policy outcomes* of radical and reformist programmes are very similar, even if the *reasons and values* underlying them are different. Very broadly speaking, the policy intention of both reformists and radicals is to protect the environment. Radical greens have long argued that this objective cannot be achieved so long as economic growth remains the leitmotiv of industrial and industrializing societies, and so long as our attitude towards environmental protection is guided by anthropocentric lights. The 'first-wave' attack on the limits to growth view came from resource cornucopians such as Herman Kahn and Julian Simon who simply argued (and still do) that there is more than enough to go round, more or less for ever: '[We]e now have in our hands . . . the technology to feed, clothe, and supply energy to an ever-growing population for the next 7 billion years' (Simon in Myers and Simon, 1994, p. 65).

These arguments continue to be put, but they have been buttressed (or in some cases supplanted) by a much more sophisticated 'second-wave' response to the limits to growth position which goes by the name of 'ecological modernization' (Jacobs, 1999b; Moll and Sonnenfeld, 2000). In his book on the politics of pollution, Albert Weale describes how ecological modernizers during the 1980s began to challenge the view that there was 'a zero-sum trade-off between economic prosperity and environmental concern' (Weale, 1992, p. 31). Ecological modernizers put three arguments: first, '[I]f the "costs" of environmental protection are avoided the effect is frequently to save money for present generations at the price of an increased burden for future generations' (ibid., p. 76); second, '[I]nstead of seeing environmental protection as a burden upon the economy the ecological modernist sees it as a potential source for future growth . . . a spur to industrial innovation' (ibid., p. 78); and third,

> With the advent of global markets, the standards of product acceptability will be determined by the country with the most stringent pollution control standards. Hence the future development of a postindustrial economy will depend upon its ability to produce high value, high quality products with stringent environmental standards enforced.
>
> (Weale, 1992, p. 77)

This decoupling of economic growth and environmental degradation has the apparent effect of drawing (at least one of) the principal sting(s) at the disposal of radical ecologists. In strategic terms, why bother with radical ecological ideas if we can, as it were, have our cake and eat it? I shall return to this question below, but first, another approach to the 'convergence thesis' needs to be canvassed. Ecological modernizers focus their attention on the economic growth equation, or what we might call the 'material' faultline within the pro-environmental caucus. But what about the arguments outlined in Chapter 2 regarding anthropocentrism and biocentrism? Surely it makes a difference to policy whether one adopts an anthropocentric rather than a biocentric stance in respect of environmental protection?

One person who thinks it does not is Bryan Norton. That Norton is a 'converger' is in no doubt, and in his search for unity among environmentalists he thinks he knows where to look: 'I have . . . tried not to use environmentalists' rhetoric – the explanations they give for what they do – but their actions – the policies they actually pursue – as the fixed points on my map' (Norton, 1991, p. x). Thus environmentalists of any persuasion might agree on the founding of a wilderness preserve, but not on *why* it should be preserved. Norton argues that whether it is preserved because the wilderness area is sacred or because of the recreational use to which it is put is immaterial from a policy point of view. He suggests that all the objects of radical ecologists can be achieved from within a broadly anthropocentric perspective:

> introducing the idea that other species have intrinsic value, that humans should be 'fair' to all other species, provides no operationally recognizable constraints on human behaviour that are not already implicit in the generalized, cross-temporal obligations to protect a healthy, complex, and autonomously functioning system for the benefit of future generations of humans.
>
> (Norton, 1991, p. 226)

More particularly, he argues for a form of 'lexical ordering' of priorities: 'productivity values have free play until their pursuit threatens the larger context, at which point limits, to be articulated in the ecological terms of system fragility, constrain choices based on a pure productivity criterion' (Norton, 1991, p. 83). He concludes that:

> A hierarchical system of value therefore opens the door to new possibilities for understanding environmental ethics. Environmentalists need not choose between the worldview of anthropocentric economic reductionism and biocentrism. Another possibility is an hierarchically organized and *integrated* system of values.
>
> (Norton, 1991, p. 239)

The attraction of Weale's ecological modernizers and Norton's policy convergers is that they offer us a 'both . . . and' solution rather than 'either . . . or' ones: *both* economic growth *and* environmental protection, *both* productivity *and* ecosystem preservation. Once again the question arises: If there is anything in these positions, why bother with radical ecology, tactically, strategically or otherwise? Does radical ecology have any 'added value', or is it – in the final analysis – an irritating distraction from the business of having our cake and eating it?

Radical ecologists might begin, of course, by disputing – or at least modulating – some of the arguments put by ecological modernizers and policy convergers. The three arguments put by Weale on behalf of the ecological modernizers are all subject to a degree of interrogation. First, why should hard-headed industrialists worry about future generations? Reasons for doing so will surely come from *outside* the ideology of ecological modernization – and one place they might come from is the camp of radical ecologists (although not only from there, of course). Radical ecology serves the purpose, on this reading, of providing grist for the ecological modernizer's mill.

Second, the view that environmental protection is a potential source of future growth is subject to two caveats. First, this is only securely true in the right environment (as it were): in societies (or groups of them) where 'quality of life' objectives are enshrined in general programmes – as they are (implicitly) in the Preamble and Article 2 (particularly the revised version) of the European Community's original Treaty of Rome (Hildebrand, 1992, pp. 17, 37). Arguably, the fact that 'environmental amenity is a superior good' (Weale, 1992, p. 76) only becomes policy-relevant when the non-provision of environmental amenity has adverse repercussions for policy-makers. Unfortunately, across vast swathes of the globe, policy-makers remain largely untouched by the effects of their folly, and this is no less true of their handling of their environment than it is of other areas of policy.

The second caveat is that not all environmental protection measures are functional for growth, and Weale himself points to evidence from the Netherlands which suggests that environmental protection might produce negative growth rates. The Dutch National Environment Policy Plan (NEPP) was published in 1989, and it contained some of the most radical policy proposals for pollution control ever countenanced by a national government. Weale describes the details and implications of the plan in full (Weale, 1992, pp. 125–53), but only one or two aspects of it are relevant to us here. First, large-scale emission reductions were factored into the plan because it was discovered that '*even with the full application of existing end-of-pipe technologies* it would not be possible to prevent a decline in environmental quality in the Netherlands' (ibid., p. 134; emphasis in original). Indeed, in order to meet the environmental objectives laid down in the plan, it was argued at the pre-planning stage that '*volume* and structural changes were needed in the economy' (ibid., p. 135; emphasis added).

This reference to changes in volume lends some succour to radical ecologists because (as I pointed out in Lewis' connection above), it is precisely a reduction in volume for which radical greens argue. The effects on Dutch GNP of implementation of the NEPP were calculated to be a fall of 2.6 per cent if the Netherlands went it alone, and a fall of 0.9 per cent if other countries followed suit (Weale, 1992, p. 135), although Weale points out that these figures do not include any savings that might accrue from implementation (e.g. through energy conservation), nor any competitive benefits that might flow from it.

Significantly, the recommendation regarding volume and structure changes 'did not seem an attractive conclusion since it threatened to put the cause of environmental protection on a collision course with economic development, and environmental policy would therefore return to the old zero-sum conflict with other policy objectives' (Weale, 1992, p. 135). At the very least, all this suggests that this aspect of the ecological modernization thesis is up for grabs, in that the decoupling of economic growth and environmental degradation may not be a painless *interruptus*. Indeed, it may not be possible at all, in which case the radical green argument returns to the surface, bloodied but unbowed.

The third ecological modernization argument was that in a world of stringent environmental standards, competitive advantage will be gained by any country whose products meet or exceed such standards. Radical greens might argue that this is only true subject to two limiting conditions. First, the products in question must be those for which 'stringent pollution control standards' are relevant – cars produced in Japan might be a case in point, but cheap plastic toys produced in China are not. Ecological modernization is partly a thesis about the 'standards of product acceptability' (Weale, 1992, p. 77), but environmental concerns are not a factor in determining the acceptability of all products, and they may not – of course – even be the overriding factor determining the acceptability of products such as cars. Ecological modernization's hold, then, over the acceptability of products may be somewhat tenuous.

The second limiting condition in this context is that 'stringent pollution control standards' must be in place for the said competitive advantage to be gained, and (globally) this is not the case for most markets of most goods. Ecological modernizers might argue that it is part of their agenda to ensure this sort of legislation, but one suspects that tough environmental standards are more likely in places where there is already an 'environmental culture'. Once again, it could be argued that such a culture is fostered *beyond* the confines of ecological modernization, and to the extent that radical ecology is a cultural critique it is tempting to suggest that the ecological modernizers need the space carved out by their more radical counterparts.

Finally, ecological modernizers will point to declining energy consumption per unit of GNP as evidence that the link between economic growth and energy consumption has been broken – thereby calling into question an apparent article of faith for radical ecologists (Weale, 1992, p. 25). It is true that this link has been broken in OECD countries over the past twenty years, but radical ecologists might point to three contributing factors, two of which at least may not be easy to reproduce worldwide: 'The decoupling of economic growth from energy consumption was encouraged by high energy prices, faster economic growth of the service sector, and the relocation of energy-intensive industries to developing countries' (World Resources Institute, 1992, p. 145). The two factors that are hard to reproduce world-wide are the second and third. Not all economies can depend on a burgeoning service sector for their survival because traditional industrial products (ships, bridges and so on) will be continually required, even if not produced in the countries that require them. Second, energy-intensive industries cannot be relocated forever; OECD energy consumption figures have improved at the cost of *displacing* consumption, not (from a global point of view) *reducing* it (ibid., pp. 144–5).

Bryan Norton's arguments regarding policy convergence are also subject to critique. In the first place, his 'lexical ordering' seems able to license some pretty fierce despoliation before the 'system fragility' constraint kicks in. At best, radicals might argue, his focus on systems rather than on individuals seems tailor-made to justify a certain amount of mayhem to individuals provided system fragility is not thereby endangered. At worst, the 'free play' of production could go on for a very long time before the 'larger context' was deemed to be under threat. How many 'non-essential' individuals, species and habitats could go under before the possibility of production itself was threatened? The very fact that this question can be so framed without misrepresenting Norton's position is, of course, the principal reason why radical greens will regard his hand extended in friendship with some caution – from their 'in principle' point of view no part of human or non-human nature can be regarded as non-essential.

Convergence theories, then, may take various forms. In some (such as Martin Lewis'), convergence amounts to liquidation of the radical perspective. Lewis and his supporters will claim that radical ecology is just plain wrong, and that the cause of environmental protection is best served by reformist ideas and policies. Other commentators (such as

Bryan Norton) will argue that policy outcomes are the same whether based upon radical or reformist values. Circumspection dictates, then, that the line of least resistance is chosen – arguing for environmental protection from within accepted paradigms. Others (such as ecological modernizers) suspect that there is a fundamental flaw in radical ecology regarding the relationship between economic growth and environmental degradation, and that economic growth is actually functional for environmental protection.

I have hinted that one radical green response to these critiques is to confront them head-on. Another response might be to accept defeat – temporarily at least – but to claim simultaneously a considerable victory. There was a time when the environment was a fringe interest, an optional extra to be taken up when all other aspects of public policy had been dealt with. The Treaty of Rome of 1957 that established the European Economic Community, for instance, contained no 'explicit reference to the idea of environmental policy or environmental protection' (Hildebrand, 1992, p. 17), and environmental enthusiasts had to rely on creative interpretation of various of the Treaty's articles to further their ambitions. By 1992 and the Maastricht Treaty, though, '[T]he traditional economic growth ethos of the community [had] been "greened" considerably' (ibid., p. 37). Environmental protection, sustainability and environment-respecting growth are all explicitly mentioned in the new Treaty's articles, and the environment has now officially 'acquired full status as a policy falling within the Union's priority objectives' (ibid.).

The political and economic history of this signal shift in intention is complex – and needs to be buttressed, in any case, by a *cultural* history. In the realm of culture a space can be carved out in which new questions regarding the politically possible and the socially desirable are put. This space is what Doug Torgerson has referred to as a 'green public sphere' (Torgerson, 1999).

Once in place, they do not go away and sooner or later 'a culture that is infused with . . . a sense of personal, civic and ecological responsibility' (Eckersley, 1992, p. 182) demands a response from professional policy-makers. This cultural arena is the one that sympathetic critics of ecologism such as Hayward, John Barry and Norton perhaps forget in their determination to make environmental politics more attractive (as they see it). Barry is surely right to say that:

> The centrality of citizenship to green arguments for democracy comes from the belief that the achievement of sustainability will require more than institutional restructuring of contemporary

Western liberal democracies. Such institutional changes are necessary, but not sufficient, from a green point of view. The green
contention is that macro- and micro-level reorganization needs
to be supplemented with changes in general values and practices.
In short, institutional change must be complemented by wider
cultural-level changes.

(J. Barry, 1999, p. 228)

The question is: Where will these changes in values and practices at
the cultural level come from? My view is that they will be produced, if at
all, at the promptings of the radical critique advanced by ecologism
itself. Radical ecology's role for the twenty-first century is as a condition for the possibility of its reformist cousin. Without radical ecology,
the convergence thesis advanced by Norton, the 'ecologising of the
Enlightenment' proposed by Hayward (1995), and the cultivation of
'ecological virtue' suggested by John Barry (1999, pp. 31–5), would be
literally unthinkable. Barry criticizes 'binary' accounts of green politics
such as the one given in this book (environmentalism 'versus' ecologism) on the grounds that they are 'a hindrance to the future evolution
of green politics' (J. Barry, 1999, p. 4). But he produces a few binary
oppositions of his own, such as that between green ideology and green
political theory (the latter is regarded as more 'mature' (ibid., p. 6)), and
between deep ecology and an 'ethic of use' for the environment. Green
political theory cannot do without green ideology and probably would
not exist without it, and deep ecology *is* an ethic of use for the environment. The point is that the reformists need the radicals just as the
radicals need the reformists. The way ahead is not to try to replace one
set of 'truths' with another, but to see that Barry's 'cultural-level
changes' require them to work in tandem.

On this reading, reformism is necessary in that it provides us with a
green platform, a new consensus on our relationship with our environment, from which we can make the leap to more radically green practices. There are, of course, radical critics, coming from the other direction, who say that reformism may constitute a barrier rather than a
platform. It may from a dark-green point of view immunize rather than
sensitize, by obscuring the informing principle of green politics: that
infinite growth in a finite system is impossible, and that therefore green
production and consumption are (in the long term) as unsustainable as
are current forms of production and consumption. On this reading,
environmentalism saps radical energy and pulls up the drawbridge
against green change.

Such a perspective suggests, in opposition to Norton (for example), that environmentalism and ecologism diverge rather than converge. Jonathon Porritt, for one, appears unsure which line to take. We have seen him 'on balance' (above), arguing in favour of the 'transitional strategy' notion, but he is equally aware of the traps it lays, especially in its green consumerist disguise:

> At best, it may mitigate the most immediate symptoms of eco-logical decline, but the short-term advantages gained in the process are almost certainly outweighed by the simultaneous immunisation of such consumers against reality. . . . Green consumerism may marginally assist environmentalists in some of their campaigns, but its very effectiveness depends on not attempting to do down or supplant today's industrial order; and on not promoting awareness of its inherent unsustainability.
>
> (in Dodds, 1988, pp. 199–200)

And so we find ourselves back at square one: the radical green demand to call today's industrial order into question. But how to do it? Friends of the Earth was faced with the fact in its CFC campaign that it 'would have made little, if any headway with an anti-aerosol campaign' (ibid., p. 201), even though calling today's industrial order into question would have involved just that. Porritt wants at least as much 'to be out there explaining why the old mechanistic world view of Bacon, Descartes and Newton is now wholly redundant . . . as to be arguing the merits of flue gas desulphurisation' (ibid., p. 203). The 'greening' of households, retailing, industry and governments, even of people – however insecure – is the signal achievement of ecologism's first three decades. Whether this will be enough to guarantee us a sustainable future remains to be seen.

Bibliography

Agyeman, J. (2005) *Sustainable Communities and the Challenge of Environmental Justice* (New York and London: New York University Press).

Agyeman, J., Bullard, R. and Evans, B. (eds) (2003) *Just Sustainabilities: Development in an Unequal World* (London: Earthscan).

Allaby, M. and Bunyard, P. (1980) *The Politics of Self-Sufficiency* (Oxford: Oxford University Press).

Anderson, F.R. *et al.* (n.d.) *Environmental Protection: Law and Policy* (New York: Little, Brown).

Anderson, V. (1991) *Alternative Economic Indicators* (London: Routledge).

Atkinson, A. (1991) *Principles of Political Ecology* (London: Belhaven Press).

Attfield, R. (1983) *The Ethics of Environmental Concern* (Oxford: Blackwell).

—— (1990) 'Deep ecology and intrinsic value', *Cogito*, 4(1).

Bahro, R. (1982) *Socialism and Survival* (London: Heretic Books).

—— (1986) *Building the Green Movement* (London: GMP).

—— (1994) *Avoiding Social and Ecological Disaster: The Politics of World Transformation* (Bath: Gateway Books).

Ball, T. and Dagger, R. (1991) *Political Ideologies and the Democratic Ideal* (London: HarperCollins).

Barry, B. (1995) *Justice as Impartiality* (Oxford: Clarendon Press).

—— (1999) 'Sustainability and intergenerational justice', in A. Dobson (ed.) *Fairness and Futurity: Essays on Environmental Sustainability and Social Justice* (Oxford: Oxford University Press).

Barry, J. (1994) 'The limits of the shallow and the deep: green politics, philosophy and praxis', *Environmental Politics*, 3 (3).

—— (1996) 'Sustainability, political judgement and citizenship: connecting green politics and democracy', in B. Doherty and M. De Geus (eds) *Democracy and Green Political Thought: Sustainability, Rights and Citizenship* (London: Routledge).

—— (1999) *Rethinking Green Politics* (London: Sage).

Barry, J. and Eckersley, R. (eds) (2005) *The State and the Ecological Crisis* (Cambridge: MIT Press).

Bauman, Z. (1987) *Legislators and Interpreters* (Oxford: Polity).

Baxter, B. (1999) *Ecologism: An Introduction* (Edinburgh: Edinburgh University Press)

Begg, A. (2000) *Empowering the Earth: Strategies for Green Change* (Bideford: Green Books).

Benson, J. (ed.) (2000) *Environmental Ethics: An Introduction with Readings* (London: Routledge).

Bentham, J. (1960) *The Principles of Morals and Legislation* (Oxford: Blackwell).

Benton, T. (1993) *Natural Relations: Ecology, Animal Rights and Social Justice* (London: Verso).

—— (ed.) (1996) *The Greening of Marxism* (New York: Guilford Press).

Bergland and Matti (2006) 'Citizen and consumer: the dual role of individuals in environmental policy', *Environmental Politics*, 15(4).

Biehl, J. (1988) article in *Green Line*, 59 (February).

—— (1993) 'Problems in ecofeminism', *Society and Nature*, 2(1).

Blühdorn, I. (2000) *Post-ecologist Politics: Social Theory and the Abdication of the Ecologist Paradigm* (London: Routledge).

Bookchin, M. (1972) *Post-scarcity Anarchism* (Montreal: Black Rose Books).

—— (1982) *The Ecology of Freedom* (Palo Alto: Cheshire Books).

—— (1986) *The Modern Crisis* (Philadelphia: New Society).

—— (1989) *Remaking Society* (Montreal: Black Rose Books).

—— (1991) 'Where I stand now', in M. Bookchin and D. Foreman (eds) *Defending the Earth* (Montreal: Black Rose Books).

—— (1995) *Re-enchanting Humanity: A Defence of the Human Spirit Against Antihumanism, Misanthropy, Mysticism and Primitivism* (London: Cassell).

Bookchin, M. and Foreman, D. (eds) (1991) *Defending the Earth* (Montreal: Black Rose Books).

Bottomore, T. (1982) *Elites and Society* (Harmondsworth: Penguin).

Bottomore, T. and Rubel, M. (1984) *Karl Marx: Selected Writings in Sociology and Social Philosophy* (Harmondsworth: Penguin).

Bramwell, A. (1989) *Ecology in the 20th Century* (New Haven, CT: Yale University Press).

—— (1994) *The Fading of the Greens: The Decline of Environmental Politics in the West* (New Haven, CT: Yale University Press).

Brennan, A. (1988) *Thinking about Nature* (London: Routledge).

British Ecology Party Manifesto (1983) (London: Ecology Party).

British Green Party Manifesto (1987) (London: Green Party).

Brundtland, Gro Harlem (1989) 'Economia ecologica', *El Pais* (Temas de Nuestra Epoca), 30 March, 4.

Brundtland Report (n.d.) *Our Common Future* (London: Earthscan).

Bunyard, P. and Morgan-Grenville, F. (eds) (1987) *The Green Alternative* (London: Methuen).

Burke, E. (1790/1982) *Reflections on the Revolution in France* (Harmondsworth: Penguin).

Caldecott, L. and Leland, S. (eds) (1983) *Reclaim the Earth* (London: The Women's Press).

Capra, F. (1975) *The Tao of Physics* (London: Wildwood House).
—— (1983) *The Turning Point* (London: Flamingo).
Carson, R. (1965) *Silent Spring* (Harmondsworth: Penguin).
Carter, A. (1993) 'Towards a green political theory', in Dobson, A., and Lucardie, P. (eds), *The Politics of Nature: Explorations in Green Political Theory* (London: Routledge).
Carter, A. (1999) *A Radical Green Political Theory* (London and New York: Routledge).
Carter, N. (2001) *The Politics of the Environment: Ideas, Activism and Policy* (Cambridge: Cambridge University Press).
Chambers, N., Simmons, C. and Wackernagel, M. (2000), *Sharing Nature's Interest: Ecological Footprints as an Indicator of Sustainability* (London, Stirling: Earthscan).
Collard, A. and Contrucci, J. (1988) *Rape of the Wild* (London: The Women's Press).
Connelly, J. and Smith, G. (2003) *Politics and the Environment: From Theory to Practice* (2nd edn) (London: Routledge).
Conroy, C. and Litvinoff, P. (eds) (1988) *The Greening of Aid* (London: Earthscan).
Cornford, P. (ed.) (1988) *The Organic Tradition* (Bideford: Green Books).
Curry, P. (2006) *Ecological Ethics: An Introduction* (Cambridge: Polity Press).
Daly, H. (1977a) 'The politics of the sustainable society', in D. Pirages (ed.) *The Sustainable Society* (New York: Praeger).
—— (1977b) 'The steady-state economy: what, why, and how', in D. Pirages (ed.) *The Sustainable Society* (New York: Praeger).
—— (1992) *Steady-state Economics* (2nd edn) (London: Earthscan).
Dauncey, G. (1988) *After the Crash* (Basingstoke: Green Print).
De Geus, M. (1999) *Ecological Utopias: Envisioning the Sustainable Society* (Utrecht: International Books).
—— (2002) *The End of Over-consumption: Towards a Lifestyle of Moderation and Self-restraint* (Utrecht: International Books).
Devall, B. (1980) 'The deep ecology movement', *Natural Resources Journal*, 20.
Dickens, P. (1992) *Society and Nature: Towards a Green Social Theory* (New York: Harvester Wheatsheaf).
—— (2004) *Society and Nature* (Cambridge: Polity Press).
Dobson, A. (1989) 'Deep ecology', *Cogito*, 3(1).
—— (1990) *Green Political Thought* (London: Routledge).
—— (1993a) 'Ecologism', in R. Eatwell and A. Wright (eds) *Contemporary Political Ideologies* (London: Pinter).
—— (1993b) 'Critical theory and green polities', in A. Dobson and P. Lucardie (eds) *The Politics of Nature: Explorations in Green Political Theory* (London: Routledge).
—— (1994a) 'Environmentalism', in M. Foley (ed.) *Ideas That Shape Politics* (Manchester: Manchester University Press).

—— (1994b) 'Ecologism and the relegitimation of socialism', *Radical Philosophy*, 67 (summer).

—— (1996a) 'Democratising green theory: preconditions and principles', in B. Doherty and M. De Geus (eds) *Democracy and Green Political Thought: Sustainability, Rights and Citizenship* (London: Routledge).

—— (1996b) 'Representative democracy and the environment', in W. Lafferty and J. Meadowcroft (eds) *Democracy and the Environment: Problems and Prospects* (Cheltenham: Edward Elgar).

—— (1998) *Justice and the Environment: Conceptions of Environmental Sustainability and Dimensions of Social Justice* (Oxford: Oxford University Press).

—— (ed.) (1999) *Fairness and Futurity: Essays on Environmental Sustainability and Social Justice* (Oxford: Oxford University Press).

—— (2003) *Citizenship and the Environment* (Oxford: Oxford University Press).

—— (2004) 'Globalization and the environment', in V. George and R. Page (eds) *Global Social Problems* (Cambridge: Polity Press).

Dobson, A. and Bell, D. (2005), 'Introduction', in A. Dobson and D. Bell (eds) *Environmental Citizenship* (Cambridge, MA, and London: MIT Press).

Dobson, A. and Eckersley, R. (eds) (2006), *Political Theory and the Ecological Challenge* (Cambridge: Cambridge University Press).

Dobson, A. and Lucardie, P. (eds) (1993) *The Politics of Nature: Explorations in Green Political Theory* (London: Routledge).

Dobson, A. and Valencia, A. (eds) (2005) *Citizenship, Environment, Economy* (London: Routledge).

Dodds, F. (ed.) (1988) *Into the 21st Century* (Basingstoke: Green Print).

Doherty, B. (1999) 'Paving the way: the rise of direct action against road-building and the changing character of British environmentalism', *Political Studies*, 47(2).

—— (2002) *Ideas and Action in the Green Movement* (London: Routledge).

Doherty, B. and De Geus, M. (eds) (1996a) *Democracy and Green Political Thought: Sustainability, Rights and Citizenship* (London: Routledge).

—— (1996b) 'Introduction', in B. Doherty and M. De Geus (eds) *Democracy and Green Political Thought: Sustainability, Rights and Citizenship* (London: Routledge).

Donald, J. and Hall, S. (1986) *Politics and Ideology* (Milton Keynes: Open University Press).

Dowie, M. (1995) *Losing Ground: American Environmentalism at the Close of the Twentieth Century* (Cambridge, MA.: MIT Press).

Doyle, T. and McEachern, D. (1998) *Environment and Politics* (London: Routledge).

Dryzek, J. (1987) *Rational Ecology* (Oxford: Blackwell).

—— (1990) *Discursive Democracy: Politics, Policy and Political Science* (Cambridge: Cambridge University Press).

—— (1997) *The Politics of the Earth: Environmental Discourses* (Oxford: Oxford University Press).

Dryzek, J. and Schlosberg, D. (eds) (1998) *Debating the Earth: The Environmental Politics Reader* (Oxford: Oxford University Press).

Eatwell, R. and Wright, A. (eds) (1993) *Contemporary Political Ideologies* (London: Pinter).

Eccleshall, R., Geoghegan, V., Jay, R., Kenny, M., Mackenzie, I. and Wilford, R. (1994) *Political Ideologies: An Introduction* (2nd edn) (London: Hutchinson).

Eckersley, R. (1987) 'Green politics: a practice in search of a theory', paper delivered at the Ecopolitics II Conference, University of Tasmania, 22–25 May.

—— (1992) *Environmentalism and Political Theory: Toward an Ecocentric Approach* (London: UCL Press).

—— (ed.) (1995) *Markets, The State and the Environment: Towards Integration* (Australia: Macmillan Education).

—— (1996) 'Connecting ecology and democracy: the rights discourse revisited', in B. Doherty and M. De Geus (eds) *Democracy and Green Political Thought: Sustainability, Rights and Citizenship* (London: Routledge).

—— (2004) *The Green State: Rethinking Democracy and Sovereignty* (Cambridge, MA.: MIT Press).

Ekeli, K. (2005) 'Giving a voice to posterity – deliberative democracy and representation of future people', *Journal of Agricultural and Environmental Ethics*, 18.

Ekins, P. (ed.) (1986) *The Living Economy* (London: Routledge & Kegan Paul).

Ekins, P. and Max-Neef, M. (1992) *Real-life Economics: Understanding Wealth Creation* (London: Routledge).

Elkington, J. and Burke, T. (1987) *The Green Capitalists* (London: Victor Gollancz).

Elliot, R. and Gare, A. (eds) (1983) *Environmental Philosophy* (Milton Keynes: Open University Press).

EFGP (European Federation of Green Parties) (2006) www.europeangreens.org/peopleandparties/results.html (accessed 15 June 2006).

Enviro Facts (2006) http://home.intekom.com/africantravel/Domains/deltaenviro/resources/envirofacts/development.html (accessed 17 July 2006).

Feinberg, J. (1981) 'The rights of animals and unborn generations', in E. Partridge (ed.) *Responsibilities to Future Generations* (New York: Prometheus Books).

Ferguson, M. (1981) *The Aquarian Conspiracy: Personal and Social Transformation in the 1980s* (London: Paladin).

Feuer, L. (1976) *Marx and Engels: Basic Writings on Politics and Philosophy* (Glasgow: Fontana).

Fischer, F. and Black, M. (eds) (1995) *Greening Environmental Policy: The Politics of a Sustainable Future* (London: Paul Chapman).

Foley, M. (1994) *Ideas That Shape Politics* (Manchester: Manchester University Press).

Foreman, D. and Haywood, B. (eds) (1989) *Ecodefense: A Field Guide to Monkeywrenching* (2nd edn) (Tucson: Ned Ludd Books).

Foreman, M. (1991) 'Second thoughts of an eco-warrior', in M. Bookchin and D. Foreman *Defending the Earth* (Montreal: Black Rose Books).

Foster, J. (ed.) 1997) *Valuing Nature? Economics, Ethics and Environment* (London: Routledge).

Fox, W. (1984) 'Deep ecology: a new philosophy of our time?', *The Ecologist*, 14 (5/6).

—— (1986a) *Approaching Deep Ecology: A Response to Richard Sylvan's Critique of Deep Ecology* (Tasmania: University of Tasmania).

—— (1986b) 'Ways of thinking environmentally', talk given to Fourth National Environmental Education Conference, Australia, September.

—— (1990) *Towards a Transpersonal Ecology: Developing New Foundations for Evironmentalism* (Boston, MA: Shambhala Press).

Frankel, B. (1987) *The Post-industrial Utopians* (Oxford: Polity Press).

Frankland, E.G. (1988) 'The role of the Greens in West German parliamentary politics, 1987', *Review of Politics*, winter.

Freer, J. (1983) 'Gaia: the Earth as our spiritual heritage', in L. Caldecott and S. Leland (eds) *Reclaim the Earth* (London: The Women's Press).

Garner, R. (2000) *Environmental Politics* (2nd edn) (Hemel Hempstead: Prentice Hall/Harvester Wheatsheaf).

German Green Party Manifesto (1983) (London: Heretic Books).

Gerrard, B. (1995) *Whose Backyard, Whose Risk: Fear and Fairness in Toxic and Nuclear Waste Siting* (Cambridge, MA, and London: MIT Press).

Goldsmith, E. (1972) *A Blueprint for Survival* (London: Tom Stacey).

—— (1988) *The Great U-turn: De-industrializing Society* (Bideford: Green Books).

Goldsmith, E. and Hildyard, N. (1986) *Green Britain or Industrial Wasteland?* (Oxford: Polity Press).

Goldstein, B. (1999) 'Combining science and place-based knowledge', in M. McGinnis (ed.) *Bioregionalism* (London and New York: Routledge).

Goodin, R. (1985) *Protecting the Vulnerable: A Reanalysis of Our Social Responsibilities* (Chicago, IL: University of Chicago Press).

—— (1992) *Green Political Theory* (Cambridge: Polity Press).

—— (1996) 'Enfranchising the Earth, and its alternatives', *Political Studies*, 44(5).

Goodwin, B. (1987) *Using Political Ideas* (Chichester: John Wiley).

Gorz, A. (1982) *Farewell to the Working-class* (London: Pluto).

—— (1985) *Paths to Paradise/On the Liberation from Work* (London: Pluto).

—— (1994) *Capitalism, Socialism, Ecology* (London: Verso).

Gottlieb, R (2001) *Environmentalism Unbound: Exploring New Pathways for Change* (Cambridge, MA, and London: MIT Press).

Gould, P. (1988) *Early Green Politics* (Brighton: Harvester Press).

Gray, J. (1993a) *Beyond the New Right: Markets, Government and the Common Environment* (London: Routledge).

—— (1993b) 'An agenda for green conservatism', in J. Gray *Beyond the New*

Right: Markets, Government and the Common Environment (London: Routledge).

—— (2002) *Straw Dogs: Thoughts on Humans and Other Animals* (London: Granta).

Greco, T. Jr. (1994) *New Money for Healthy Communities* (Tucson: Thomas H. Greco).

Green Party (England and Wales) Manifesto for a Sustainable Society (1999) (London: Green Party, http://www.greenparty.org.uk).

Grubb, M., Koch, M., Munson, A., Sullivan, E. and Thomson, K. (1993) *The Earth Summit Agreements: A Guide and Assessment* (London: Earthscan/ RIIA).

Hailwood, S. (2004) *How to be a Green Liberal: Nature, Value and Liberal Philosophy* (Chesham: Acumen Publishing).

Hamilton, M. (1987) 'The elements of the concept of ideology', *Political Studies*, 35(1).

Hampson, N. (1979) *The Enlightenment* (Harmondsworth: Penguin).

Harper, P. (n.d.) 'Life at the quarry' (unpublished).

Harvey, D. (1993) 'The nature of environment: the dialectics of social and environmental change', *The Socialist Register*.

Hay, T. (1988) 'Ecological values and Western political traditions: from anarchism to fascism', *Politics*, 8(2).

Hayward, T. (1994) 'The meaning of political ecology', *Radical Philosophy*, 66 (spring).

—— (1995) *Ecological Thought: An Introduction* (Oxford: Polity Press).

—— (1997) 'Anthropocentrism: a misunderstood problem', *Environmental Values*, 6(1).

—— (1998) *Political Theory and Ecological Values* (Cambridge: Polity Press).

Heilbroner, R. (1974) *An Inquiry into the Human Prospect* (New York: HarperRow).

Henderson, H. (1983) 'The warp and the weft: the coming synthesis of ecophilosophy and ecofeminism', in L. Caldecott and S. Leland (eds) *Reclaim the Earth* (London: The Women's Press).

Heywood, A. (1992) *Political Ideologies: An Introduction* (London: Macmillan).

Hildebrand, P. (1992) 'The European Community's environmental policy, 1957 to "1992": from incidental measures to an international regime', *Environmental Politics*, 1(4).

Hülsberg, W. (1988) *The German Greens* (London: Verso).

Humphrey, M. (ed.) (2001) *Political Theory and the Environment: A Reassessment* (London: Frank Cass).

Inglehart, R. (1977) *The Silent Revolution: Changing Values and Political Style Among Western Publics* (Princeton, NJ: Princeton University Press).

Irvine, S. (1989) *Beyond Green Consumerism* (London: Friends of the Earth).

Irvine, S. and Ponton, A. (1988) A *Green Manifesto: Policies for a Green Future* (London: Macdonald Optima).

Jacobs, M. (1997) 'Environmental valuation, deliberative democracy and public decision-making institutions', in J. Foster (ed.) *Valuing Nature? Economics, Ethics and Environment* (London: Routledge).

—— (1999a) 'Sustainable development as a contested concept', in A. Dobson (ed.) *Fairness and Futurity: Essays on Environmental Sustainability and Dimensions of Social Justice* (Oxford: Oxford University Press).

—— (1999b) *Environmental Modernisation* (London: Fabian Society).

Jahn, D. (1994) 'Unifying the Greens in a united Germany', *Environmental Politics*, 3(2).

Johnson, L. (1991) A *Morally Deep World: An Essay on Moral Significance and Environmental Ethics* (Cambridge: Cambridge University Press).

Jordan, A., Wurzel, R. and Zito, A. (eds) (2003) *'New' Instruments of Environmental Governance? National Experiences and Prospects* (

Kenny, M. (1994) 'Ecologism', in R. Eccleshall, V. Geoghegan, R. Jay, M. Kenny, I. Mackenzie and R. Wilford *Political Ideologies: An Introduction* (2nd edn) (London: Hutchinson).

King, Y. (1983) 'The eco-feminist imperative', in L. Caldecott and S. Leland (eds) *Reclaim the Earth* (London: The Women's Press).

—— (1989) 'The ecology of feminism and the feminism of ecology', in J. Plant (ed.) *Healing the Wounds: The Promise of Ecofeminism* (London: Green Press).

Kollmuss, A. and Agyeman, J. (2002) 'Mind the gap: why do people act environmentally and what are the barriers to pro-environmental behaviour', *Environmental Education Research*, 8(3).

Kovel, J. (2002) *The Enemy of Nature: The End of Capitalism or the End of the World?* (London: Zed Books).

Kumar, K. (1987) *Utopia and Anti-Utopia in Modern Times* (Oxford: Blackwell).

—— (1991) *Utopianism* (Milton Keynes: Open University Press).

Kumar, S. (ed.) (1984) *The Schumacher Lectures: Volume II* (London: Blond & Briggs).

Laferrière, E. and Stoett, P. (1999) *International Relations Theory and Ecological Thought: Towards a Synthesis* (London: Routledge).

Lafferty, M. and Meadowcroft, J. (eds) (1996a) *Democracy and the Environment: Problems and Prospects* (Cheltenham: Edward Elgar).

—— (1996b) 'Democracy and the environment: congruence and conflict – preliminary reflections', in M. Lafferty and J. Meadowcroft (eds) *Democracy and the Environment: Problems and Prospects* (Cheltenham: Edward Elgar).

Latour, B. (2004) *Politics of Nature: How to Bring the Sciences into Democracy* (Cambridge, MA, and London: Harvard University Press).

Layard, R. (2003) 'Happiness: has social science a clue?' (Lionel Robbins Memorial Lecture), (http://cep.lse.ac.uk/events/lectures/layard/RL030303.pdf) accessed 11 July 2006.

—— (2005) *Happiness: Lessons from a New Science* (London: Allen Lane).

Leach, R. (1991) *British Political Ideologies* (New York and London: Philip Allen).

Lee, K. (1989) *Social Philosophy and Ecological Scarcity* (London: Routledge).

Leland, S. (1983) 'Feminism and ecology: theoretical connections', in L. Caldecott and S. Leland (eds) *Reclaim the Earth* (London: The Women's Press).

Leopold, A. (1949) *A Sand County Almanac* (Oxford: Oxford University Press).

Lewis, M. (1992) *Green Delusions: An Environmentalist Critique of Radical Environmentalism* (Durham, NC: Duke University Press).

Light, A. (ed.) (1998) *Social Ecology after Bookchin* (New York and London: Guilford Press).

—— (2002) 'Restoring ecological citizenship', in B. Minteer, and B. Pepperman Taylor (eds) *Democracy and the Claims of Nature: Critical Perspectives for a New Century* (Lanham, Boulder, CO, New York, and Oxford: Rowman & Littlefield).

Light, A. and De Shalit, A. (eds) (2004) *Moral and Political Reasoning in Environmental Practice* (Cambridge, MA, and London: MIT Press).

Lomborg, B. (2001) *The Skeptical Environmentalist: Measuring the Real State of the World* (Cambridge: Cambridge University Press).

Lovelock, J. (1979) *Gaia* (Oxford: Oxford University Press).

—— (1986) 'Gaia: the world as living organism', *New Scientist*, 18 December.

Low, N. and Gleeson, B. (1998) *Justice, Society and Nature: An Exploration of Political Ecology* (London: Routledge).

Lutz, W. (ed.) (1994) *The Future Population of the World: What Can We Assume Today?* (London: Earthscan).

McGinnis, M. (ed.) (1999) *Bioregionalism* (London and New York: Routledge).

MacGregor, S. (2006) *Beyond Mothering Earth: Ecological Citizenship and the Politics of Care* (British Columbia: University of British Columbia Press).

McLellan, D. (1986) *Ideology* (Milton Keynes: Open University Press).

Macridis, R. (1992) *Contemporary Political Ideologies: Movements and Regimes* (5th edn) (New York: HarperCollins).

Marien, M. (1977) 'The two visions of post-industrial society', *Futures*, October.

Martell, L. (1994) *Ecology and Society: An Introduction* (Cambridge: Polity Press).

Martinez-Alier, J. (2002), *The Environmentalism of the Poor: A Study of Ecological Conflicts and Valuation* (Cheltenham, and Northampton, MA: Edward Elgar).

Mason, M. (1999) *Environmental Democracy* (London: Earthscan).

Mathews, F. (1991) *The Ecological Self* (London: Routledge).

—— (ed.) (1995) 'Ecology and democracy', *Environmental Politics*, Special Issue, 4(4).

Max-Neef, M. (1992) 'Development and human needs', in P. Ekins and M. Max-Neef *Real-life Economics: Understanding Wealth Creation* (London: Routledge).

Meadows, D., Meadows, D., Randers, J. and Behrens III, W. (1974) *The Limits to Growth* (London: Pan).

—— (1992) *Beyond The Limits: Global Collapse or a Sustainable Future* (London: Earthscan).

—— (2005) *Limits to Growth: The 30-year Update* (London: Earthscan).

Mellor, M. (1992a) *Breaking the Boundaries: Towards a Feminist Green Socialism* (London: Virago).

—— (1992b) 'Green politics: ecofeminist, ecofeminine or ecomasculine?', *Environmental Politics*, 1(2).

—— (1997) *Feminism and Ecology* (Cambridge: Polity Press).

—— (2006) 'Socialism', in A. Dobson and R. Eckersley (eds) *Political Theory and the Ecological Challenge* (Cambridge: Cambridge University Press).

Merchant, C. (1990) *The Death of Nature* (New York: Harper & Row).

Meyer, J. (2001) *Political Nature: Environmentalism and the Interpretation of Western Thought* (Cambridge, MA, and London: MIT Press).

Midgley, M. (1983a) *Animals and Why They Matter* (Harmondsworth: Penguin).

—— (1983b) 'Duties concerning islands', in R. Elliot and A. Gare (eds) *Environmental Philosophy* (Milton Keynes: Open University Press).

Miliband, R. (1994) The plausibility of socialism', *New Left Review*, 206 (July/ August).

Mill, J.S. (1859/1972) *Utilitarianism, On Liberty and Representative Government* (London: Dent and Dutton).

Miller, D. (1999) 'Social justice and environmental goods', in A. Dobson (ed.) *Fairness and Futurity: Essays on Environmental Sustainability and Social Justice* (Oxford: Oxford University Press).

Minteer, B. and Pepperman Taylor, B. (eds) (2002) *Democracy and the Claims of Nature: Critical Perspectives for a New Century* (Lanham, Boulder, CO, New York, and Oxford: Rowman & Littlefield).

Moll, A. and Sonnenfeld, D. (2000) *Ecological Modernisation Around the World: Perspectives and Critical Debates* (London and Portland: Frank Cass and Routledge).

Monbiot, G. (2004) *The Age of Consent* (London: HarperPerennial).

Müller-Rommel, F. and Poguntke, T. (eds) (2002) *Green Parties in National Governments* (London and Portland: Frank Cass).

Myers, N. (1985) *The Gaia Atlas of Planet Management* (London: Good Books).

Myers, N. and Simon, J. (1994) *Scarcity or Abundance? A Debate on the Environment* (London: Norton).

Naess, A. (1973) 'The shallow and the deep, long-range ecology movement. A summary', *Inquiry*, 16.

—— (1984) 'Intuition, intrinsic value and deep ecology', *The Ecologist*, 14(5/6).

—— (1989) *Ecology, Community and Lifestyle* (Cambridge: Cambridge University Press).

North, P. (1998) ' "Save our Solsbury!": the anatomy of an anti-roads protest', *Environmental Politics*, 7 (3).

Norton, B. (1991) *Toward Unity Among Environmentalists* (New York and Oxford: Oxford University Press).

O'Connor, J. (1996) 'The second contradiction of capitalism', in T. Benton (ed.) *Natural Relations: Ecology, Animal Rights and Social Justice* (London: Verso).

Oelschlaeger, M. (1991) *The Idea of Wilderness* (New Haven, CT: Yale University Press).

O'Neill, J. (1993) *Ecology, Policy and Politics: Human Well-being and the Natural World* (London: Routledge).

Ophuls, W. (1977) The politics of a sustainable society', in D. Pirages (ed.) *The Sustainable Society* (New York: Praeger).

Ophuls, W. with Boyan Jr., A. (1992) *Ecology and the Politics of Scarcity Revisited: The Unraveling of the American Dream* (New York: W.H. Freeman).

O'Riordan, T. (1981) *Environmentalism* (London: Pion).

O'Riordan, T. and Cameron, I. (1994) *Interpreting the Precautionary Principle* (London: Earthscan).

Owen, D. (1980) *What is Ecology?* (Oxford: Oxford University Press).

Paehlke, R. (1988) 'Democracy, bureaucracy and environmentalism', *Environmental Ethics*, 10.

—— (2003) *Democracy's Dilemma: Environment, Social Equity and the Global Economy* (Cambridge, MA, and London: MIT Press).

Partridge, E. (ed.) (1981) *Responsibilities to Future Generations* (New York: Prometheus Books).

Paterson, M. (2000) *Understanding Global Environmental Politics: Domination, Accumulation, Resistance* (Basingstoke: Macmillan).

Pearce, D., Markandya, A. and Barbier, B. (1989) *Blueprint for a Green Economy* (London: Earthscan).

Pellow, D. and Brulle, R. (eds) (2005) *Power, Justice, and the Environment: A Critical Appraisal of the Environmental Justice Movement* (Cambridge, MA, and London: MIT Press).

Pepper, D. (1984) *The Roots of Modern Environmentalism* (Beckenham: Croom Helm).

—— (1991) *Communes and the Green Vision: Counterculture, Lifestyle and the New Age* (London: Green Print).

—— (1993a) 'Anthropocentrism, humanism and eco-socialism: a blueprint for the survival of ecological polities', *Environmental Politics*, 2(3).

—— (1993b) *Eco-socialism: From Deep Ecology to Social Justice* (London: Routledge).

Pirages, D. (ed.) (1977a) *The Sustainable Society* (New York: Praeger).

—— (1977b) 'Introduction: a social design for sustainable growth', in D. Pirages (ed.) *The Sustainable Society* (New York: Praeger).

Plant, J. (n.d.) 'Women and nature', *Green Line*, offprint.

—— (ed.) (1989) *Healing the Wounds: The Promise of Ecofeminism* (London: Green Press).

Plumwood, V. (1986) 'Ecofeminism: an overview and discussion of positions and arguments', in 'Women and Philosophy', supplement to *Australasian Journal of Philosophy*, 64 (June).

—— (1988) 'Women, humanity and nature', *Radical Philosophy*, Spring.

—— (1993) *Feminism and the Mastery of Nature* (London: Routledge).

—— (1997) 'Androcentrism and anthropocentrism: parallels and polities', in K. Warren (ed.) *Ecofeminism: Women, Culture, Nature* (Bloomington, MD: Indiana University Press).

—— (2006) 'Feminism', in A. Dobson and R. Eckersley (eds) *Political Theory and the Ecological Challenge* (Cambridge: Cambridge University Press).

Poguntke, T. (1993) 'Goodbye to movement polities', *Environmental Politics*, 2(3).

—— (2002) 'Green parties in national governments: from protest to acquiescence?', in F. Müller-Rommel and T. Poguntke (eds) *Green Parties in National Governments* (London and Portland: Frank Cass).

Politics.co.uk   (2006)   http://www.politics.co.uk/issue-briefs/public-services/road/congestion-charge/congestion-charge-$366631.htm (accessed 21 June 2006).

Ponting, C. (1991) A *Green History of the World* (Harmondsworth: Penguin).

Porritt, J. (1984a) *Seeing Green* (Oxford: Blackwell).

—— (1984b) Interview in *Marxism Today* (March).

—— (2005) *Capitalism as if the World Matters* (London and Sterling, VA: Earthscan).

Porritt, J. and Winner, D. (1988) *The Coming of the Greens* (London: Fontana).

Pulido, L. (1996) *Environmentalism and Economic Justice* (Tucson: University of Arizona Press).

Rawls, J. (1973) A *Theory of Justice* (Oxford: Oxford University Press).

Redclift, M. (1987) *Sustainable Development* (London: Methuen).

Reed, C. (1988) 'Wild men of the woods', *Guardian*, 13 July.

Rees, W. (1996) 'Revisiting carrying capacity: area-based indicators of sustainability', *Population and Environment: A Journal of Interdisciplinary Studies*, 17 (2).

Regan, T. (1988) *The Case for Animal Rights* (London: Routledge).

Richards, F. (1989) 'Can capitalism go green?', *Living Marxism*, 4 (February).

Riechmann, J. (1997) 'Ecologismo y ambientalismo', *Revista de Libros*, 9 (September).

Roderick, R. (1986) *Habermas and the Foundations of Critical Theory* (London: Macmillan).

Rolston, H. (1983) 'Are values in nature subjective or objective?', in R. Elliot and A. Gare (eds) *Environmental Philosophy* (Milton Keynes: Open University Press).

Rousseau, J-J. (1762/1968) *The Social Contract* (Harmondsworth: Penguin).

Rüdig, W. (2002) 'Germany', in F. Müller-Rommel and T. Poguntke (eds) *Green Parties in National Governments* (London and Portland: Frank Cass).

Ryle, M. (1988) *Ecology and Socialism* (London: Radius).

Sagoff, M. (1988) *The Economy of the Earth: Philosophy, Law and the Environment* (Cambridge: Cambridge University Press).

Sale, K. (1984) 'Mother of all: an introduction to bioregionalism', in S. Kumar (ed.) *The Schumacher Lectures: Volume U* (London: Blond & Briggs).

—— (1985) *Dwellers in the Land: The Bioregional Vision* (San Francisco, CA: Sierra Club).

Salleh, A. (1984) 'Deeper than deep ecology: the eco-feminist connection', *Environmental Ethics*, 6.

—— (1997) *Ecofeminism as Politics: Nature, Marx and the Postmodern* (London: Zed Books).

Sarkar, S. (1999) *Eco-socialism or Eco-Capitalism? A Criticial Analysis of Humanity's Fundamental Choices* (London: Zed Books).

Saward, M. (1993a) 'Green democracy?', in A. Dobson and P. Lucardie (eds) *The Politics of Nature: Explorations in Green Political Theory* (London: Routledge).

—— (1993b) 'Green theory', *Environmental Politics*, 2 (3).

Schlosberg, D. (1999) *Environmental Justice and the New Pluralism* (Oxford: Oxford University Press).

Schumacher, F. (1976) *Small is Beautiful* (London: Sphere).

Schwarz, W. and Schwarz, D. (1987) *Breaking Through* (Bideford: Green Books).

Scruton, R. (2006), 'Conservatism', in A. Dobson and R. Eckersley (eds) *Political Theory and the Ecological Challenge* (Cambridge: Cambridge University Press).

Seabrook, J. (1988) *The Race for Riches* (Basingstoke: Green Print).

Seel, B. (1997) 'Strategies of resistance at the Pollok Free State road protest camp', *Environmental Politics*, 6(4).

—— (1999) 'Strategic identities: strategy, culture and consciousness in the New Age and road protest movements', unpublished Ph.D. thesis, Keele University, UK.

Sessions, G. (ed.) (1994) *Deep Ecology for the 21st Century* (Boston, MA, and London: Shambhala Press).

Seyfang, G. (2005) 'Shopping for sustainability: can sustainable consumption promote ecological citizenship?', *Environmental Politics*, 14(2).

Seymour, J. and Girardet, H. (1987) *Blueprint for a Green Planet* (London: Dorling Kindersley).

Shiva, V. (1988) *Staying Alive* (London: Zed Books).

Simms, A. (2006) 'An environmental war economy: the lessons of ecological debt and global warming' (London: New Economics Foundation) http://www.neweconomics.org/gen/z_sys_PublicationDetail.aspx?PID=65 (accessed 23 May 2006).

Simon, J. and Kahn, H. (1984) *The Resourceful Earth: A Response to Global 2000* (Oxford: Blackwell).

Simonon, L. (1983) 'Personal, political and planetary play', in L. Caldecott and S. Leland (eds) *Reclaim the Earth* (London: The Women's Press).

Simons, M. (1988) article in *Green Line*, 64 (July–August).

Singer, P. (1975) *Animal Liberation* (New York: Review Books).

Smith, G. (2003) *Deliberative Democracy and the Environment* (London: Routledge).

Smith, M. (1998) *Ecologism: Towards Ecological Citizenship* (Buckingham: Open University Press).

Spinoza, B. de (1677/1955) *On the Improvement of Understanding, The Ethics, Correspondence* (New York: Dover).

Spretnak, C. and Capra, F. (1985) *Green Politics* (London: Paladin).

Stephens, P. (2001a) 'Green liberalism: nature, agency and the good', *Environmental Politics*, 10(3).

—— (2001b) 'The green only blooms among the Millian flowers: a reply to Marcel Wissenburg', *Environmental Politics*, 10(3).

Stoett, P. (1994) 'Cities: to love or to loathe?', *Environmental Politics*, 3(2).

Strong, D.M. (1988) *Dreamers and Defenders: American Conservationists* (Lincoln: University of Nebraska Press).

Sylvan, R. (1984a) 'A critique of deep ecology' (part one), *Radical Philosophy*, 40.

—— (1984b) 'A critique of deep ecology' (part two), *Radical Philosophy*, 41.

Szasz, A. (1994) *Ecopopulism: Toxic Waste and the Movement for Environmental Justice* (Minneapolis: Minnesota University Press).

Talshir, G. (2002) *The Political Ideology of Green Parties* (Basingstoke: Palgrave Macmillan).

Thomas, C. (1983) 'Alternative technology: a feminist technology?', in L. Caldecott and S. Leland (eds) *Reclaim the Earth* (London: The Women's Press).

Thomas, C. (1992) *The Environment in International Relations* (London: RIIA).

Thomashow, M. (1999) 'Towards a cosmopolitan bioregionalism', in M. McGinnis (ed.) *Bioregionalism* (London and New York: Routledge).

Thompson, J. (1983) 'Preservation of wilderness and the Good Life', in R. Elliot and A. Gare (eds) *Environmental Philosophy* (Milton Keynes: Open University Press).

Tokar, B. (1988) 'Social ecology, deep ecology and the future of green thought', *The Ecologist*, 18(4/5).

—— (1994) *The Green Alternative* (2nd edn) (San Pedro: R. and E. Miles).

Torgerson, D. (1999) *The Promise of Green Politics: Environmentalism and the Public Sphere* (Durham, NC: Duke University Press).

Tudge, C. (1996) *The Day Before Yesterday: Five Million Years of Human History* (London: Pimlico).

Various (1994) *Pod* (active newsletter, no recorded publisher).

Vincent, A. (1992) *Modern Political Ideologies* (Oxford: Blackwell).

—— (1993) 'The character of ecology', *Environmental Politics*, 2 (2).

Wackernagel, M. and Rees, W. (1996) *Our Ecological Footprint: Reducing Human Impact on the Earth* (British Columbia: New Society Publishers).

Wall, D. (1999) *Earth First! and the Anti-roads Movement* (London: Routledge).

—— (2005) *Babylon and Beyond: The Economics of Anti-capitalist, Anti-globalist and Radical Green Movements* (London and Ann Arbor, MI: Pluto).

Ward, B. and Dubos, R. (1972) *Only One Earth: The Care and Maintenance of a Small Planet* (London: André Deutsch).

Warren, K. J. (1987) 'Feminism and ecology: making connections', *Environmental Ethics*, 9.

—— (ed.) (1997) *Ecofeminism: Women, Culture, Nature* (Bloomington, MD: Indiana University Press).

Weale, A. (1992) *The New Politics of Pollution* (Manchester: Manchester University Press).

Wells, D. (1982) 'Resurrecting the dismal parson: Malthus, ecology, and political thought', *Political Studies*, 30(1).

Wenz, P. (2002) 'Justice, democracy and global warming', in B. Minteer and B. Pepperman Taylor (eds) *Democracy and the Claims of Nature: Critical Perspectives for a New Century* (Lanham, Boulder, CO, New York, and Oxford: Rowman & Littlefield).

Weston, I. (ed.) (1986) *Red and Green* (London: Pluto).

Whiteside, K. (2002) *Divided Natures: French Contributions to Political Ecology* (Cambridge, MA, and London: MIT Press).

Williams, R. (n.d.) *Socialism and Ecology* (London: SERA).

—— (1986) *Towards 2000* (Harmondsworth: Pelican).

Wissenburg, M. (1998a) *Green Liberalism: The Free and the Green Society* (London: UCL Press).

—— (1998b) 'The rapid reproducers paradox: population control and individual procreative rights', *Environmental Politics*, 7(2).

—— (2001) 'Liberalism is always greener on the other side of Mill: a reply to Piers Stephens', *Environmental Politics*, 10(3).

—— (2006) 'Liberalism', in A. Dobson and R. Eckersley (eds) *Political Theory and the Ecological Challenge* (Cambridge: Cambridge University Press).

Witherspoon, S. (1996) 'Democracy, the environment and public opinion in Western Europe', in W. Lafferty and J. Meadowcroft (eds) *Democracy and the Environment: Problems and Prospects* (Cheltenham: Edward Elgar).

World Resources Institute (1992) *World Resources 1992–93: A Guide to the Global Environment* (Oxford: Oxford University Press).

Young, S. (1992) 'The different dimensions of green polities', *Environmental Politics*, 1(1).

Index